Asmat Shield

CHINA

Hong Kong

S.E.
ASIA

Manila • PHILIPPINES

Bangkok

PACIFIC
OCEAN

NETHERLANDS
NEW GUINEA

BORNEO

Hollandia Equator

SUMATRA I N D O N E S I A

Djakarta • JAVA

Asmat

AUSTRALIAN
NEW GUINEA
ADMIN. UNIT

INDIAN
OCEAN

LIA

Sydney

Map by Nick Springer. Copyright © MMXIV Springer Cartographics LLC

SAVAGE HARVEST

SAVAGE HARVEST

A TALE OF CANNIBALS, COLONIALISM, AND MICHAEL
ROCKEFELLER'S TRAGIC QUEST FOR PRIMITIVE ART

CARL HOFFMAN

wm

WILLIAM MORROW

An Imprint of HarperCollinsPublishers

All photographs appear courtesy of the author, with the following exceptions: pages 3, 22, 87, 157, 172, 181: Library of Congress; page 55: Mieke van Kessel; pages 76, 149, 166, 186: MSC/OSC Brotherhood, Order of the Sacred Heart.

Book epigraph from *The Other* by Ryszard Kapuscinski (Verso Books, 2009), reprinted by permission of Verso Books.

HarperCollins books may be purchased for educational, business, or sales promotional use. For information please e-mail the Special Markets Department at SPsales@harpercollins.com.

FIRST EDITION

Endpaper map copyright ©2014 Springer Cartographics LLC.

Designed by Lisa Stokes

Library of Congress Cataloging-in-Publication Data has been applied for.

ISBN 978-0-06-211615-4 (hardcover)
ISBN 978-0-06-232531-0 (international edition)

14 15 16 17 18 OV/RRD 10 9 8 7 6 5 4 3 2 1

For Lily

Every encounter with the Other is an enigma, an unknown quantity—I would even say a mystery.

—RYSZARD KAPUSCINSKI

CONTENTS

SAVAGE HARVEST

PART I

1

November 19, 1961

THE SEA FELT warm as Michael Rockefeller lowered himself in from the overturned wooden hull. René Wassing peered down at him, and Michael noticed René was sunburned and needed a shave. Their exchange was brief. They'd been drifting on the ocean off the coast of southwest New Guinea for twenty-four hours now, and there wasn't much that hadn't been said.

MICHAEL ROCKEFELLER IN NEW GUINEA.

I really don't think you should go.

No, it'll be okay. I think I can make it.

Michael cupped his hands and swung his arms, swiveling around. It was eight a.m. The tide was high. He was wearing white cotton underpants and thick, black-rimmed glasses. He had two empty gasoline cans tied to his webbed, military-style belt. He hugged one tightly and started swimming, kicking toward the coast, a hazy

line of gray, barely a smudge. He estimated they were five to ten miles off the coast. He kicked slowly and ran the numbers. A mile an hour and he'd be there in ten hours. A half-mile an hour and he'd reach shore in twenty. No problem. The sea was almost as hot as a bath, and it was just a matter of setting his mind to the task. Plus, he and René had the tide charts for the coast and he knew something else in his favor: the tides weren't evenly spaced right now. Between four p.m. and the next morning, there would be a high tide at midnight, a brief low tide at two a.m., and then another high tide at eight a.m. Which meant that for twelve of the fourteen hours between four p.m. and the next morning, the water would be pushing him toward the coast when he was the most tired.

It wasn't long until there was no more René on the overturned catamaran behind him. He knew that feeling from swimming off the coast of Maine every summer, how the shore behind you receded quickly even when the destination didn't seem any closer. And the Arafura Sea here was shallow. He ought to be able to stand, to touch the muddy bottom, when he was still a mile from shore. He rolled onto his back and kicked, long, slow, steady kicks, dragging the cans. He could hear his heart thumping and the sound of his own breathing.

He never would have said it out loud, but he carried a sense of destiny. A bigness. A self-confidence he was barely aware of. Twenty-three-year-olds don't think about death; life seems eternal, the same as when he would speed along the Maine Turnpike in his Studebaker doing eighty. *Now* was everything to a twenty-three-year-old. Plus, he was a Rockefeller. Sometimes it was a burden, sometimes a gift, but it defined him, even when he didn't want it to. "Can't" wasn't part of the family lexicon. Everything was possible. He had grown up being able to go anywhere, do anything, meet anyone. His great-grandfather had been the richest man in the world. His father was governor of the state of New York, had just run for president of the United States. In epic survival situations, will is everything,

and Michael's was as big as a will could be. He carried a responsibility, every Rockefeller did, to do good things, big things, to make something of himself. "Stewardship" was the word the family used. He wasn't just swimming for his life. He was swimming for René, who needed to be rescued. He was swimming for his father, Nelson. For his twin sister, Mary. For the Asmat themselves, in a way, because he had collected so much of their beautiful art that he wanted to share with his father, with Robert Goldwater at the Museum of Primitive Art, with his best friend, Sam Putnam, with the world. He didn't exactly articulate this, he just knew it, felt it. So he swam and stroked and kicked with confidence. It was a big world, but he was in a bubble. Him and the sea, the big Arafura.

He wasn't in a hurry. Fear, panic, those were what killed people, made their minds crazy, frantic, exhausted precious energy. He remembered that from army basic training. And he even smiled a little, recalling how he and his Harvard classmates had rolled their eyes at the Widener swim—the requirement that every Harvard graduate complete a fifty-meter swim before graduation, stipulated by the mother of former alum Harry Elkins Widener, who'd died on the *Titanic,* when she gave $2.5 million for the school's new library. This was a matter of steadiness. When he felt his calves starting to cramp, his shoulders tiring, he rested, floating, clinging to the gasoline cans, staring at the big sky full of shifting, changing clouds overhead. Luckily the wind and the sea were calm, and they grew calmer as the afternoon passed. At sunset, the ocean was as still as a swimming pool on a summer's eve. He swam on. He thought about the exhibition he wanted to mount in New York. The feast poles twenty feet tall he'd collected—no one had ever seen anything like that in the United States before; they would dwarf anything else in his father's new museum. The stars came out, billions of them. Heat lightning flashed along the horizon. The moon rose, three days from full, and he wasn't in total darkness.

He swam on.

He wasn't sure where he was, but probably somewhere between the Faretsj and the Fajit Rivers, between the villages of Omadesep and Basim. By dawn there'd be people along the shore, for sure—they were always there fishing. He was happy with how well he already knew these people; Asmat, this remotest corner of the world, had become his. His universe, an alternative world that he'd discovered, was untangling, and this swim to shore was like a baptism, deep in Asmat, and it would be a good story to tell. It was dark and had been for a long time when he saw strange reflections on the water. Behind him the sky lit, white, the light of phosphorescent flares dropping toward the sea. He saw them, but he didn't know what they were.

Around four a.m. the sky started to turn faintly purple, first light. Out here Michael could feel those subtle shifts. He had been swimming for eighteen hours, but it was almost done, he knew, if he could keep going. His waist was raw where the belt holding the floats was chafing. He was exhausted, but the dawn gave him some added strength. He could see the trees more clearly now. They were a dark line, but they were there. He rested again. Floated again. His whole body hurt. He was thirsty and hungry, and the salt water stung. He'd do anything for a long drink of cold, fresh water. He shivered. Best keep going. As the day got lighter, brighter, he got closer. He tried to touch bottom and he could. Barely. It was mud, though, slippery and sticky, and it was easier to swim. But he could stand and rest, and just knowing that was everything. He knew he would make it. He untied one of the empty gasoline cans and let it go; it was easier without it. He swam, he stood, he swam some more—on his back now, really the only way to make progress, even though it hurt. He was almost safe. Nipa palms and mangrove rose seemingly right from the water, and among them canoes, a flotilla of them nestled in the trees.

And men.

2

November 20, 1961

AN ASMAT ANCESTOR SKULL.
THE LOWER JAW IS ATTACHED,
INDICATING THAT THE DECEASED
WAS NOT THE VICTIM OF A
HEADHUNTING RAID.

THEY SAW HIM, fifty of them, resting in eight long canoes along the mouth of the Ewta River. It was six a.m. The sun was already rising above the trees, the saturated glow of the early morning tropics soon to be washed out by the stark tropical light. The tide was almost high, and there was no definitive shoreline to speak of—just flooded, scattered shrubby trees where water and land came together and the swamp and dense jungle began. Here they could float in the shade, have a smoke with long cigarettes rolled in the yellow husk of nipa palm, and munch balls of sago flour after a night of paddling toward home, just three miles up the Ewta.

"Look, an *ew*!" said Pep, in the Asmat language. A crocodile!

The men reached for their spears, ten feet long, carved with vicious, inch-long barbs, some of them tipped with the claw of a cassowary.

They watched the crocodile, which didn't move like any croco-
dile they'd ever seen before. Michael was swimming on his back,
but he rolled over and saw the men and the canoes and smelled the
smoke from their cigarettes and the smoldering coals nestled in mud
at their sterns, and he waved, shouted. Unbelievable. He'd made it!

"No," said Fin, "it is a man!"

"Wo!" they grunted. Pep and Fin and Ajim and the others
stood and bent forward at the waist and dug their long paddles
into the water with powerful strokes, their canoe surging toward
the swimming man. The other men in their canoes did the same.
The canoes were forty feet long, narrow and low to the water, and
some bore faded ochre and white vertical stripes. They surrounded
him. Michael was smiling and panting, his beard wet, his lips
chapped, blistered. Pep reached down and tried to pull him in,
but Michael was too exhausted to help them. Fin and Pep held his
arms and began towing him toward shore. They recognized him.
In a world without photographs or writing, they had sharp memo-
ries, and they had seen him before; he had been in the village. His
name was Mike.

The men in the canoes were black-skinned, strong-featured,
with high cheekbones and holes in their septums the size of dimes.
Beyond the occasional wild pig or human being, they ate no fat,
no oil, and they didn't know sugar. Absent was the subcutane-
ous layer padding even thin Americans. They were hard muscle,
vein, and skin, their chests and shoulders broad from a lifetime of
paddling. Their waists were narrow, their abs ripped. They were
naked but for tight, finely woven bands of rattan just above their
knees and elbows and fiber bags decorated with the seeds of Job's
tears and cassowary and cockatoo feathers. The bags of the older,
more important men hung over their chests; those of the younger
hung over their backs. Ajim's, Pep's, and Fin's bags hung over their
chests, and their left wrists were bound in thick, six-inch-wide
bracelets, protection against the powerful snap of the coarse rattan

strings of their seven-foot-long bow. Some had a carved pig bone through their septum.

Ajim looked at Pep. "Now is your chance," he said. It wasn't just a statement—it was a taunt. Ajim was the head of one of the five *jeu,* or men's houses, that made up the Asmat village of Otsjanep. He had killed more people than any of them, had taken more heads. He was quick of mind, fierce, bold, belligerent, full of passionate extremes, and he'd earned his status through fearlessness and risk-taking. He exuded what the Asmat called *tes,* charisma.

Pep didn't hesitate. He was surrounded by relatives and fellow villagers, and his status was built on how bold he was, how many people he killed, how many heads he took. He howled and arched his back and drove his spear into the white man's floating ribs. Michael screamed, groaned a deep, inhuman sound. They hauled him up into the canoe, blood spurting from the wound. They knew what they were doing, had done it dozens of times before, were following sacred rules that prescribed every step of what they were about to do, rules that defined them. Made them men. Made them whole. For they were about to take his power, *become* him, and restore balance to the world.

The fifty men rowed south on the Arafura Sea, standing up in a line in each canoe, the most important men at the stern and bow, the places of hardest work. Their shoulders and triceps rippled; sweat poured off their chests and foreheads; their backs glistened in the sun. They sang, shouted "Wo! Wo! Wo!" as they clacked their paddles on the sides of the canoe and blew bamboo horns that sounded like eerie foghorns. They laughed. They chanted "Wo! Wo! Wo!" over and over again. They were filled with adrenaline and purpose, the white man's hot blood mixing with the water in the canoe, sloshing around their bare feet.

A few miles south of the Ewta River, they turned left, into a barely perceptible cut in the shoreline. Here the ocean was silvery over the black mud, long banks of which ran along the shore. The jungle was

thick green on all sides, nipa palm and mangrove roots like claws in the water. Flocks of sulfur-crested cockatoo flew overhead, screaming. The cockatoos ate fruit, and Pep and Fin and Ajim were like them, for they, too, ate fruit—human heads. Human heads were the fruit of men and powerful symbols of fertility, precious seeds that blossomed, grew, died, and from which new men sprouted.

As they turned into the inlet—a deserted, beautiful place with small white waves rolling in, the mud shining in the sun and the river water brown, a place that had never seen an engine or a radio, a place where the spirits dwelled—they were about to acquire a powerful new seed: Michael Rockefeller's head.

There was no beach, just a brief shoreline of thick, soft mud the color of ash. They dragged the white man out of the canoe and slapped him on his skull. "This is my head!" screamed Fin, as the others gathered around, shouting and taunting. Michael was limp, gravely injured, blood oozing from his mouth, matting his wet beard. Fin and Pep and Ajim held his chest off the ground and pushed his head forward and with one blow of an ax in the back of his neck, Michael Rockefeller was dead. Ajim turned him over and thrust into his throat with a bamboo knife, then pressed the head back until the vertebrae cracked. Man, pig, it was all the same now—Michael was sacred meat. As others gathered dead branches from the forest and lit them with coals from the canoe, Fin made a deep cut from Michael's anus to his neck, through one side of his trunk to his armpit, across the collarbone to his throat, and down the other side, exactly as the ancestors had instructed them how to butcher a man. Blood ran everywhere, soaking their hands, clotting on their arms, spattering their legs. Flies too, buzzing and swarming by the thousands.

Fin broke Michael's ribs with an ax, put his hand underneath his sternum, ripped it loose, and put it aside. Ajim twisted his legs and arms and cut them off and then pulled out Michael's entrails with a vigorous jerk. Fifty voices chanted and sang in unison, a

powerful, earthy rhythm that might have been the pulse of the mud and the trees themselves. It was sacred violence. The fire was crackling and smoking and hot, and the pieces of meat were placed in it to roast. When it was done, they pulled the charred legs and arms out of the fire, tore the meat off the bones, and mixed it with crumbly whitish-gray sago into long sticks for everyone to eat. Their hands were slippery with precious grease and fat, some of which they saved in small woven bags.

If this had been a normal killing of a fellow villager just a few years earlier, they would have taken the body back to the village for the elaborate, shameless ritual that should ensue. But times were changing. This was a white man, and this had to be done now, here, in secret. They held the head over the fire just long enough to scorch the hair. Fin took the burned hair and mixed it with the blood they'd saved, which they all smeared over each other's heads, shoulders, and bodies, even their anuses. They were coated in Michael Rockefeller.

When the head was cooked, they scalped it, cut across its face from the root of the nose to the nape of the neck, and as they did this they talked about what Michael had been doing when he was alive.

"He was eating fish yesterday," said Pep.

"He was swimming," said Fin, "and now he is dead."

Ajim cut a hole about two inches in diameter into Michael's right temple with a stone ax. The ax had a name, a new one. Its name was Mike. They shook the brains out onto the leaf of a palm, scraped inside the skull with a knife to get every last bit, then mixed the mass with sago, wrapped the leaf up, and roasted it on the fire. This food was special. Only Pep, Fin, Ajim, and Dombai, the most senior men there, ate it. It tasted rich. It was hard to be full in Asmat, and they were all now full. Finally they could rest, sleep without fear. They wrapped the skull in banana leaves, tucked it into Fin's canoe, and paddled home.

3

February 2012

WE CRESTED a wave, the thirty-foot, fiberglass longboat slamming into a narrow trough. As the waters of the Arafura Sea crashed over me, I wondered if that was how Michael Rockefeller had died. The swells were short and steep, and my mind had been racing, picturing Michael as a victim of the sacred Asmat ritual of killing and butchering described in detail in the *American Anthropologist* in 1959. If they'd killed Michael, that was how it had been done.

If they'd killed him—that's what I was here to find out. Thankfully, the waves brought me back. We were taking them beam on, Wilem throttling up their faces before they could break, then de-

AMATES, MANU, AND WILEM (*FRONT TO BACK*) IN THE LONGBOAT ON THE ARAFURA SEA.

celerating to minimize the downward slam on the other side. He'd
been bottle-fed on these waters, and he knew what he was doing,
but the boat was becoming uncontrollable. It was just growing
light; in Asmat you travel with the tides, and we'd left the vil-
lage of Atsj at 3:30 a.m. The moon had been huge and full and
so bright it was a dull sun in the darkness, making shadows off
the trees and the bow waves silver. The Southern Cross had been
directly overhead, as sharp as a string of Christmas lights. Small
bats had jerked back and forth over the boat. Now, though, we
were getting hammered on the open sea, with water pouring over
the gunwales, and the beauty of the night had given way to terror.
I crawled forward, reached under a plastic tarp, fumbled blindly
for my duffel, found it, found the Ziploc bag holding the satellite
phone, slipped it into my pocket, and was soaked by another wave.

I hadn't wanted to bring the phone, but at the last minute I'd
thought how stupid it would be to die for want of a call. Had Mi-
chael Rockefeller had even a radio when his boat overturned in
1961, he never would have disappeared. It was as simple as that.

We were crossing the mouth of the Betsj River, off the south-
west coast of New Guinea. Here, north of Australia, the Arafura
rolls across a thousand miles and then hits the swamps of Indo-
nesian Papua. Where the water ends and the land begins is hard
to know. The Arafura is the color of pale opal, heavy with silt
carried by a thousand brown rivers that course from central New
Guinea's great mountains, jagged, steep sawteeth reaching sixteen
thousand feet. The peaks trap the heavy, moisture-laden tropical
clouds, and every rivulet feeds another and another, and they grow
larger and intertwine and curve as the land flattens, and it flattens
quickly, suddenly, and for a hundred miles to the sea this land is
without a hill, a rock, or even a pebble.

The Arafura is an ocean of fifteen-foot tides, epic shifts of wa-
ter, an invisible swelling that daily slides into this flat swamp. It
inundates the land, which becomes a netherworld of water and

trees through which you can navigate a canoe, as if you're float-
ing within a hydroponic garden. Mangroves with tangled, mossy
roots hang with vines and epiphytes. Stands of bamboo rise high
and tight in green clusters. The fronds of prehistoric-looking nipa
palms are thirty feet long and rustle in the breeze, their roots
twisted and black and bulging. Towering ironwood trees grow out
of water as brown as a strong cup of tea. When the tide runs out,
it leaves behind great swaths of glistening mud so fine you sink up
to your knees if you step in it. The mud feels as soft as liquid satin.
And cool to your skin. It's alive with wiggling mudskippers and
tiny yellow crabs the size of your fingernails.

From above, in an airplane, it is nothing but a flat, impenetra-
ble green carpet cut with the interconnected veins of brown water
snaking in every direction. From a boat or the banks of a river,
the land is so flat the sky is always huge overhead, changing, full
of layers and shapes, patches of blue mixed with angry pewter-
colored clouds. Torrential curtains of rain fall from the sky, so
much water in drops so big, hammering with such force, you can't
believe the air could hold it all. Often the sun is shining and it's
raining at the same time. It's hot. Humid. Sometimes glimmer-
ingly bright. Quiet, the sound of leaves rustling and water trick-
ling, the plop of a fish jumping or a cockatoo's screech or the dip
of a paddle. At night the stars are bold and bright, the Milky Way
overhead as swirly white and thick as tapioca pudding. And even
on those wonderfully clear nights heat lightning flashes along the
horizon, as if somewhere out there big things are happening, just
not here. The Arafura is a whole, big sea; sometimes it's flat and
still and almost blue, and sometimes it's wild and angry, a steady
hot wind pushing it against the opposing current of river mouths
three miles wide, creating a boiling turbulence. It feels primal.
Biblical. Distant from everything.

Asmat is, in its way, a perfect place. Everything you could pos-
sibly need is here. It's a petri dish, teaming with shrimp and crabs

and fish, clams and mussels and snails. Crocodiles fifteen feet long prowl its riverbanks, and jet-black iguanas sun on uprooted trees. In the jungle there are wild pig, the furry, possumlike cuscus, and the ostrichlike cassowary. And sago palm, whose pith can be pounded into a white, edible starch and which hosts the larvae of the Capricorn beetle, both key sources of nutrition. The rivers are navigable highways. There are flocks of brilliant red-and-green parrots. Hornbills with five-inch beaks and blue necks. White sulfur-crested cockatoo and coal-black king cockatoo sporting elaborate crests.

And secrets, spirits, laws, and customs born of men and women who have been walled off by ocean, mountains, mud, and jungle for longer than anyone knows.

Until fifty years ago, there were no wheels here. No steel or iron, not even any paper. Today there's still not a single road or automobile. In its ten thousand square miles, there's but one airstrip, and outside of the main "city" of Agats, there isn't a single cell tower.

The waves slammed and the boat rolled, and I tried to form a plan. The craft was fiberglass; presumably it would float. Would I be able to climb anywhere out of the water enough to use the phone? Who would I call, and what would they be able to do if I reached them back in the United States in what was the middle of their night? For that matter, habituated to my cell phone, I didn't even know most people's numbers by heart anymore. We were nearing the southern mouth of the river, close to shore, but there wasn't really any shore—just flooded coastline and swamp. Could I climb one of the flimsy mangroves? And craziest of all, this was the exact spot that Rockefeller had been trying to navigate fifty years earlier.

He was twenty-three years old, just out of Harvard, the privileged son of New York governor Nelson Rockefeller, seven months into the adventure of a lifetime that had transformed him from clean-cut student to scruffy photographer and art collector. One

moment his boat was being tossed by the waves, just as ours was, and the next it was upside down. And then Rockefeller had swum for shore and was gone. Vanished, no trace of him or his body ever found, despite a two-week search involving ships, airplanes, helicopters, and thousands of locals prowling the coasts and jungle swamps. The fact that such a simple, banal thing had happened to him made what was happening to us feel all the more real. There'd be no foreboding music. One bad wave and I'd be clinging to a boat in the middle of nowhere.

The official cause of Rockefeller's death was drowning, but there had long been a multitude of rumors. *He had been kidnapped and kept prisoner. He had gone native and was hiding out in the jungle by choice. He'd been consumed by sharks or crocodiles. He'd made it to shore, only to be killed and eaten by the local Asmat headhunters.* The story had grown, had become mythical. There had been an off-Broadway play about him, a novel, and a popular rock song, even a three-part television series in the 1980s hosted by Leonard Nimoy. I'd been fascinated with the story ever since I first saw a photo of Michael. In it he is bearded, kneeling, holding his thirty-five-millimeter camera under the close eyes of natives in what was then Dutch New Guinea, while working on a film in the highlands of the Great Baliem Valley. That film, *Dead Birds,* had been a groundbreaking and controversial ethnographic examination of a barely contacted, Stone Age culture that engaged in constant ritual warfare. The mountains, the mist, the naked men yelling and screaming and attacking each other with spears and bows and arrows, had fascinated and entranced me, as had the whole idea of contact between people from dramatically different worlds. In my twenties, I'd tried to get to what was then called Irian Jaya, but it was too expensive for my young budget, and I'd ended up, briefly, in Borneo instead. I had a photograph that mirrors the one of Rockefeller—we are about the same age, and I am holding my camera up to the eyes of a Dayak child in Indonesian Borneo.

I was a half-Jewish middle-class mutt with a public education, not a blue-blooded scion, but Rockefeller's journey resonated with me. I knew what he was doing and why he was there, at least in part. It wasn't just to collect what was then called "primitive art," but to taste, smell, see, touch that world for himself. An older, less "civilized" world, one as different from his own as it was possible to find. An encounter with the Other. And I wondered if he, like me, wanted to know what the Other could say about him, about us. Whether he wanted not just to interact with it, but to see if these naked men whose pursuit of sacred heads that resulted in spectacular carvings might be a mirror of a younger, more elemental self, a self before all the complications of technology and civilization. To see if there might even be something Eden-like about it—a world before Eve tasted the apple. To see himself, Michael Rockefeller, before privilege and social convention. Were they the same, or different?

And how could he make his "primitive art"–collecting father prouder than by going to its source and plunging in deeper than the forceful governor and presidential candidate had ever dreamed? Michael wouldn't just acquire primitive art from galleries or flea markets, but collect it from the creators themselves, understand it, introduce a whole new group of artists to the world.

I spent hours looking at that photo, wondering what Michael had seen and felt in Asmat, wondering what really happened to him, wondering if I might be able to solve the mystery. That he had been kidnapped or had run away didn't make sense. If he had drowned, well, that was that, except he'd been attached to flotation aids and no trace of his body had ever been found. As for sharks, despite their fearsome reputation, they rarely attacked men in these waters. Which meant that if he hadn't perished during his swim, there had to be more. Someone had to know something. And that "more" was the nightmare of every traveler—to be drawn to a place from which you never returned. There had to be

some collision, some colossal misunderstanding. The Asmat were warriors drenched in blood, but Dutch colonial authorities and missionaries had been in the area for almost a decade by the time Michael disappeared, and the Asmat had never killed a white. If he had been murdered, it struck to the heart of a clash between Westerners and Others that had been ongoing ever since Columbus first sailed to the New World. I found it compelling that in this remote corner of the world the Rockefellers and their power and money had been impotent, had come up with nothing. How was that even possible?

Michael's disappearance was a mystery, and mysteries by their nature are open wounds, events without closure. We long to have answers, and the idea of vanishing is particularly unsettling. The great existential questions, after all, are about who we are, where we come from, where we end up. Ceremonies, from birthdays to weddings to graduations to funerals, are rituals that address those questions in a public and symbolic way, a way that lets us process them, deal with them, accept the passing changes of life and time. But Michael Rockefeller had vanished. Though his family had declared him dead, had held a memorial service for him, and maintained a gravesite on the family compound, there had been no body; no one could say with certainty what had happened to him, and no newspaper had ever run an obituary. A ghost was the spirit of a man or woman who'd died but couldn't move on, a death that had been unsettled. As a fellow traveler, a journalist who'd traveled frequently to the fringes of the world, who'd taken the bus across Afghanistan and encountered angry, jacked-up soldiers in the Congo and been in a hundred other crazy situations, I knew something had gone wrong, and I was unsettled, bothered, by the fact that we'd never known what. Michael Rockefeller was a sort of ghost. His twin sister, Mary, had spent her lifetime struggling with the grief and loss and lack of closure, a journey that had taken her from psychotherapy to healing ceremonies. Solving

the mystery, I decided, wouldn't be just solving one of the world's most famous cold cases; it would be performing a ritual, telling the end of the story, bringing closure to a life.

I started poking around in Dutch colonial archives and the records of Dutch missionaries, and one document led to another. I found more than I'd ever imagined. After the ships and planes and helicopters had gone home, new information surfaced in the weeks immediately after Michael disappeared, and a series of new investigations had taken place. There were pages and pages of reports, cables, and letters discussing the case and the events leading up to it, sent by the Dutch government, Asmat-speaking missionaries on the ground, and Catholic Church authorities, and none of it had ever been made public. Men who had been key participants in those investigations had remained silent for fifty years, but they were still alive, and I found that they were finally willing to talk.

CRASH. ROLL. The wind was picking up, and even though we were nearing shore, Wilem couldn't find a rhythm. The waves were too choppy and steep and fast and close together. Wilem and Amates Owun, my translator and guide, conferred, then Amates said in his painstakingly slow English: "Many boats have problems here in the winter. But there is a bus here, under the water."

"A bus?" Half the time I couldn't figure out what Amates was talking about. It wasn't just his limited English, but his Asmat mind, which was privy to a world I could never enter or even know about. In the main Asmat town of Agats was a small but wondrous museum packed with ancestor poles, shields, drums, spears, paddles, skulls, and masks. At night, to me, it was dark and locked tight, but to the Asmat the museum was filled with the cacophony of the drumming and chanting spirits who were embodied in the carvings there. So, a bus? There wasn't even a car or road within hundreds of miles, much less a bus.

"A bus, like with wheels that carries people?" I said.

Amates pointed toward the water with the stub of his right forefinger—the first two inches had been bitten off in a fight the month before. His face was narrow, his eyes close-set, with huge lips and the high cheekbones that characterize many Asmat. He was missing a few teeth, and those visible were brown from chewing betel nut. He was six feet tall, as thin as wire. I looked where he pointed and saw waves and sky and heavy black clouds and patches of blue, but no bus.

"Yes," he said. "The Bimpu Bis. It is a big bus that lives under the water right here, and when people have trouble it comes up and they ride it to shore. Many people have been saved by it. Michael Rockefeller did not know about this bus."

I lit a clove cigarette—we were all smoking incessantly—and gripped the satellite phone in my pocket like it was a talisman. I had no idea what Amates was talking about. I was shivering in the spray, and hungry—a diet of rice and stray bits of fish was never enough calories. I would do anything for a steak. My feet and legs were covered with red bites. We turned toward shore, surfing fast with the waves, and a narrow opening in the wall of swampy green appeared. The moment we entered the cut, the wind fell away. The water smoothed. I smelled smoke and piss, the smell of men. We rounded a slight bend and another hundred yards ahead stood eight houses—palm-thatched roofs and walls, ten feet over the water on slender poles, each with a three-foot-wide veranda. Women, some naked from the waist, and children perched on one, men gathered on the one next to it. No one said anything; there was no greeting. It was always like this when I came to a village on my first trip to Asmat, no words exchanged as we slid up to the hut with the men. We tied up, I grabbed a pouch of loose-leaf tobacco and some rolling papers and clambered onto a porch made of split pieces of bamboo fastened with rattan. There wasn't a nail in the place. No running water. No power, no connection to anywhere else in the universe except by human touch and the distance over

which a voice could shout. It was silent, only the sound of birds and those voices. The men on the veranda were shirtless and wearing battered gym shorts. I shook their hands, leathery and tough and dry, and they touched their hearts, a gesture picked up from Indonesia's Muslims. Wet and dirty and tired, I plunked down and passed out the tobacco. We sat and smoked and stared into the new morning green. I had a thousand questions to ask, but no way to ask them.

4

February 20, 1957

ON FEBRUARY 20, 1957, in a city of concrete and steel six thousand times bigger than the largest hamlet in Asmat, a village big man named Nelson Rockefeller introduced the world to a new kind of seeing. Temperatures in New York City peaked that day at thirty-seven degrees, and Rockefeller was dressed in the height of New York tribal finery: black tie. He was forty-nine years old, square-jawed, and ambitious, the grandson of Standard Oil founder

MICHAEL ROCKEFELLER AND HIS FATHER, NELSON, AT MICHAEL'S GRADUATION FROM HARVARD, JUNE 1960.

John D. Rockefeller. At Nelson's birth, which was announced on the front page of the *New York Times,* John D. was the richest man on earth, with a fortune estimated at $900 million. Nelson's wealth and political and social influence would be hard to comprehend for most Americans, let alone a tribe of hunter-gatherers. In one year he would become the governor of New York. In two he would run for the presidency. In 1974 he would become vice president of the United States under Gerald Ford.

He had a Down East patrician drawl and was known for clasping the hands of voters and saying "Hiya, fella." He "exuded an exuberant self-assurance so unshakable that it must have been instilled from birth," wrote his former press secretary Joseph Persico. "Not a social arrogance, but rather an almost child-like openness which he assumed before anyone or anything." It seemed like he and his family owned half of Manhattan. On that day in February, inside a newly renovated, Rockefeller-owned, four-story townhouse with elegantly curving bay windows at 15 West Fifty-Fourth Street—just off Fifth Avenue in the heart of midtown and directly behind the Museum of Modern Art—guests began arriving at 8:30 p.m. to a private reception heralding the first exhibit of the Museum of Primitive Art, which would open to the public the following day.

The sleek, modern, and minimalist space, which one critic said was "so tasteful and restrained" that it "hardly seems like a museum at all," couldn't have contrasted more with the objects it displayed or the people celebrating its opening. Some of the most powerful men and women in the arts and society were on the guest list. There was Rene d'Harnoncourt, the director of the Museum of Modern Art. Robert Woods Bliss, whose fifty-four-acre estate in Washington, DC, Dumbarton Oaks, is now a museum and library belonging to Harvard University. New York socialite Gertrud Mellon. Henry Luce, who founded *Time* and *Life* magazines. Henry Ochs Sulzberger, the owner of the *New York Times.* And of

course, Nelson's nineteen-year-old son Michael. The things they were celebrating came from a world away. A carved paddle from Easter Island. The elongated, exaggerated face of a wooden mask from Nigeria. Aztec and Mayan pre-Columbian stone figures from Mexico and Hopi Kachina dolls and an engraved reindeer bone from the Pyrenees, all created by nameless craftsmen in the nooks and crannies of the world. Around these objects were no ethnographic dioramas, no depictions of African huts or canoes and fishing nets, and no maps. They rested atop stark white cylinders and cubes, illuminated by track lighting against white walls, a "severely simple setting," wrote the *New York Times*. As everything about their presentation said, they were to be viewed as works of art in and of themselves.

As the guests nibbled on canapés and sipped their wine, Nelson reminded them that his new museum was "the first . . . of its kind in the world"—the first museum dedicated exclusively to primitive art. While a frigid wind swept up Fifth Avenue outside, d'Harnoncourt and Luce marveled at the beauty of form and line and listened to Nelson speak. Museums of history and ethnology, he said, had long shown objects like the ones here, but he reminded his guests that they'd always done so to document their studies of indigenous cultures. "It is our purpose to supplement their achievement," he said with Rockefellerian assurance. "We do not want to establish primitive art as a separate kind of category, but rather to integrate it, with all its missing variety, into what is already known to the arts of man. Our aim will always be to select objects of outstanding beauty whose rare quality is the equal of works shown in other museums of art throughout the world, and to exhibit them so that everyone may enjoy them in the fullest measure."

IT WAS a bold proclamation, the word choice explicit. Ever since Western explorers had begun conquering the world they had re-

turned with souvenirs, which they displayed in special rooms or curiosity cabinets. A description of one of those cabinets in 1599 lists its contents: "an African charm made of teeth, a felt cloak from Arabia, an Indian stone ax, a charm made of monkey teeth." To travel is to want to remember and to acquire. It is from the Latin "to recall" that we get the word "souvenir," as every airport trinket shop knows well; I haven't yet been on a trip from which I've not returned bearing coveted objects. My house is adorned with blowpipes from Borneo and Buddhist charms from Thailand and an opium pipe from China, and you can be sure that every European sailor and his captain from Columbus onward tucked exotic keepsakes into their pockets and the holds of their ships. But that's just how they were seen—as exotic trinkets. The native people of Africa, the Americas, Asia, and Oceania were unformed savages, people without religion, and the objects they created were anything but art. Every seed, leaf, and plant collected on Captain James Cook's third voyage, for instance, was recorded individually, while most of the human artifacts weren't listed at all. Ethnographic objects in the collection of Sir Hans Sloane, which formed the basis of the British Museum, were classed merely as "Miscellanies."

At the turn of the twentieth century, a handful of Western artists became deeply influenced by the primitive. Paul Gauguin's paintings of naked Tahitians shocked the world. Pablo Picasso began depicting the masks he found in Parisian flea markets, and his cubist figures resembled the rough, exaggerated forms of indigenous African carvings. But artists like Gauguin and Picasso were radicals by their nature. It was one thing for a Western artist to be inspired by "the primitive," quite another for the primitive objects themselves to be exhibited as works of art equivalent to a da Vinci or a Matisse.

THE STORY OF ART is as much the story of the men and women who collect it, and there were no collectors more important than the

Rockefellers. Nelson Rockefeller grew up surrounded by art. His father, John D. Rockefeller Jr., loved porcelain; in fifty years he would spend more than $10 million to amass what some critics called the most important collection of its kind in the world. His mother, Abby Aldrich Rockefeller, had a passion for Asian and French Impressionists, and her and John D. Jr.'s mansion on West Fifty-Fourth Street overflowed with it—along with medieval tapestries and Chinese porcelains and a rotating display of works by French and American modernists. The Rockefeller influence cannot be overstated. Abby's passion led to the creation of the New York Museum of Modern Art, which opened in 1929, nine days after the crash of Wall Street. As a child, Nelson was schooled in art like most boys are schooled in baseball, an education that included trips to the studios of prominent modern artists. When he wrote his mother a note from Dartmouth in 1927 about one of those journeys, she replied: "If you start to cultivate your taste and eye so young, you ought to be very good at it by the time you can afford to collect."

In 1930 Nelson and his new bride, Mary Todhunter Clark, received a $20,000 wedding gift from John D. and a honeymoon journey around the world that lasted nine months. As would happen with Michael thirty years later, Rockefeller employees paved the way, setting up connections at the highest levels of government wherever they went. In India, Nelson even met with Mahatma Gandhi. On that journey he bought a knife in Sumatra adorned with a sculpted head and human hair, a purchase that began his lifelong love for primitive art. "I started to see art as widely varying expressions of individuals," he once said, "individuals from all parts of the world and from all ages, with strong feelings and great creative capacities to express their feelings. No longer was my appreciation confined to classical forms of art as taught in our schools and shown in our great museums." Appointed the second president of the Museum of Modern Art that year, he at-

tempted to persuade the museum to mount an exhibit of primitive art. Nelson was ahead of his time, however, and the trustees rejected the idea.

Twenty years later, Nelson had surpassed his parents. Picasso, Braque, and Léger canvases and Matisse murals hung in his New York apartment. The gardens at the family estate in Pocantico Hills, named Kykuit, twenty-eight miles north of midtown Manhattan, bloomed with Calders, Giacomettis, Noguchis, and even an Aphrodite once thought to be the work of Praxiteles. The inside, said Persico, "had the ambience of a museum after hours. George Washington gazed down from a Gilbert Stuart original, and in an arched window stood a full-sized male nude, the *Age of Bronze*, Rodin's first major work. One half expected to see red ropes across the chairs to ward off actual use." At the Rockefeller summer home in Seal Harbor, Maine, Nelson maintained a separate gallery in a former coal wharf renovated by the architect Philip Johnson, full of contemporary painting and sculpture. Contemporary Latin American art filled his ranch in Venezuela.

In 1955 the Museum of Modern Art held a photographic exhibit called *The Family of Man.* "Everywhere," wrote Carl Sandburg in the show's catalog, "the sun, moon and stars, the climates and weathers, have meanings for people. Though meanings vary, we are all alike in all countries and tribes in trying to read what sky, land and sea say to us. Alike and ever alike we are on all continents in the need of love, food, clothing, work, speech, worship, sleep, games, dancing, fun. From tropics to arctics humanity lives with these needs so alike, so inexorably alike."

Times were changing. The arts, politics, culture—there was no way to separate them, and what was happening in the world of art reflected what was happening in global politics. People who had existed to be dominated, converted, enslaved, and exploited in far-flung colonies were asserting their right to independence.

The British surrendered India in 1947. The Netherlands turned over all of the Indonesian archipelago, except for its half of New Guinea, in 1949. The Belgian Congo became free in 1960, Kenya three years later. As Nelson Rockefeller's new museum opened, the 1960s were about to explode forth: The civil rights movement. Feminism. Vatican II and the liberalization of the Catholic Church. The Peace Corps. A shift in thinking about those mythical savages was perfectly captured by the timing of the museum's opening. New York art critic Hilton Kramer's review of the Museum of Primitive Art's first exhibition, based almost entirely on Nelson's collection, reads like a manifesto for the end of colonialism.

"Far more striking than any common denominator of form or craft or cultural origin," he wrote, "is the staggering abundance of artistic ideas and the vitality which marks the execution of every piece. It shatters even some very sophisticated assumptions about the meaning of what is primitive; for this writer, at least, it shatters the term itself. . . . One is suddenly appalled that rather than telling us anything, it only masks our ignorance. It reminds us of the extent to which our conception of history has locked out some of the most brilliant civilizations. . . . It underscores the imperiousness of our Western sensibilities, and exposes a kind of historical provincialism."

There is something darker, though, and ironic, about this love of the primitive. Who knows what inner cravings and demons, passions, and curiosities lay behind a Michelangelo or a Matisse or even a Hockney? Van Gogh killed himself. Picasso had an insatiable sexual appetite. Who cares? We can like the colors. We can admire the form and line. A Western artist's personal life might inform his painting, but it's an individual expression to which we may or may not relate, and we can enjoy the painting or sculpture, or not, without caring about or knowing the artist's intention.

Primitive art, however, is mostly sacred art, the individual artist

subsumed in the symbolic language that is instantly understood by the community and the religious power carried within it. For the creators of primitive art there is no separation of form and function. An Asmat shield might be carved to stop an arrow, but the penis protruding from the top, the fruit bat wings or boar tusks etched into it, have spiritual utility and meaning, and the spirit of a known man lives within it. For the Western collector, the Asmat shield is a thing of beauty; for the Asmat, it is a thing of supernatural power. An Asmat might look at a shield and drop with fear. "The ancestor's spirit lives in the shield," wrote Tobias Schneebaum, a writer and artist who spent more than five years in Asmat, "and is a presence that endows the living relative not only with fearlessness and courage in the face of all odds, but also with the omnipotence to overpower the enemy and become the victor."

Nelson Rockefeller recognized the beauty and form of the Sumatran knife that he acquired on his honeymoon. With his refined eye—and to his credit—he saw a work of art. But he was seeing only its surface. A human head, genuine human hair—those indicated something far deeper going on, a meaning vastly different for the Sumatran who'd made it than for Nelson Rockefeller.

As primitive art moved from ethnographic curio to art in and of itself, to be appreciated on a white pedestal under track lighting in a Manhattan townhouse, it was disassociated from its original meaning and purpose. Nelson himself told an interviewer in 1965: "My interest in primitive art is not an intellectual one. It is strictly esthetic. Don't ask me whether this bowl I am holding is a household implement or a ritual vessel. . . . I could not care less! I enjoy the form, the color, the texture, the shape. I am not in the least interested in the anthropological or the ethnological end of it. That is why I founded the museum: to show that the art of primitive people could be treated on purely esthetic and formal grounds."

Those who began swarming into the exotic world, however,

were not just acquiring inanimate objects, but walking into something else entirely: a potentially dangerous world of spirits who could make them sick or even kill them, of secrets and meanings whose language they didn't speak, whose symbols they didn't understand, and where life and death, literally, hung in the balance.

IN SCIENCE FICTION stories there's often some mad scientist who creates a portal between our world and a distant world through which our epic hero travels. Unexpected things happen when those doors are opened. So it was that evening in 1957. Nelson Rockefeller had thrown open a door to a distant swamp in New Guinea, a world where spirits roamed and there were no boundaries between life and death, between the I and the Other, between man as eater and man as food—a world representing as alternative and parallel a universe to midtown Manhattan as it's possible to have. Some people (most people probably) are content to look at an Easter Island paddle or a Nigerian mask on a pedestal. Or to look at something their father puts on a pedestal. But not everyone, especially a boy who had a lot to prove to a father with a pair of very big shoes.

Michael Rockefeller was just nineteen years old on that opening night, and it's easy to imagine the power the event had for him. His powerful father's pride and joy over the new museum, the strange and exotic beauty and pull of the objects, the cream of New York's elite admiring them. Across thousands of miles, forces were being unleashed and connecting lines drawn. It's hard not to wonder if Nelson Rockefeller ever regretted the words he wrote Robert Goldwater, the museum's director, the next day: "Last night was a really perfect evening—the realization of a dream which all of us have shared. The creation of this new museum and the association with you which it has afforded are the source of infinite pleasure and happiness to me."

5

.

December 1957

SEVEN MONTHS AFTER Nelson Rockefeller opened the Museum of Primitive Art, Pip, Dombai, Su, Kokai, Wawar, and Pakai dipped their paddles in the Arafura Sea and stroked long and smooth. Dip and stroke. Dip and stroke. They were united by complex family ties and years of practice, and their paddles moved as one.

Their dugout canoe was barely twelve inches wide and eighteen deep, tipsy and unstable, and yet they rowed in a line standing up, balancing on toughened, splayed feet that had never worn shoes. Their paddles were ten feet long, with narrow, short, oval

CANOES FROM THE VILLAGE OF OMADESEP ON THE FARETSJ RIVER.

blades and long handles tapering to sharp points. From the tops
of some dangled the white feathers of a sulfur-crested cockatoo,
the badge of a successful headhunter. Carved about three-quarters
of the way up each of the paddle's handles, right at eye level, was
the small image of a dead relative's face. With every stroke, each
rower saw the face on his paddle and remembered the death of his
brother, uncle, cousin. Their canoe had a penis—its bow—carved
with an upturned face: a dynamic, beautifully rendered image of a
man. The canoe bore his name.

They carried in their canoes lumps of dried sago flour wrapped
in banana leaves, bows seven feet long that shot barbed bamboo
arrows without fletching, long spears with a multitude of points,
and axes with heads of stone and steel. The stone came from the
highlands along ancient trading routes, the steel from Dutch mis-
sionaries who had begun to filter into Asmat in 1952. In the damp
swamps and rivers the rowers had no way to make fire, so they
brought it with them: in the stern of each canoe smoldered a few
hot coals on a bed of mud.

Dip and stroke. Dip and stroke. And with every stroke the pad-
dles struck the sides of the canoe like a drumbeat. A heartbeat.

They were all from the village of Otsjanep, and soon most of
them would be dead.

If they felt any uneasiness, they wouldn't have shown it. Mov-
ing south with them were 118 other men in eleven canoes, all
from the neighboring village of Omadesep. Some hamlets in the
swamps and rivers had a hundred people, some less, some a few
more. But Otsjanep and Omadesep were each more than a thou-
sand people strong. They were big, powerful, deeply traditional
communities on parallel rivers just a few miles apart as the crow
flies. The men in each village fought together, killed together,
protected their wives together—sometimes even traded them for
a night. Their lives were so closely bound to village and jeu that
they were more single organism than a collection of individuals.

But to say they were fearless would be wrong. The Asmat lived in a complex world of spirits kept in balance by elaborate ceremonies and constant reciprocal violence. No death just *happened*. Even sickness came at the hand of the spirits. Every villager could see them, talk to them. There were spirits in rattan and in the mangrove and sago trees, in the whirlpools, in their own fingers and noses. There was their world, and there was the world of Safan, the realm of the souls and kingdom of the ancestors across the seas. The worlds were equally real, sickness and death kept in check by constant appeasement and scaring of the spirits of their ancestors back to beyond the sea where they belonged, where they could do no harm. The spirits often came at night, and to keep them away the Asmat used the skulls of their ancestors as pillows.

The canoes of Pip, Dombai, Su, Kokai, Wawar, and Pakai and the men from Omadesep were bunched together, slipping over the water almost as though they were part of it, as naturally as men walk along a path. Their canoes, their paddles, their ornaments, everything came from the jungle. Sometimes they rowed in silence, and sometimes they broke into song, each word long and slow, drawn out, dirgelike.

Seabird coming
How are you coming?
You can help keep me company.

"Wo!" shouted Wawar, for emphasis, as the six paddles drummed on the flanks of the canoe. "Wo!"

We believe you
Everyone believes you
Because you live in the sea.
Where are you coming from?
I will follow you.

They made fun of each other. They joked about women; half their battles concerned them, villages often came to blows over them, and warfare was in part linked to winning their favor. Although an outsider might struggle to see even the mouths of small creeks, they noticed everything. In an unending geography of green sameness that held no seasons, not even divided into rainy and dry, they knew whose sago stands were whose, where the territory for Otsjanep, for instance, ended and that of Omadesep began.

They had a rich oral tradition, which they'd learned as boys sitting at the knees of their fathers in the long, smoky jeu. As hunter-gatherers in this world without seasons, they knew no time. Sometimes they drummed and sang all night and slept most of the day, sometimes they fell asleep at dusk. They paddled their canoes according to the tides. Pakai mentioned the village of Biwar Laut, and they remembered when Biwar had stolen two women from Otsjanep, and they'd killed men in return, the "they" being their fathers, brothers, brothers-in-law, uncles. That had been thirty years ago, but it might have been yesterday. At the mouth of the Jawor River, barely a perceptible cut on the muddy beach, they all shuddered a little, for the Jawor was a powerful place full of spirits.

And they all knew some version of the story of Desoipitsj and Biwiripitsj, the first brothers in the world, who taught them how to headhunt and how to butcher a human body and how to use that meat and the skull to make new men from boys and to keep life flowing into the world. As an Asmat creation myth, its origins are unknown, as is an easy explanation for the origins of cannibalism itself, a complex subject that has often provoked fierce debate among anthropologists. Why have some cultures practiced something that others see as one of the most fundamental taboos in human society? Cause and effect, the chicken and the egg, can be hard to pin down, but in Asmat, at least, food—especially food rich in fat and protein—has never been abundant or regular. Besides the crocodile, there are no large animals to eat or hunt—even wild pigs are not

indigenous to New Guinea. There is no gardening, and nowhere to go—when the first humans arrived on the island forty thousand years ago, it was the end of the line. The Asmat competed fiercely with each other, village against village, for access to sago and fishing grounds; the anthropologist David Eyde believed that all Asmat warfare resulted from that existential struggle. In a study of cannibalism across a hundred traditional cultures, the anthropologist Peggy Reeves Sanday found that in those who practiced some form of anthrophagy, "ecological stress" was present in 91 percent of them. Even at its peak, the murder rate in Asmat was hardly enough to provide large amounts of nutrients to the population as a whole, but it may have been important to the war leaders and their families. Humans create myth and story to bring meaning to their lives, to explain their lives, and over thousands of years the Asmat created story and ritual that transcended basic nutrition or eating and provided both genesis and justification for their actions. By the 1950s, Asmat cannibalism was seen as a by-product of headhunting and its sacred rituals, rather than as its primary purpose.

Linked with Asmat cannibalism was a whole consciousness, a world of opposites, and the story of Desoipitsj and Biwiripitsj reveals the close link between victim and perpetrator, the I and the Other, in Asmat. Recorded by Gerard Zegwaard, a Dutch priest, in the 1950s, it is *the* detailed account of the rituals associated with headhunting and cannibalism. The story had fueled my visions of Michael's death, for if he had been killed, it would have closely followed the tale's script.

DESOIPITSJ WAS OLDER and unable to hunt, so Biwiripitsj had to do all the work. One day the boy brought home a wild pig. He cut off the head and thrust a cassowary bone dagger into its throat, pinning the head to the floor. "Bah, a pig's head is but a pig's head," said Desoipitsj, watching. "Why not replace it with a human head? That would be something, I think."

Biwiripitsj didn't agree, and anyway, where was he to get a human head?

Desoipitsj was fixated on the idea and said, "Well, you can have my head." After a lot of cajoling, he convinced Biwiripitsj to kill him with a spear, cut into his throat with a bamboo knife, and press the head forward until the vertebrae cracked. Even as Biwiripitsj removed his brother's head, Desoipitsj continued to speak, describing the correct technique of butchering humans and initiating boys into manhood, instructions that had to be followed to the letter. Time and space shift in this story, for it is also a charter, a set of instructions on how all Asmat men and women were to act in the future, even though there weren't yet any other people in the world.

When he returned with the men from a successful headhunt, Biwiripitsj blew a bamboo hunting horn to announce their triumphant return.

"How did you do?" the women yelled from the riverbanks. "What did you accomplish?"

"I, Biwiripitsj, have been to the Islands River this night. I killed a man, a big man. The flesh lies in the canoe."

"What is his name?" the women called.

"His name is Desoipitsj."

The women cheered and danced and jumped and howled as the warriors in their canoes paddled fast toward the shore.

Once in the jeu, Biwiripitsj had to sit on the floor, his head lowered in a position of shame. He was then given the name of the victim, his older brother Desoipitsj—the *nao juus*, or decapitation name. Later, having become the man he had killed, he could be welcomed back into the victim's family as if he were the victim himself.

The mother's oldest brother then held the head over the fire just long enough to scorch the hair. Mixed with blood collected from the victim's decapitation, the fluid was smeared on the head, shoulders, and body of the initiate, cementing the identity between him and the victim.

The boy, now named Desoipitsj, told them to paint his body

with red ochre, wet ash, and chalk. His hair was lengthened with sago leaf fibers, a piece of mother of pearl hung on his forehead. On the back of his head were placed two tassels of black cassowary feathers; in his septum was placed a nose pin from carved pig bone. His arms, wrists, calves, and ankles were wrapped in belts of finely split rattan, and in one arm belt was placed a dagger carved from the thigh of a cassowary. Later, when he had become a man and had killed other men, the dagger could be made from a human thigh or crocodile jaw. From his abdomen hung a triton shell, around his hips a sago leaf apron, and down his back a bamboo plate. He was now dressed as a man.

Then Desoipitsj gave instructions for what the initiate's maternal uncles had to do with the decapitated head. They were balancing the world, becoming the Other.

The skull was painted with ash, ochre, and chalk and decorated with tassels of cassowary feathers and beads. The nose was filled with resin, and a net was drawn over the whole head to facilitate attaching the ornaments. The decorated head was placed between the spread legs of the initiate. This head, the fruit of a man, would nourish his genitals, the place from which new men came, and ensure his maturity, just as the fruit nourished the tree by making new trees that men ate. The head would remain for two or three days between his legs, and the initiate had to stare at it the entire time.

After a few days, Desoipitsj instructed the villagers how to adorn themselves and how to paint the canoes in stripes of chalk and ochre. Then everyone boarded them. The boy being initiated stood in the canoe of his relatives with the skull in front of him. As they drummed and sang and paddled toward the sea—to the west where the sun set and the ancestors lived—he leaned on a stick acting like an exhausted old man. The farther west they traveled, the weaker and older he got, until he was leaning on the shoulder of an uncle. Finally, he was so old that he died and collapsed onto the bottom of the canoe.

One of his mother's uncles then immersed him in the sea with

the skull. Lifted out, his ornaments were removed and placed in a magic mat. He was reborn, a child of women now born anew as a man, from men this time.

While singing, the men in the canoe carrying the initiate turned back toward land, to the east, to where the sun rises, to the land of the living. First the young man acted like a newborn baby, and then as a child who didn't know the names of the river, the trees, anything. Gradually he learned more, and at each tributary his name was called and he answered with a bamboo horn. Returning to the village, he spent the night with his family and was again decorated head to foot. After resting awhile, the family gathered sago in the jungle. Then more dancing and sago pounding, and the skull was hung in the center of the men's house. Finally, the initiate left the jeu, carrying the magic mat under his arm and in his hand the richly decorated skull. The men carried shields, which they pumped up and down while they sang. They danced again, and this time the initiate joined the men, swinging the skull. The songs that had been sung during the preparation of the head and during the sago pounding were repeated.

And once more the skull of Desoipitsj emphatically ordered that in the future all should obey his instructions.

IN MANY WAYS, the Asmat world at the time of European contact was reversed, a mirror image of every taboo of the West. In parts of Asmat, men had sex with each other. They occasionally shared each other's wives. In bonding rituals, they sometimes drank each other's urine. They could perform acts of deep intimacy and submission; once all of the men of the village of Tambor sucked the penis of the chief of Basim. They killed their neighbors, and they hunted human heads and ate human flesh, and there was nothing strange about this to Pip and his brothers. It is from the Latin word for "woods," *silva,* that we get the word "savage," and the Asmat men from Otsjanep paddling that day on the Arafura

might as well have been characters in some European medieval fantasy—men who, in the words of historian Kirkpatrick Sale, lived in woods full of "monsters and hell creatures that abduct women and devour children; of whole races of accursed near human peoples who are animalistic and savage . . . a huge, powerful hairy figure, carrying a wooden club, with large genitals exposed, draped with strands of rank foliage, mute and therefore without reason, possessed of the secrets of nature, slave to natural desires and passions uncontrolled, always lurking there, over there, in the arboreal darkness—and as well in the dark, repressed corners of human desire and anxiety and fear."

Pip and his jeu mates weren't savages, however, but complex, biologically modern men with all the brain power and manual dexterity necessary to fly a 747, with a language so complex it had seventeen tenses, whose whole experience, whose whole world, was here, constituted in this isolated universe of trees, ocean, river, and swamp, cut off from other resources, other men, other ideas, other technologies. They were pure subsistence hunter-gatherers. They had no crops, no food source that lasted more than a few days. Headhunting and cannibalism were as right to them as taking communion or kneeling on a carpet facing Mecca. There was no Empire State Building, no America or Shakespeare, no atom bomb or rocket ships or cars or radios, no Jesus Christ or telephone. They had other symbols, other things that ordered their world and their place within it. They knew that a red sunset meant a big headhunting raid was taking place somewhere. They knew that the moon changed shape every night because it was annoyed by the sun, which retreated to the underworld, the land beyond the sea, every evening. They knew that they were descended from the trees because both trees and men had feet, legs, arms, a fruit on top. A man was a tree; a tree was a man. They knew that they were like the fruit bat, the cuscus, the King Cockatoo, because they all hunted and ate the same thing: fruit, whether it was the

fruit of trees or the fruit of men. They were like the wild boar
and the crocodile, because boars and crocodiles killed men and
ate flesh and so did they. And they were like the praying mantis,
because it was just like them: it, too, ate heads—in the very act of
reconstituting itself.

They knew that a man who had taken many heads was a pow-
erful man, admired by other men and wanted by women. They
knew the tides and every creek and where the fish and shrimp ran
and how to find cassowaries and wild pig in the forest with their
hunting dogs. They knew how to make canoes and how to con-
struct a house in a few hours from whatever was at hand. And they
knew how to carve wood, how to instill an inanimate piece of tree
with life, in a language of form and symbol that every man and
woman in the swamps could read. That was, after all, how they
had come to be—the first man had carved men from wood and
then drummed them to life. The drum, the spear, the canoe prow,
the shield and bisj pole, their songs—that was their literature.

"There is a bird on the sea," the men from Otsjanep sang, clack-
ing their paddles on the sides of the canoe.

Watching me,
because I am here in this boat.
Don't push a big wind in my way
Until I return.

The water splashed against its gunwales. The coast appeared as a
line to their left—nothing but ocean and sky and green. They were
bound for the village of Wagin on the Digul River, seventy miles
down the Casuarina Coast. For Asmat, this was a long journey, and
it would take them past half a dozen villages, all of them hostile.

The warriors from Otsjanep didn't know it yet, but they had
been lured into a trap. Deception was common in Asmat. The en-
emy had to be deceived to be taken, the spirits had to be deceived

if they were to be driven back to Safan, all to keep the balance so essential to Asmat life. Otsjanep and Omadesep were enemies. They had been tricking each other and killing each other for years, and Otsjanep had often been the victim. But they were neighbors, and they were also closely connected by death and marriage.

Faniptas, a master wood-carver and head of one of the jeus in Omadesep, for instance, was related to three men in Otsjanep. He was tall, with long strands of sago leaf braided into his hair and a carved pig bone in his nose. A few days before, he'd paddled up the Faretsj River, which at high tide meandered into navigable swamps and connected to the Ewta, leading to Otsjanep, a two-hour journey. "Hello, my brothers and sisters," he had said to the men in the village. "Don't attack me. Come to Wagin with me." Some years back, a contingent of families from Omadesep had moved there. "There are many dogs' teeth in Wagin; we will go there and get rich."

In the jungle near Wagin, on a tributary of the Digul, lay a whirlpool, and every Asmat knew that whirlpools were entries to the underworld; they were places where the spirits dwelled. This particular doorway had a guardian, a dog, and the well produced *jursis*—dogs' teeth. There was no money in Asmat, and necklaces of dogs' teeth strung together like bandoliers had symbolic power and great value; they were the preferred currency used to acquire a bride. But for the whirlpool to produce the dogs' teeth required offerings of fresh skulls wrapped in banana leaves. Where were the men from Omadesep to get those skulls? Faniptas and his mates from the jeu Desep hatched a plan: they would convince some men from Otsjanep to accompany them and then kill them and give their heads to the pool.

It wasn't going to work out so simply. A mutual massacre was about to take place, the first in a series of interwoven events that would lead to the death of Michael Rockefeller. And Pip, Dombai, Su, Kokai, Wawar, and Pakai were paddling right into it.

6

· · · · · · · · · · · ·

February 2012

THE ENGINES OF the Tregana Airways Twin Otter droned. I was strapped into a bench seat in the front row with so little legroom that my knees were pressed against my chest. The plane was threadbare, the floor bare plywood. Ten thousand feet below us lay a carpet of green with so many rivers zigzagging through it that it looked like a training area for backhoe drivers who'd gone wild. The engines slowed, we dropped altitude, and the plane banked hard to the left as a slash in the jungle below opened—a few

THE AIRPORT IN EWER, THE ONLY AIRSTRIP IN ASMAT'S TEN THOUSAND SQUARE MILES OF JUNGLE AND SWAMP.

houses and corrugated roofs and a green grass-and-dirt airstrip covered with World War II–era aluminum mats. We banked again, swooped low over the river, and touched down, braking hard at the end of the runway. The rear door popped open, and heat and humidity poured in, a moist, hot thickness. I was barely down the two rungs of the ladder when the Otter revved and roared airborne, and I stood alone in Asmat.

It had taken me nine days and a lifetime to get here.

I DON'T QUITE know where my obsession with the primitive, as it used to be called, started. Clichéd though it may be, I have vivid memories of Tarzan movies on our old Philco black-and-white television, some of my earliest TV memories—I couldn't have been older than four or five. Thick jungle. Drumming. Howling. Fires. As I grew older, themes emerged. I couldn't subsume myself to a group consciousness; I stuck out, or always felt like I did. I was bullied. I got in fights. In fifth grade I found karate, an old-fashioned kind of karate taught by an outsider that was punishing, full of endless repetition and physical contact and brutality. I loved it. Me, the small guy, the guy who couldn't catch the ball, could do straight kicks till everyone around me dropped and could take hits and pain until I was black and blue and green and my nose was squished and bloody, and it wasn't long until I could make those big tough talkers drop to their knees.

I read a lot. Hours and hours on summer hammocks and porch swings and late into the night. I loved the idea of alternative worlds, universes. At some point I saw David Lean's epic *Lawrence of Arabia,* too young to understand the subtleties of T. E. Lawrence's internal struggles, but old enough to sense them, to recognize a fellow outsider.

Fantasies gave way to the great nonfiction adventure narratives. I read the real Lawrence—*Seven Pillars of Wisdom.* Wilfred Thesiger's *Arabian Sands,* about his punishing treks across the

Arabian Empty Quarter with the Bedouin. The great sailing classics, loners all: Joshua Slocum. Francis Chichester, who, passing Cape Horn while circumnavigating the earth alone, heard a noise, stumbled on deck, and saw an airplane buzzing overhead to check on his progress and wish him luck. Instead of a momentary feeling of companionship, he felt only annoyance, his solitude interrupted. Or Bernard Moitessier, who would have won the *Sunday Times* Golden Globe race, the world's first single-handed sailing race around the world, if he hadn't approached the finish line and then just kept going. He couldn't bear to stop; he sailed halfway around the world again to Tahiti before he finally came to shore.

After college, I went traveling. I remember stepping out of Cairo's airport and smelling a smell I'd never smelled before, acrid and sweet. Smoke. Dust. A hint of rotting fruit mixed with car exhaust. A darkness barely illuminated by too few and too weak streetlights. A bus with no window glass, rusted and beaten down, rattling and spewing gray smoke, and a charming, persuasive man with rotting teeth insisting that the hotel to which my girlfriend and I were headed was closed. We ended up in a ramshackle but friendly hotel off Tahrir Square, and I have never loved a place like I loved Egypt. I left fear behind. In Luxor we spent hours on the banks of the Nile negotiating with a felucca captain, not for a normal three-hour sail but for a five-day voyage to Aswan, a thing of beauty and meals of tomatoes and Nile fish and strange fires burning on the sterns of boats at night.

From Egypt forward, I wanted to plunge into the world, not the normal parts, but the dusty corners and crevices. America felt wrapped in plastic. Controlled. I wanted that drumming and howling, those fires in the Tarzan movies. The fear and loneliness of the long-distance sailor. The passion and pageantry of Thesiger's and Lawrence's Bedouin. Sudan. Congo. India. Afghanistan. The Arctic. Siberia. Bangladesh and Mali and Indonesia. I ranged far and wide over two decades. I liked intense flavors. And that meant

the intense feelings and emotions of our humanness—love and hate and violence and pain and suffering, emotional and physical. I liked the idea of peeling back the layers of all the things that I imagined civilized us. And as an outsider, I often felt less alienated in those distant places where no one expected me to belong, where it was obvious I didn't and probably never could.

All of which led me to the idea that traditional tribal societies living in the jungle might show me the root of something. Of who we are. Contemporary anthropologists long ago abandoned the idea that there is some steady, linear march from primitive to civilized and now discount the very notion that modern, technically advanced cultures are any more "civilized" than ones like the Asmat, with all its complexities. Nelson Rockefeller's museum, in raising the art of illiterate and isolated tribesmen to the equal of anything produced by overeducated Westerners, was a nod to this idea. But boyhood dreams die hard. Primitive, tribal, call it what you want, but I hungered to see a humanity before the Bible, before the Koran, before Christian guilt and shame, before clothes and knives and forks. Indeed, a world like the one described by Kirkpatrick Sale, inhabited by medieval wild savages, men possessed of the secrets of nature, a place where natural desires still reigned. A world where a boy in a wolf suit could dance with creatures who gnashed their terrible teeth and roared their terrible roars.

Along the way I found Tobias Schneebaum's book about the Asmat. Living in one of the remotest corners of the world, away from everything modern, they held out the possibly naive and idealized hope that in them I might find this raw, unfiltered world. Schneebaum had rolled in the mud with them and traveled in their canoes and slept with their men. I wasn't gay, but everything else about his experience resonated with me, and it was through Schneebaum that I'd first heard the Michael Rockefeller story.

Now, finally, I was here.

I'D BEEN DELVING deep into Asmat for months, immersed in files from Dutch colonial archives and missionaries. It was a slow process. I'd sat with Father Hubertus von Peij one cold winter's night in Tilburg, Netherlands, leaning close over his hand-drawn map, and I'd spent hours on the Canary Island of Tenerife listening to Wim van de Waal, a former Dutch patrol officer who'd been stationed in Asmat in 1961 and had been closely involved in the Rockefeller case. Both men had fed me names and dates that my Dutch researcher and I could chase down. This trail of documents had never been made public, and it illustrated a vivid narrative that was surprisingly straightforward. But to understand what had happened to Michael, I had to know Asmat; unraveling his story was also personal.

Getting there had been a different matter. Plenty of websites offered photos and bits and pieces of information, but it was all either out of date or so vague as to be useless. Google Maps showed a big green blank. There was nothing to do but go and figure it out. I had no reservations, no real plan, only one name—a "Mr. Alex," a man who was said to own a hotel in Agats and speak English and who could facilitate travel.

I'd flown from Washington, DC, to London to Singapore to Jakarta, then overnight on a flight to Jayapura (the former Hollandia, the capital of what had been Dutch New Guinea), where I had to get a permit from the police to travel within Indonesian Papua. Michael had been through Jayapura too, as had most of its colonial administrators, and I imagined communing with their ghosts amid its old colonial buildings. But Indonesia's strategy for dampening a long-simmering Papuan independence movement was to flood the territory with Indonesians, and Papuans were now a minority in their own land. Jayapura was just another big Indonesian city, crowded with motorcycles and cars and minivans and concrete buildings, and it was hard to spot a single native.

I flew on to Timika, a mad little city of heat and dust, where I hoped to find a boat to Agats. Except there was no boat. There was

not even a river—the "port" was thirty miles away. I drove there anyway, with a taxi driver named Ainum, an Indonesian from Makassar, and we found wooden cargo vessels with indeterminate schedules and a ship that left once every two weeks. There was a plane, Ainum said, that left on Thursdays and Saturdays, but there was only one place to get tickets—at the terminal. Timika is home to the Grasberg Mine, the largest copper mine in the world and the third-largest gold mine, owned and operated by a subsidiary of an American company, Freeport-McMoRan. Timika's airport terminal was brand-new, modern and shiny and sweet-smelling, bold testaments to Freeport's environmental stewardship lining every wall, clocks showing the time in Jakarta, London, New Orleans. The domestic terminal on the other side of the parking lot was a shed, its concrete floor covered in blazing orange betel nut spit, cigarette butts, plastic straws, empty yogurt containers, ripped plastic bags. Liquid overflowed from the bathroom—but here, at last, were Papuans. Short black men and women in tattered T-shirts, with calloused bare feet, reeking of body odor.

The plane for Thursday was sold out. "Don't worry," Ainum said. "I have a friend at the airport, and I can get you a ticket." Which he did, arriving at my hotel to hand me a ticket under someone else's name. I paid him double its face value.

Back in the terminal four days later, there was the same chaos, the same crowds. It was a hundred degrees. Two red-and-green parrots chained to each other perched on a bench. The women had small tattoos of a black dot on their cheeks, the men had beards, though none of them were Asmat, I would later realize. No one had any idea where the plane was, much less when it would leave. We sat. I felt weak, a fever coming on, my stomach cramping. After three hours, the plane appeared. We filed out, squeezed in, and forty minutes later I was in Asmat.

This was the village of Ewer, though, the only place in thousands of square miles with enough dry ground to land a plane. I

shouldered my bag and followed the other passengers along a rick-ety boardwalk toward a river, past a few wooden houses. I spot-ted a huge, long jeu, an Asmat men's house. Men lounging on its veranda. I couldn't process it; it all might have been pictures in a book. At the end of a crumbling concrete pier with rebar sticking out helter-skelter were tied brightly colored red and yellow and green fiberglass speedboats. I handed my bag to an Indonesian man and jumped in the tiny vessel, and we sped off with three other people, all Indonesian.

I had little idea where I was going or how long it would take to get there. We barreled down a river a quarter-mile wide, thick jungle on either side, the other speedboats racing with us. The river opened—we were close to the sea, the Arafura wide and big before us—and a longboat coming from the other direction swept close, its passengers waving their hands in a frantic up-and-down motion, pointing. Their message was soon obvious to me as we hit the mouth—a wild roiling and boiling of waves and whirlpools and currents. The captain throttled back, but still water sprayed over us. He navigated his way to the opposite bank through the turbulence, and we turned left, up the Asawets River. Fifteen minutes later, we motored into Agats.

It felt like the end of the known world. A mile of rickety docks and shacks on stilts hanging over floating plastic water bottles and empty ramen wrappers and packs of clove cigarettes. Dozens of shiny, naked children jumping into the brown, frothy river. A bro-ken boardwalk slanted into the water. A barefoot man grabbed my bag, I followed blindly, and a few minutes later we were at the Pada Elo Hotel. Four windowless rooms of plywood over the river around a courtyard of oil barrels filled with water, laundry on a clothesline. A young woman in blue jeans showed me my room—two single beds, a hole over the river for a bathroom. No running water. No electricity. A cockatoo paced around the rim of a barrel, gazing at me with a black, liquid eye.

"I'm looking for Mr. Alex," I said.

She shook her head, shrugged her shoulders. She didn't speak English.

Then the skies opened up, and I collapsed. Rain thundered down, more than I ever thought possible, and my fever raged. The room was dark and suffocatingly hot. A parade of ants crawled up and down my bedposts, and water dripped through the roof, gathering into a small river flowing across the floor. For two days the rain drummed on the corrugated roof and I tossed and turned. What was I doing here? What was I chasing? How was I to pierce this place when I couldn't even speak the language?

Then I woke to a cacophony of roosters and intense brightness coming through the cracks in my door, my walls, my roof. I doused myself with cold water from a bucket and stepped out. Steam rose from mossy, broken boardwalks over an omnipresent muddy carpet of those empty plastic water bottles, thousands and thousands of them. There were boats everywhere—dugout canoes and sixty-foot longboats and colorful little speedboats—crowding the creeks and streams. Agats was a city of seven thousand, but there wasn't a single street, not a single car. Along the waterfront, open shops lined the boardwalk, crowded with Javans and Bugis and Torajans and Indonesian traders and opportunists from throughout the archipelago. The town square and soccer field was made of wooden planks raised over the muck. This was the frontier of the growing republic, the Indian country of Indonesia, Manifest Destiny as powerful here as it had been in America a hundred years ago. When Michael Rockefeller had arrived in Agats, it was a Dutch administrative center with a handful of Dutch priests and nuns and colonial officers next to the Asmat village of Sjuru, and he had been hosted by the Dutch government. Now there wasn't another Westerner to be seen, and Agats was growing by the day as Jakarta pumped money into the region and paid civil servants six times what they'd make back on Java.

The market teemed with Asmat, though. Dark black, broad-chested men and bony, short-haired women sold clams and crabs wrapped in palm leaves, strings of two-foot-long shark, skates, and catfish gasping for air, strange-looking lumps of white—the pith of the sago palm, which was Asmat's most important food. I was getting closer; the pure world of Asmat was out there.

After an hour of rambling, I discovered another hotel. It had rooms with toilets and sheets and windows opening onto a court-yard of black mud and, best of all, a desk clerk who spoke a bit of English. When I asked about a guide, he whipped out his cell phone, made a call, and a few minutes later in walked Harun.

He was Asmat, inscrutable, quiet. He spoke in a whisper, his eyes downcast, his left arm in a dirty, unraveling plaster cast. "I am a guide," he said. "Many tourists come to Asmat."

"How many?" I said.

"Maybe four this year," he said.

I wanted to get a boat and explore the rivers and villages, I said, not mentioning Rockefeller, though I had a plan: to make a general reconnaissance journey and work my way south through the villages that Michael had visited and that had figured promi-nently in the story, and then end up in Omadesep and Otsjanep.

I brought out a map of Michael's route during his two trips and showed it to Harun. "A week, two weeks, I'm not sure," I said. "I just want to explore."

Harun nodded. "I can take you anywhere."

We threw around some prices. His arm hurt, he said—he had fallen off one of the boardwalks in the darkness one night. He was going to the hospital, and he said he'd come back in a few hours.

Which he did, this time with two other men, Amates and Wilem. "The doctor said I cannot go with my arm, but my friends will take you."

Amates looked tense, tightly wound. He was dripping with sweat, his body lost in baggy pleated slacks, his mouth an ugly

dark cave. He had a suppurating carbuncle on his neck that he couldn't stop touching. And there was that half a finger, the stub still swollen. Wilem was his opposite. Round for an Asmat, in flip-flops and gym shorts and a red-and-white-striped soccer jersey, and there was something haughty about him. Amates's English was slow, labored. "I am from Biwar Laut," he said. "I have been to university. I teach English. This is Wilem, he is the boat driver."

We haggled over prices some more, settled on a number, and it was done. They would provide food, fuel, everything.

WE PULLED AWAY from the dock just after six the next morning in a narrow, thirty-foot longboat powered by a fifteen-horsepower Johnson outboard. The air was still, the Asawets River a half-mile wide. There were five of us in the boat: Amates and Wilem and me, plus Manu, Wilem's assistant, and Filo, Amates's brother. We carried two hundred liters of fuel and a pile of rice and ramen and water and enough loose-leaf tobacco and clove cigarettes to give the whole of Asmat cancer—hundreds of dollars' worth. We hugged the left bank, passed Sjuru, the original Asmat village next to which Agats had been built (now all trash and shacks and billowing smoke), and turned left, into the Famborep River.

One second there were boats and big coastal traders and the smell and clamor of Agats and Sjuru, the next silence and water and green. The Famborep was barely twenty feet wide, a drowned world of hanging vines and epiphytes and moss-covered mangroves. The dark water mirrored the trees and sky above it as shafts of sunlight streamed through the overgrowth, the river flooding the land as far inland as I could see. Birds called. It was beautiful and ethereal, removed. There was no trash, nothing man-made—it looked the same as it had at the dawn of time.

Amates pointed to a Seussian fan of leaves. "A tree of sago!" he said. "One day I slept here. I was coming back to school in Agats from Biwar." He was thirty-two, had six kids, had been smart

enough to be shipped off to Catholic boarding school in Agats and then university in Bali. He had no job, though, no money, and even with Biwar Laut just a few hours downriver by powered longboat, he hadn't been home in five years. It was just too far and expensive.

We passed into the Banduw River. "This is a crocodile place." We zigged and zagged, hit the Jet River, and turned north. The waterway widened, and it began to make sense—why there were people here, and why the few Westerners who'd made it this far had been so infatuated with it. Asmat was otherworldly. Compelling. A strange and fecund universe utterly removed from the grip of the world. The jungle was thick, but the rivers were highways, and they kept it from feeling cloying, oppressive. It was a drowned Eden, full of birds and fish and freshwater and a giant sky that was always in motion. We passed villages you could smell before you got to them, smoke and laughing children's voices and canoes drawn up on muddy banks. Dugouts lined with standing men paddled by, smoke rising from the coals in the stern.

After four hours, we came to Atsj, one of the largest and most developed villages outside of Agats. Under way, there was always a breeze, but as soon as we stopped the sun bore down on us as we tied up at some rickety poles and climbed to an unpainted wooden house belonging to Amates's sister. The front porch was crowded with men and women in T-shirts and gym shorts. Its boards were shiny and polished smooth from years of bare feet. A thin woman with short hair rushed out. "Oh, oh, oh!" she cried. "Oooh," she moaned, clasping Amates by the elbow, the arm, hugging and clutching him, rocking back and forth, sobbing, rubbing her tear-covered face over his arms and cheeks, a dramatic outpouring of emotion that ended as quickly as it began, when she simply turned and walked away. This was my first glimpse into the Asmat way—a place of intense emotional extremes and the very consciousness and sense of self that had been inextricably

bound with cannibalism—though it would take me a long time to understand it.

The house had four rooms, bare plank walls, and two red velour sofas. A pig's jaw hung over the door. A seven-foot-long bow and a thick bunch of bamboo arrows dangled from a nail in the corner. Plastic tubs of rainwater lined the back porch. A hand-woven fishing net hung on the wall. And beyond, more rooms, dark, windowless, and smoky, one with a mud hearth full of glowing coals and blackened pots. Uncles, cousins, nephews—Amates identified each as "my brother," one of them albino—were everywhere, lying, sitting, squatting on the bare floor. By the fire, a woman took handfuls of pinkish-white sago, pressed it into a mold, covered it with a banana leaf, then lay the mold on the fire. After a few minutes, she lifted it out and shook the rectangular cakes onto a tin plate. The sago tasted warm, nutty, but dry, like eating sand; it was hard to imagine surviving off it. Even though they lived here in Atsj, Amates's family was from Biwar Laut, and so, Amates said, "this sago comes from the jungle of Biwar Laut. Not Atsj. If we go to the Atsj jungle for sago, there will be boxing, fighting. It will be very bad."

As the hours ticked by and hardly anyone moved, I felt an unsettling dislocation of time and place. Atsj had a hotel, stores, and little restaurants run by Indonesian traders, a big concrete dock, mosques, and we were sitting in a house with a corrugated metal roof and those incongruous velour sofas. A TV rested in a corner, reverently covered by clear plastic. But the principal food was still sago cooked on an open fire, and it still came from a source that couldn't be deviated from. I had traveled all over the world, and I'd always felt more than welcome—I'm usually an object of attention, people are curious and fascinated by where I'm from and why I'm in their midst, me a little doorway to the mythical America. But here no one asked any questions. I felt like a ghost, a feeling that would only grow the deeper I went. No one spoke English except for Am-

ates, and there was nothing to do but sit and listen and watch other people sitting and sweating and smoking and talking. I felt a wall that had another side I couldn't get to, couldn't see, except for a few tantalizing clues, and I wasn't even sure what that wall was or what lay behind it. This wasn't the Asmat that Michael Rockefeller had seen. Layers had been added, layers of Christianity and Indonesia, but how much had changed and who they really were, what they were thinking, I couldn't tell. At least not yet.

To go to the bathroom I had to exit a plank door, negotiate a ten-foot-long board over mud, tightrope across a three-inch-wide log at a steep angle down into another house filled with people cooking and lying on the floor, then go out on another plank to a wooden outhouse with a hole over a stream.

As it got dark, Filo rustled up some white rice and instant ramen by candlelight and the skies burst open, unleashing dramatic sheets of rain that thundered on the roof and sent a fine mist curling through the eaves. I retreated to the master bedroom, which had been turned over to me, a furniture-less room full of fishing nets and an ax and bow and arrow and hyperbolic, colorful pictures of Jesus. I blew up my thin, inflatable air mattress in the flickering candlelight and lay down, exhausted.

December 1957

FATHER CORNELIUS VAN KESSEL WEARING
BOAR TUSKS ON HIS LEFT ARM, A CUSCUS
FUR HEADBAND, AND TRADITIONAL ASMAT
MARKINGS.

AS THE 124 MEN from Otsjanep and Omadesep paddled south along the coast toward Wagin, Pip and Faniptas knew that strange people had lately been appearing from across the sea, as if by magic. But in 1957 those beings were still dim apparitions to them, with little impact on their lives, and they weren't thinking about the white men at all. The warriors stayed well offshore, but as they neared the Digul the weather turned. Big, low green-black clouds covered the sky, and the wind whipped the sea into whitecaps. A fierce winter storm blew in, piling the Arafura against the shallows in short, steep waves that threat-

ened to swamp the canoes. Water poured in over the gunwales. The men couldn't balance any longer, couldn't make headway, couldn't keep the waves from filling their canoes. Torrents of cold rain fell from low gray clouds. In the roiling surf and breaking waves, they were forced to shore at the coastal village of Emene.

In New York, art critics were celebrating humanity's oneness, our commonality of love and games and dancing and sunsets. In Asmat, men who would soon be heralded as some of the greatest artists of the world attacked each other with spears, bows and arrows, and axes. In the driving, chill rain, Emene attacked the men from Omadesep and Otsjanep. They fought hand to hand, howling and screaming and covered in mud. It was awful, but glorious too, for they were warriors. One man from Omadesep died and four from Emene, and the men from Omadesep and Otsjanep scattered into the jungle swamp.

In the morning they found their canoes destroyed. Faniptas led them north. They trudged through the mud, fighting their way home through one hostile territory after another. In Baiyun six died, three from Omadesep and three from Baiyun. Near Basim, the men from Omadesep turned on their own traveling companions, the men from Otsjanep, planning to kill them all. Pip took a steel ax blow to his abdomen and fell to the mud. Everisus Birojipts was a small child, maybe six, maybe seven, and he saw Pip fall. "Father," he said, staring at the dead man, "I saw Pip's eyes open; maybe he's not dead."

"No, he's dead," said Birojipts's father. "Don't worry."

He wasn't dead. After three hours, he stood, nursing his wound, and made his way toward the Ewta River and Otsjanep, his home. Alone, he moved fast, outpacing the others.

The mouth of every river belongs to the village that lies upstream. At the Ewta, Pip encountered his kinsmen, and they paddled immediately back to the village, where he spoke of Omadesep's treachery. The warriors drew Xs across their chests

and rings around their legs and arms with ochre and black ash, adorned themselves with cuscus fur headbands and cockatoo feathers, and put curving shells in their noses that resembled the tusks of the wild boar, giving themselves strength, power. They wanted to look fierce, to strike fear in the hearts of their enemies. They became the animals that lived in the jungle, eaters of fruit, eaters of men. In the jeu they drummed and sang and chanted through the night, sweat pouring off their chests and arms and legs, filling the jeu with their smell, a smell that gave them added strength, bravery. They danced and howled and screamed, pushing themselves to the limits of fearlessness. They danced with their bows and arrows, their spears. There were straight spears with inch-high barbs, spears that branched off to six points, spears with points that broke off in their prey. Just before dawn, they gathered their shields—six feet long and intricately carved with the symbols of the forest and headhunting, fruit bats and boar tusks and praying mantises—and each bore a protruding penis in the shape of a man from its top. They carried powdered lime (a female element that made men hot) to throw into the air and frighten their opponents, and they looked like what they were—wild creatures from the jungle. Two hundred men in twenty canoes paddled silently down the Ewta in the dawn light and waited at the narrow, tangled mouth of the river.

THAT THE ASMAT remained so untouched by the rest of the world for so long was remarkable. It was one thing to live deep in the jungle a thousand miles up tributaries of a river like the Amazon, but Asmat was on the coast, the rivers were roads, and Europeans had been cruising by for centuries. The Portuguese touched the island in 1526, the Spanish a few years later. In 1595 the Netherlands sent an expedition to the Moluccas—nine hundred miles to the northeast of Asmat—to secure its supply of spices and soon established the United East Indies Company, which began ruling over the Indonesian archipelago. But New Guinea was an enormous mystery,

its shores hot and moist and its interior an impenetrable land of
steep mountains and valleys, the southwest coast even more so;
indeed, it remained outside the control of governments for longer
than any other non-Arctic coast in the world. Crops didn't grow
there. Asmat nourished no large mammals to domesticate or hunt,
possessed no known mineral resources, and was so shallow and
tidal it was hard to navigate. The place seemed untamable. When
Jan Carstenz landed in 1623, "the natives attacked without warn-
ing," wrote Gavin Souter in his history of New Guinea, and "tore
one man to pieces, killed eight others with arrows and spears, and
wounded the remaining seven."

Captain James Cook paused at the entrance to the Cook
River—now the Kuti—in 1770 and sent two boatloads of men
upriver, where they encountered canoes full of Asmat armed with
spears and bows and arrows, enveloped in clouds of white smoke—
the lime the Asmat threw—which Cook's men took for gunfire.
"Their Arms were ordinary darts about four feet long made of
a kind of reed and point at one end with hard wood, but what
appear'd most extraordinary to us was something they had which
caused a flash of fire or smook, very much like the going off of a
Pistol or Gun without any report, the deception was so great that
the People in the Ship actually thought they had fire arms." When
that first contact was over, twenty of Cook's men and an unknown
number of Asmat were dead, and Cook felt no need to remain or
encourage others to return.

In 1800 the Dutch government took over the archipelago from
the United East Indies Company, and a century later it began a
series of forays up the rivers of Papua's southwest coast, but made
little contact with the Asmat. In 1902, under pressure from British
authorities, whose territories were being invaded by headhunting
Marind warriors from the Dutch side of the island, the Nether-
lands established a police post in Merauke, 150 miles southwest
of Asmat. The Dutch colonial capital of Hollandia, three hundred

miles to the north, across the high mountains, was so far away it might as well have been on a different planet.

The Asmat existed in their own world, as if these outsiders were nothing but occasional spirits passing by. When World War II hit the Pacific, huge battles raged across the northern coast, culminating in large American bases in Hollandia and on the island of Biak. The Japanese briefly established a post in what would become Agats and killed twenty-two men there on a single day, but their influence on the rest of Asmat was small.

After the war, in 1947, the Dutch Catholic priest Gerard Zegwaard arrived in Mimika, a culturally and linguistically different region of much firmer land northwest of Asmat. Zegwaard belonged to the Order of the Sacred Heart, a missionary brotherhood that had been working in the Pacific since the late 1800s. OSC priests were highly educated and devout tough guys. They practiced self-flagellation, flaying their own backs with a knotted whip. Besides their native Dutch, they spoke Latin, English, French, and German. They were steeped in the philosophy of Aristotle, Thomas Aquinas, and Nietzsche. Zegwaard was twenty-eight when he arrived, with an anthropologist's sense of wonder and curiosity, and it wasn't long before he acquired a scruffy beard and deep tan. He smoked a pipe and plunged deeply into Asmat culture, stumbling into ceremonies and headhunting raids, which no white man had ever seen—and recording them in his journals.

Raids could happen at any time, anywhere. Villages were constantly on the move, the larger, more powerful ones extending their range by destroying their smaller neighbors and appropriating their hunting, fishing, and sago-gathering grounds. Face-to-face battles between warriors were few. When canoes of men from two warring villages met on the rivers, the men howled and hurled insults across the water, calling their opponents wives or women. They drew their bows, they fired arrows overhead or into

the water, and they threw fistfuls of lime at each other. But being evenly matched, there was little reason to fight.

Far preferable were sudden ambushes on villages or the taking of a stray man, woman, or child with the bad fortune to be caught unprotected in the open. Whole villages or men's house groups fished or gathered sago in the jungle as protection. Warriors formed a cordon upstream and down from where a group was working, and others accompanied women into the forest to harvest sago. This, of course, often left old people or children alone, and they, too, were fair game.

Even among warring villages, some people related by blood or bond, like Faniptas from Omadesep, had safe passage and could be received as guests. By the exchange of children or marriage or the taking of names of those they had killed, there was always some connection that left villages able to travel and communicate with each other. But the Asmat were opportunists and tricksters, and sometimes those visitors were killed anyway in their sleep, or given presents and killed as they were leaving, or lured as suckers on voyages like the one to Wagin.

Village ambushes were associated with ceremonies meant to restore order in a world of opposites, including the creation of elaborate wooden poles carved from a single piece of mangrove that could be as tall as twenty feet, known as *bisj*. Each pole depicted a column of stacked ancestors; the pole carried the name of its topmost person. Canoes, snakes, and crocodiles were carved into the base of the pole, and symbols of headhunting extended out in a three-foot-long protrusion from its top. The poles were haunting, alive, often sexually suggestive.

For the Asmat, ancestors are involved in every aspect of their existence. The carvings are memorial signs to those ancestors, and to the living, that their deaths have not been forgotten, that the living's responsibility to avenge them is still alive and strong, and that the living should not be punished if those deaths haven't yet

been avenged. *Bisj* itself comes from the word *"mbiu"*—the spirit or soul of the dead—and the bisj pole, more than any other object, is an embodiment of the dead person, whose spirit lives inside it. The pole is a symbol of his presence, a reminder of the obligation to revenge, and, possessing both a penis and a vagina, a symbol of fertility. Death into life and life into death, inextricable opposites of a unified whole.

To the west lies Safan, the home of the spirits of the ancestors. Man is born in Asmat, lives and dies there, and then enters a secondary level of earthly existence, a sort of limbo. In order to pass through it to Safan, he depends on the help of the living. They must celebrate with bisj festivals that can last seven months, beginning with the warriors attacking a mangrove tree in the jungle just as they would a man. They yell and scream and shoot it with arrows, before cutting it down and bringing it to the village just as they would a man killed in battle. Only a great man can afford to sponsor such a process—the carvers must be fed, for instance, and much food is necessary for all of the feasting.

The completion of a pole usually unleashed a new round of raids; revenge was taken and balance restored, new heads obtained—new seeds to nourish the growth of young men—and the blood of the victims rubbed into the pole. At the end of the feast and the bisj celebration, the spirit in the pole was made complete and could return to help the living. The villagers then engaged in sex, and the poles were left to rot in the sago fields, fertilizing the sago itself and completing the cycle. If no remembrance was made, no bisj celebration held, no new heads taken, life and happiness could not flow into human existence from the ancestral world.

Raids usually took place just before dawn. After a night of planning, the raiding party was divided into three groups: the leaders, who gave advice; the archers, who opened the attack; and the spearmen and shield-bearers, who did the killing. The warriors approached as close as they could by canoe, then surrounded the

village. The leaders, all older, distinguished warriors, took the rear. The archers crept to the front, between the village and the river, and the spearmen to the rear, between the village and the jungle, for all Asmat houses have hidden rear doorways.

One of the attackers would make a noise.

"Who is that?" someone in the houses would call.

"Your husband, Sjuru!" he would reply, using the name of the attacking village.

Then panic. Women and children would try to escape into the jungle or by canoe. Sometimes they were spared, the women taken as wives if there was a shortage of women in the attacking village, the children adopted. As soon as a victim was overpowered, he was pushed and beaten, especially his head, as the killer yelled, "My head, my head won in the raid!" The victim's name was discovered, if it wasn't already known. Preferably, if there was time, the victim wasn't killed immediately, but taken to the canoe and made to sit with his hands and chest hanging over a pole.

At the confluence of rivers or river bends, the victims were decapitated (sometimes even by women—the wife of a great headhunter could become great too), and the horns were sounded upon their return to the village for the ensuing ceremonies and feasts.

WHEN ZEGWAARD ARRIVED in Mimika in 1947, this had been going on for as long as the Asmat could remember. In 1928, ten canoes of a hundred Asmat came ashore at the Mimikan village of Atuka, near a Dutch outpost. The Atukans fled, and the Asmat stripped the village, particularly anything made of steel. They tore apart the desks and benches in the Atuka school and pulled out the nails, which they flattened and used as carving tools. By 1947, the raiding and warfare in Asmat had become so fierce that as many as six thousand Asmat fled their villages to escape the violence. They ended up next door, in Mimika, where Zegwaard encountered them for the first time. This was a refugee crisis; the Dutch

government forced them to return to their villages, and Zegwaard and the Dutch Resident, the local official in charge, began making regular voyages into the swamps and rivers.

Zegwaard remains the best authority on the Asmat in their purest state, at the time of first sustained contact with Europeans, and his writing draws a bloody portrait. "There is a tendency to minimize what we have heard about the violence in Asmat's culture," he wrote. "I frequently sense that government officials are very skeptical about the 'wild stories' they have heard about Asmat. I do not blame them as I, too, had this initial impression when I knew the Asmat only in superficial contact situations. As I mentioned above, the Asmatters are such good actors that they can give favorable impressions and suggest that things are 'not really too bad.'

"The Asmat language," he continued, "has an abundance of words for such concepts as 'fight,' 'argue,' 'quarrel,' 'murder,' and 'headhunting.' Any conflict between two persons will usually escalate into involvement of all members of their immediate families, then their clans and finally can involve the entire village. A conflict with a related or friendly village usually ultimately involves a major battle. Asmatters fight with all weapons they possess: clubs, bow and arrow, spears, paddles, etc. They try to maintain a balance in conflicts with 'friendly' or related villages but anything is fair in battle or warfare with non-related or enemy villages. Some examples from this post–World War II period will serve to clarify this state of affairs. Two men from Sjuru were killed by Jasakor's arrows in a fight over tobacco and women. Another six men from Ewer were killed, as well as five men and a woman from the village of Sjuru. In 1950 two children were beaten to death in a conflict over a woman. This was countered by the other party. . . . I know of three men killed in Jamasj during 1952 and another three in March 1953. These were revenge for [the] 1952 killings. The fights may continue for hours and even spill over into days without pause.

If a man feels that he has been wronged in any way he will quietly bide his time looking for revenge. Sometimes this means waiting for the opportunity and the killing place. This pattern of revenge through the children was used as an explanation for the scarcity of children in Asmat when I was taking a census there. I know of similar child-revenge-killing in Erma in 1952. This child was killed because his parents had gathered sago in someone else's sago area. The child's parents in turn took revenge on a man from Joni who was a relative of the man who killed their child. These conflicts (frequently culminating in killings) are the usual reason for the division of clans (i.e. JEW units) [sic] or the disintegration of village units. The history of almost every Jew [sic] begins in conflict."

In the village of Sjuru in 1947 and 1948, Zegwaard recorded "sixty-one known deaths resulting from this ever-present violence. Fifty-six of this total were headhunting victims who were eaten by their enemy and who gave their name, in death, to their 'murderer.' Thus Sjuru's total population was reduced from 675 to 610 during this two-year period—an absolute decrease of 10 percent and annual decrease of 4 percent."

Figuring the average for the villages of Sjuru, Ewer, Ayam, Amborep, and Warse for the same two-year period, Zegwaard extrapolated that "we can presume a population decrease approximately 2% to 3% per year due to death by violence." This was one of the highest murder rates ever recorded anywhere. In the years in which Washington, DC, was known as the murder capital of the United States, its rate was less than 1 percent.

In 1952 Zegwaard opened a rectory in Sjuru, and the government soon followed by opening a police post adjacent, which it named Agats. The pacification of the Asmat began, though it was a long and slow process that would take more than twenty years. A handful of government officials and priests would voyage by canoe or motorized launch up the rivers making contact, using fishhooks, axes, and tobacco, to which the Asmat soon became ad-

dicted. For a people with nothing but wood, shell, and a few pieces of stone that came from the highlands, these objects were revolutionary pieces of technology. Felling sago trees, their primary source of food; hollowing out canoes; carving their shields, drums, bowls, and bisj poles—the most essential tasks of their lives—were done with stone. A piece of steel was as transformational as a tractor.

Though small in numbers, the whites had an impact hard to understate. They arrived in a place and among a people to whom the visible and invisible worlds were connected into one vast unity, a consciousness formed purely by the physical world around them—the jungle, the rivers, the sky, the mud, themselves. And for most Asmat, that meant their village, their hunting and gathering grounds, any neighboring villages, and their war territory. What they could see was the whole universe. Anything outside of that tangible immediacy had to come from the spirit world—it was the only comprehensible explanation. Those spirits were omnipresent, always jealous of the living, always wanting to return and make trouble. Upon a death in the village, women rolled in the mud, covering their bodies with it, so the spirit of the deceased couldn't smell them, couldn't find them. An airplane was *opndettaji*—a passing-over-canoe-of-the-spirits—and white men were super-beings who came, mysteriously, from the land beyond the sea, the same place the spirits lived. Arriving strangers meant an invasion of reincarnated souls, their ancestors who were never content with their fate and always wanted to return and were thus aggressive with the living. The Asmat greeted them with fear and often aggression, armed with spears and bows and arrows and skulls, to impress and scare these invading spirits, for the sight of their own hollowed-out skulls ought to make them fly away.

These new superbeings were also rich. Nails and steel ax heads were marvels of eye-popping value, made from the scarcest and most valuable resource the Asmat had ever seen. To see a whole ship

of metal—it was unimaginable. The wealth! The creatures bearing these marvels possessed an immediate and awe-inspiring power.

For Asmat men, their wives were sacrosanct; violence would erupt, and whole villages be split, over adultery. Yet they also carried out *papisj*—the sharing of wives between male bond mates—a practice meant to be so disruptive, so bad, that it frightened the spirits, driving them back to Safan. Papisj happened under times of stress in a village, and almost without fail, the arrival of priests or government officials in those years precipitated the mass exchange of sexual partners.

In 1955 Zegwaard moved back to Merauke and was replaced by the Dutch priest Cornelius "Kees" van Kessel. He was tall and lanky, with a narrow face and a long, unruly beard. He had a deep wanderlust, and he'd dreamed about being a missionary since he was seven years old. At twelve, he entered the seminary, and in 1947 he was sent to New Guinea. Eight years later, he was posted to the southern Asmat village of Atsj, one of the most powerful and violent in the territory.

"The mission had no motorized vessel," he wrote in an unpublished memoir, "so all the luggage was loaded in ten canoes. The jungle telephone worked very fast: on the Siretsj we got an extensive escort of all the leaders from Atsj. Close to the village the big armada made a special formation according to the Asmat protocol—apart from the calm splashing of the paddles no sound was made. But close to the village a cantor started a solemn song interrupted by a massive yell out of this whole group and echoed by the village. When we came in front of the houses the women threw lime into the air."

Van Kessel built a house, traveled the rivers by canoe, and made sure he kept the cargo coming. And of course, he learned the language. "In each village I left one or two [axes], but in Atsj I gave out hundreds . . . to distract them from going headhunting. Daily I had to exchange food and art objects to still their hunger for knives and choppers, razorblades and fishing hooks and tobacco!"

Van Kessel was an unusual man. He had a huge heart. He was deeply pious, but that faith was built on the idea that men are good, that the world and life are beautiful and full of wonder, that God is a warm, loving presence who tolerates our human eccentricities and imperfections. He believed unequivocally in heaven. He loved cigars—his family in Holland kept him supplied with his favorite Dutch brand, La Paz. He didn't think religion could be enforced, and he proselytized slowly. He believed in getting to know the Asmat, so he talked with them, ate with them, slept with them, and was slow to bring up his God. He was a striking figure, this gangly white man in shorts and sneakers, with a wild beard and the stub of a cigar between his lips. He was often streaked with white and ochre bands on his chest, arms, and legs, white feathers sticking from his beard, sometimes even a cuscus fur headband enveloping his bald head. He was a free, joyous spirit, and for this the Asmat loved him and his superiors mistrusted him. They were forever at odds. He chafed at authority, could only speak his mind. The files of the Order of the Sacred Heart are filled with letters from his superiors, wringing their hands over this ebullient child who would not be bridled. He was reprimanded for not baptizing enough people fast enough, reprimanded for speaking his mind and not following orders from officials in Holland who, he felt, knew nothing about the realities of the place and its culture.

Van Kessel was a priest for the best reasons, the right reasons, an optimistic romantic who, years later, would fall in love, leave the priesthood, and marry—and yet remain ever close to the Church, his faith never wavering. This divide between van Kessel and his superiors would have serious repercussions when Michael disappeared.

Slowly, the priests began inserting Papuan laypeople into villages as catechists, who could begin teaching the Asmat about Christianity and report back to the Church and the government

about headhunting forays. Still, some villages were more recep-
tive than others, and Otsjanep was particularly skittish. Its first
contact with outsiders hadn't gone well. In October 1953, a group
of Chinese Indonesian crocodile hunters, employing villagers
from Omadesep as guides, attacked a group of Otsjanep women
fishing near the mouth of the Ewta River. The Chinese hunters
killed six women and two children, four of them shot to death—
Otsjanep's first experience not just with Others but with Others
carrying firearms. When Dutch official F. R. J. Eibrink Jansen vis-
ited Otsjanep in 1955 to investigate the Chinese murders, a classic
story of cultural misunderstanding unfolded. Although Eibrink
Jansen was arriving on the village's behalf, he sailed up the river
for the first official contact with Otsjanep with a heavily armed
police patrol accompanied by a group of warriors from Omadesep.
The men of Otsjanep saw the white Dutchman, the weapons, they
saw their enemies from Omadesep, and they freaked; the police
were surrounded in the narrow river by hundreds of screaming,
lime-throwing, and well-armed warriors. Eibrink Jansen had the
sense to back down, turn around, and retreat. "I could have mown
them down," he told van Kessel the next day, "but I would have
hit dozens of innocent people. So I decided to go back without
even having been in contact."

Two months later, van Kessel himself visited Otsjanep for the
first time. "We were welcomed most heartily. But then we were
unarmed and (of course) not accompanied by police." He returned
again on April 15, 1956, "was heartily welcomed," and left two
catechists, but they fled after twenty-four hours. "The village be-
came wildly enthusiastic about the tobacco of the catechists, who
misinterpreted the intrusive enthusiasm and made a run for it!"

THE KILLING THROUGHOUT Asmat went on. In September 1956,
Omadesep killed another four from Otsjanep, bringing the num-
ber whose deaths had not yet been avenged to ten.

Van Kessel traveled to Amborep and found the village had just "beaten off an attack from Jasokor and Kaimo, and that Jasokor had something in mind." He raced to Jasokor and found the village empty, save for his two catechists, "who told me in a laconic way 'the people had just gone on a raid to Damen.' So in a hurry I rushed to Damen, but too late: the houses were still burning and the villagers still lamenting their dead—eight men, eight women and eight children were killed and loaded into the canoes of Jasokor for the cannibalistic ritual."

In the village of Ajam, in May, twenty-eight men and boys visiting from Japaer were slaughtered, and van Kessel himself was almost caught in the violence. "Rowing on the Asawetsj [sic] toward Ajam I came in a rain of arrows from a Jepaer [sic] armada. I traveled with three canoes of Atsj people and Jipaer [sic] ran after us. By throwing tobacco into the river I obstructed the speed of my pursuers (free tobacco works miracles!) and finally they stopped the persecution because we came close to Ajam where a strong police force was settled, so I escaped an uncertain fate, for Japaer was still loaded with feelings of revenge to anybody."

Van Kessel kept a list of the violence. In 1955, 300 dead. In 1956, 120, including the four from Otsjanep killed by Omadesep and two from Otsjanep killed by Basim. In 1957, 200. This was in southern Asmat alone, and it's impossible to know how many deaths he wasn't even aware of.

In October 1956, van Kessel was joined by a colleague, Father Hubertus von Peij. He was twenty-six years old, a recently ordained OSC minister, like van Kessel. Von Peij, too, had heard the calling early, wanting to be a priest since the age of twelve, and he could have gone to Brazil, the Philippines, or elsewhere in Indonesia, but he chose New Guinea. He wanted adventure. "We heard the stories," he said. "It was attractive to me." After four months of learning Malay in Merauke, Zegwaard, his superior, escorted von Peij to Ajam, where he was to be posted. "Ajam was very bad," he

said when I found him alive and well and eighty-four years old in Tilburg, Netherlands, "and there was a lot of killing in revenge for the raids in the 1940s." More than ten years might have passed, but as von Peij said, "They never forget. Ever."

Zegwaard installed von Peij in Ajam and said, "So, I leave," and he was gone. "I had no radio. No phone. I couldn't communicate with anyone." Von Peij stayed in Ajam for three years, and then spent another two in Atsj. He was much more conservative than van Kessel. While van Kessel looked like some wild man in the jungle, with his war stripes and the feathers in his beard, von Peij never went native and looked like what he was—a white missionary, always cleanly shaven and scrubbed, dressed in white shorts and a white T-shirt. He tried to visit every village in his parish once a month, placed non-Asmat Papuan catechists in them to "testify about what's happening and if necessary tell the government." He learned Asmat fluently. And like van Kessel, he was in no hurry to baptize anyone. "We had a lot of time, and they weren't able to understand."

AND SO, on that day toward the end of 1957, the men from Otsjanep hid in the scrubby green tangle at the mouth of the Ewta to avenge the murder of Dombai, Su, Kokai, Wawar, and Pakai, the men killed by Omadesep a day earlier. They were aware of the superbeings entering their world. They knew van Kessel and von Peij, accepting their occasional presence in their villages because, over time, they got to know them and wanted their tobacco and modern tools, and they knew the government men and the police who backed them up, but it's fair to say that at that moment all of these people remained cloudy presences on the periphery of their lives. The Asmat of Otsjanep hadn't changed yet. Their sense of purpose and the very balance of their world were built around war and headhunting and rituals. Now, here, waiting for the men from Omadesep, they were fulfilling their purpose as men. To attack.

To fight. To restore balance in a dualistic world. If we could be inside their minds, if we could film what they saw, feel what they felt and be them, we might understand their need. The violence was the very fabric of their lives—it made them whole, constituted them, gave them identity and literally nourished them, helping the semen flow and the sago grow. And from it they created the shields and spears, the drums and masks and bisj poles, that was their language, their art, their symbolic and creative expression— ironically the very "art" beginning to attract the notice of Western collectors like Nelson Rockefeller.

As the last stragglers from Omadesep passed the river on their way home from the coastal fighting of the trip to Wagin, the men from Otsjanep attacked in force, hurtling down on them in swiftly paddled canoes. The exhausted men from Omadesep, with no canoes of their own, were vulnerable. Otsjanep shouted and screamed and clouds of lime burst over the water and bamboo horns sounded, and Otsjanep beat their canoes with the sides of their paddles. The warriors slaughtered their counterparts from Omadesep with arrows and spears, without remorse. The river ran red with blood. They beat the heads of their captives, dragged them back to their canoes, tied them onto crosspieces so they could be decapitated. Of the 124 men from the two villages who set out together to Wagin a few days earlier, only 11 made it home alive.

Van Kessel called it the Sylvester Massacre, because it happened at the end of December.

February 2012

WILEM SHOOK ME awake at three a.m. I tiptoed around bodies sprawled asleep on the living room floor in the darkness, climbed into the boat, and soon we were under way with the outflowing tide. It was still deep night, a few lanterns flickering yellow on the opposite bank, but the sky was alive with a trillion stars, the full moon so bright that long shadows of trees spread over the river, easily a mile wide. And that Southern Cross, an arrow pointing south. We were all sleepy, silent, lost in our own reveries as the bats flew and dipped overhead, Amates passing around cigarettes for all of us.

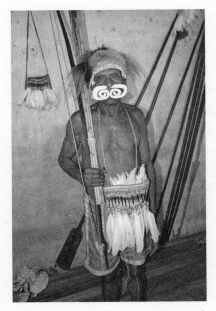

KOKAI, THE FORMER HEADMAN OF PIRIEN VILLAGE, WEARING A TRADITIONAL ASMAT CUSCUS FUR HEADBAND, NOSE ORNAMENT, BAG, AND BOW AND ARROWS.

After an hour the sky began to lighten, and we crossed to the opposite bank as waves

grew and the longboat started bucking. The morning was gray, still without sun, as we entered the Arafura. The wind picked up, pushing against us from the south, and we followed a quarter-mile off the coast, crossing the mouth of the Betsj on the same route Michael Rockefeller had taken that fateful day. The sun rose, the wind and waves grew stronger, the boat rolled and water crashed over the gunwales, I went for my satellite phone, and we ran for shelter up the Aping River.

AT THE MOUTHS of rivers and small creeks are often one or two huts—bivouacs built as temporary fishing camps. Which is what I thought this group of huts was too. But drying out inside, as Filo boiled water for rice and I stretched across a floor of split bamboo covered in sweet-smelling palm fronds, Amates said this was a new, permanent village, broken off from Omadesep, which itself had broken from Biwar Laut long ago. "Why?" I asked.

"Woman trouble," he said.

We ate, we smoked, we snoozed and swatted flies, and when Wilem decided the wind had died enough, we moved on, arriving at the Fajit River and the village of Basim in the early afternoon. Basim was spread out, had a handful of stores along the waterfront boardwalk. The day was burning hot, windless, and still. As always, we climbed onto a dock surrounded by silent, staring men and women and children in rags. Amates would mumble a few words and stride off, and the next thing I knew we'd taken over the schoolmaster's house, four bare wooden rooms across from the elementary school.

At first, these villages felt as if they'd been stripped of something, as if they were waiting, empty, as if some reason for being was gone. Basim's jeu was empty and crumbling, though magnificent in the way they all were—long and huge and tied together with rattan, nail-less. But there were no carvings anywhere, and if people weren't out gathering sago or fishing, they sat around.

Listless. Waiting. All except for the children, who played wildly, rambunctiously, loudly, climbing palm trees and covering themselves with mud and jumping off docks into the brown river. The sound of an Asmat village is the sound of a crowded playground, of children laughing and shouting and playing.

That night we were sitting on the floor when an older man walked in. He was thin, small, five-foot-seven and 140 pounds or so, with a prominent jaw, a big nose, and deep-set eyes. Veins popped from his neck and his temples. He had a hole in his septum. His polyester T-shirt was stained, spotted with small holes, and emblazoned with the image of a Papuan with shells through his nose and the word NOSESLIDE! A woven bag adorned with Job's tears seeds and cockatoo feathers hung from his neck across his chest—a sign of his importance. He had quick, darting eyes and spoke fast in a voice that sounded like gravel rolling across glass, exuding a wildness I hadn't seen yet in Asmat. "This is Kokai," Amates said. "He is my elder brother, my papa, the headman from Pirien," meaning that he was a chief in Pirien, a village named after one of the jeus in Otsjanep that had violently split to form a new village sometime after Rockefeller's disappearance. "He has a new wife in Basim, so he's here a lot." Kokai sat down on the floor with us, Amates brought out a pouch of tobacco and rolling papers. It was too good an opportunity: I confessed to Amates that I was interested in some old stories from Otsjanep and Omadesep, especially about a Dutch raid on the village in 1958, in retaliation for the killings during the trip to Wagin. In fact, from Dutch government archives, I had the original colonial reports filed at the time, describing the events.

"How old is he?" I asked Amates.

They talked, I waited. "He doesn't know," Amates said, "but maybe in his sixties."

"Does he remember a story about a Dutch raid, men being killed?"

Amates spoke to Kokai with what would soon become familiar to me—a long-winded, winding indirectness, a simple, ten-word question taking ten minutes to ask. Amates's interrogatory concluded, Kokai looked at me. Rolled a cigarette, a long one, using two pieces of rolling paper. The candlelight flickered. It was hot, my legs ached from the hard wooden floor, and I hadn't sat on a piece of padding since arising from my air mattress at three that morning. Then Kokai started talking.

"He remembers," Amates said. "He was a child, and he saw it." On and on it went in a disjointed swirl of story, Amates pausing to translate. The Asmat, I would learn, are splendid storytellers in a world without TV or film or prerecorded media of any kind. Kokai pantomimed the pulling of a bow. He slapped his thighs, his chest, his forehead, then swept his hands over his head, illustrating the back of his head blowing off. His eyes went big to show fright; he showed running with his arms and shoulders, then slinked, crept into the jungle. He held his cigarette between his middle finger and thumb, wiping his forefinger across the glowing coal to brush off the ash. I heard the names Osom, Faratsjam, Akon, Samut, and Ipi, and a tale that was the second link in the chain of events surrounding the mystery of Michael Rockefeller and that had been nothing but typewritten pages from a dusty Dutch archive came to life.

February 1958

ON FEBRUARY 6, 1958, as he boarded the government launch *Een-dracht* and headed for Otsjanep, the sun burned overhead with such intensity it made Max Lapré wilt. The *Eendracht* was thirty feet long, shallow draft, with a high bow and a curving sheer line that ended in a low waist just a foot above the water. At the bow was a small cuddy cabin with two portholes, and a white canopy covered the open deck. Lapré was wiry and tightly wound. Accompanying

THE VILLAGE OF OTSJANEP AND THE EWTA RIVER AT LOW TIDE AROUND THE TIME OF MAX LEPRÉ'S RAID.

him were eleven Papuan policemen dressed in khaki military-style uniforms and armed with Mauser M98 bolt-action rifles and one Schmeisser submachine gun, and Lapré carried a sidearm.

Lapré felt afraid. Following behind were three canoes of warriors from Atsj, and looking at them paddling naked in the sun, he couldn't shake a nagging feeling of smallness; he was a white dot in an utterly foreign, black-skinned world. And yet it was his country's to rule, this jungle, this swamp, these people, his to govern and tame, and he was determined to teach the natives a lesson in the power of civilized government.

The days of colonialism may have been ending, but Lapré, the new government controller who had taken over Asmat in 1956, was a man from another era. Max Lapré's relatives had been in the Dutch East Indies since the 1600s, and he was born in 1925 on the island of Sumatra. His father was a soldier in the Royal Netherlands Indies Army. When he was three, the family moved to Malang on the island of Celebes. There Max grew up in a community as insular as only a group of colonists can be, a place where people depended on each other against the majority and toasted the queen on her birthday. Even more so because, from the 1930s on, it was a community under threat as Indonesians agitated for independence and Japan began expanding throughout the Pacific. Years later, Max would remember his first encounter with Japanese soldiers in an interview. "There was this Japanese store in the Chinese area of Malang," Lapré said. "These were really long buildings and all the way in the back, you always had some sort of living area with a patio. I kept on walking further and further into the back of the store. Right there at the patio there were Japanese having a meeting. They sat there in uniforms, their samurai swords leaning against their seats. They saw me and I ducked away. It frightened me."

Still, the Dutch were shocked when Japan invaded Singapore in 1942. Lapré's father was sent to the front, and his seventeen-

year-old son never forgot the words he told his father: "You go teach them a lesson."

Instead, William Lapré stepped on a land mine and was taken prisoner from his hospital bed. He wouldn't see his family until 1946. As the war deepened, the Laprés lost their income and their servants, and the Dutch schools closed. Max became a hustler, selling watches, fabric, clothes, and beauty products to prostitutes. His girlfriend's father was executed. He was beaten by Japanese soldiers in 1944 and had to report to a working prison camp. His head was shaved, he was made to chop down trees with a dull ax, he slept in a wooden shed and was fed a meager diet of tea and a cup of corn in the morning, and more corn and raw vegetables in the evening. He grew weak with dysentery and had wild dreams; his mind drifted like it was floating away from his body.

Lapré's dysentery may have saved his life, because he was soon transferred to a hospital and released from the work camp to live with his grandparents. When the war ended, however, his troubles did not, for Indonesians were seeking independence. Houses and cars were appropriated by Indonesian republicans. Dutch were stoned and beaten with sticks. The Laprés' servants, back on the payroll, were blocked from entering the house. Max was arrested again, this time by young Indonesians with machine guns and swords, and locked in a prison cell in Malang. One day a prisoner started singing "The Wilhelmus," the Dutch national anthem, and all the prisoners joined in and were pelted with rocks and struck with sticks. When a half-Indonesian, half-European came to persuade them to become Indonesian citizens, they booed him.

After being released in June 1946, Lapré sailed for the Netherlands.

NOW, TEN YEARS LATER, he was back, working for the government in the last Dutch colony in the East. A death here, a death there, could be overlooked, but the recent mayhem between Omadesep

and Otsjanep was too much. Holland was a civilized country try-
ing to make something out of its half of New Guinea, and it was
time to step in. Did he carry animosity toward the Asmat? He
would say in later interviews that he didn't. But his whole life had
been formed as a colonist, as an overlord, and then he'd suffered
years of abuse and was ripped away from the only world he knew.
Did he have any knowledge about the Asmat as a culture? Did he
care? There is no evidence in his writings or reports that he had
any empathy for them, and he seems to have stepped into his post
with an agenda. After meeting him, van Kessel lamented that
Lapré was "planning to rule the Asmat with a strong hand."

Soon after Lapré arrived in Asmat, the small village of Atem-
but took a head from the village of Biwar Laut, in retribution for
two men and two women from Atembut who had been killed
three years before on a visit to Biwar. Lapré sped to the village,
which he found deserted. Still, he would teach them a lesson. He
set the jeu on fire, destroyed all the canoes he found, and emptied
a machine gun into the air, an action that van Kessel called "un-
proportionate."

When he'd first heard the news about the fight between
Omadesep and Otsjanep, Lapré had simply dispatched a police-
man named Dias, himself a colonial mutt, half-Indonesian, half-
Dutch. Dias and a force descended on Omadesep on January 18,
1958. They arrested eleven, confiscated as many of the weapons in
the village as they could find, and burned canoes and at least one
of the men's houses. Reports reached Dias, however, that Otsjanep
wouldn't be so pliable. Fearing trouble, he sent three Papuan po-
licemen with a Dutch flag and some steel axes to the village. The
police returned quickly. Otsjanep wanted nothing to do with the
government and were willing, Lapré would write in his official
report, "to use violence to make themselves clear. The Dutch flag
was not accepted."

Lapré went himself ten days later. He'd first stopped at Atsj,

where he asked the people for help—a curious thing to do since the villages were barely known to each other and canoes of warriors from Atsj would hardly be a calming influence on Otsjanep. "Maybe they saw it as an opportunity to smack someone's head off," Lapré admitted of the rowers from Atsj. "You never know with these people, and if there were fights, yeah, they liked that." Again he'd sent three Papuans with a flag, and again they'd returned reporting that the flag was rejected and that Otsjanep was "fully armed and waiting for them."

Years later, Lapré would say that he went to Otsjanep only to "investigate" and to see if he could find anyone who might "identify the perpetrators." If that was true, however, he could have waited for things to cool off. He could have arrived unarmed in a canoe with von Peij or van Kessel bearing tobacco. In fact, in 1958 no white men had ever been attacked by the Asmat, who either feared the white strangers in their midst or regarded the few who came without weapons and bearing fishhooks, axes, and tobacco—like van Kessel—with tolerance.

THAT HAD ALMOST always been the case with tribal people in the first stages of contact. When Christopher Columbus reached the New World in 1492, he wrote in his journal on December 16: "They are the best people in the world and above all the gentlest. They became so much our friends that it was a marvel. . . . They traded and gave everything they had, with good will. I sent the ship's boat ashore for water, and they very willingly showed my people where the water was, and they themselves carried the full barrels to the boat. They are very gentle and without knowledge of what is evil, nor do they murder or steal. Your highnesses may believe that in all the world there can be no better or gentler people."

Four hundred years later, Tobias Schneebaum arrived in the last mission outpost in the Peruvian Amazon. Out there, beyond

the mission, he was told, were uncontacted tribes who bashed the heads of their enemies and attacked any attempts at contact from outsiders. But Schneebaum had an insatiable curiosity and deep affinity for indigenous people—they didn't scare him. One day he left the mission and headed alone into the jungle. After four days of walking, he spotted a group of men on the banks of the river. Had he been armed, fearful, on edge, or in a big group, who knows what would have happened. But Schneebaum surrendered totally: he shed his clothes and walked naked into their midst. The violent savages' response? They hugged him and touched him and kissed him all over and marveled at him and led him back to their village, where he lived for months.

Inevitably, those early peaceful encounters between whites and natives soon turned to violence. The cultural collision was too great, the power imbalance too extreme, between men who knew nothing beyond their immediate world and men who thought they knew everything. They weren't, after all, just people with different technologies, but people living in completely different worlds— and the whites invariably had no inkling of this other world. They couldn't see the spirits, didn't know they existed, and were blind, deaf, and dumb to the symbols and meanings of the cultures they were entering.

In the 1930s, explorers began a series of foot journeys into the highlands of what is now Papua New Guinea, almost always in large parties of several whites and with extensive retinues of porters and policemen, all of them armed with modern firearms. And always the response was the same: the Papuans were petrified, believing that the whites were ghosts, spirits of the dead. The white creatures' boot prints, to those used to reading footprints, indicated a being that had its toes cut off, and the tread patterns implied a skeleton of some kind.

These creatures had to be either avoided, driven away from their homes, or placated with sweet potatoes and pigs, and the accounts

offer a long tale of one misunderstanding after another. When Australians Jack Hides and Jim O'Malley entered the Great Papuan Plateau in 1935, they appeared to the local Etoro people as if coming from outer space. "We jumped with surprise," recalled an Etoro who'd witnessed them. "No one had seen anything like this before or knew what it was. When they saw the clothes on the Sowelo—Europeans—and the others, they thought they were like people you see in a dream; 'these must be spirit people coming openly, in plain sight.'" About fifty Etoro warriors eventually appeared, armed with bows and arrows. They pranced and whooped and to disrupt them Hides let out a loud, two-fingered whistle. In that moment two worlds—three, really, the world of the whites, the world of the Etoro, and the world of the spirits, a fourth dimension that Hides couldn't see, didn't know existed—collided. For the Australian it was just a sound, a loud noise to get the natives' attention. To the Etoro it was something else altogether: the sound a witch made when it approached. By the time an escalating series of cultural miscommunications came to an end, Hides and his porters had fired three shots, killing two.

AS LAPRÉ ENTERED the Ewta River, geography didn't help. The river is narrow: seventy-five feet wide at its mouth at high tide, it quickly diminishes to less than half that upstream. Three hundred yards upriver, they encountered a fleet of canoes full of armed warriors from Otsjanep. They screeched and "bawled," as Lapré put it, but pulled back as Lapré came closer. He chased them for a bit, but got nervous, and then decided to retreat.

Not wanting to take any chances, Lapré increased his strength. On the sixth of February, he dispatched a mobile police force out of Merauke to the mouth of the Faretsj, where it linked up with Dias and another ten policemen, and together with four canoes full of warriors from Atsj they again arrived at the mouth of the Ewta.

It was afternoon and the tide was incoming, but the river was still too shallow to enter with the launch. They waited, the tension increasing with the afternoon heat. Finally, late in the day, there was enough water to proceed, and they entered what must have seemed like the heart of darkness. As the Ewta narrowed to thirty feet, sometimes twenty, the banks pressed in, a tangle of nipa palms and reeds and mangrove roots rising out of black mud. And then it started to rain, a driving, pelting tropical deluge. Lapré felt unsure, frightened. Where van Kessel would have arrived in shorts and sneakers, sitting in the bottom of a native canoe, Lapré was steaming upriver in a powered steel motor launch packed with gun-toting, uniformed policemen. Even worse, he was leading a party of warriors from Atsj, historic enemies of Otsjanep. Behind every tree he believed lurked a savage warrior, and he was worried about how to get out—the upper Ewta was too narrow to turn around quickly.

Lapré grabbed the tiller himself. It took an hour for them to creep toward the village. The heat. The overhanging trees and dangling vines, all dripping and moist. A twisting, narrow passageway. The sound of their engine bouncing off the wall of green. The agonizingly slow voyage toward an armed confrontation with naked men smeared with war paint and adorned with feathers and the tusks of pigs and teeth of dogs, shells and pig bone in their noses, who followed no conventions regarding prisoners, who were as different as it was possible for human beings to be.

Lapré's concern was self-fulfilling. After an hour, they rounded a bend and the world opened. The clearing was thick with men, and Lapré noted seeing no women, children, or dogs—"always a bad sign." The villagers were as scared as Lapré, maybe more so. Word had traveled fast in the jungle; they knew what happened in Omadesep, the canoes destroyed, the men arrested. And they knew about guns, the violence they were capable of. But they were confused. They didn't know what Lapré and his patrol would do,

what they should do, maybe not even who, or what, he really was. They were proud and independent in their world, and Lapré might even be a ghost. What to do?

On the left a group approached, Lapré believed, in capitulation. But on the right stood a group armed with bows and arrows and spears and shields. Lapré looked left, he looked right; he was equally unsure of what to do. Women and children streamed out of the houses and fled into the jungle. Behind the houses a third group of men broke into what he described as "warrior dances." Lapré and a force of police scrambled onto the left bank, Dias and his men took the right. A few men from Otsjanep bolted for the bush, and the armed men backed toward the rim of the forest.

"Come out!" Lapré yelled, through interpreters, "and put down your weapons!"

A few men edged forward and then tried to run away, and Lapré's policemen tried to restrain them.

Then pandemonium. A man came out of a house bearing something in his hand, and he ran toward Lapré. What was he holding?

Shots rang out from all directions. Bang. Bang. Bang. An Asmat named Faratsjam was hit in the head and the rear of his skull blew off. Four bullets ripped into Osom—his biceps, both armpits, and his hip. Akon took shots to the midsection, Samut to the chest. Ipi's jaw vanished in a bloody instant. As in stories of similar encounters in the highlands, the villagers would remember every detail of the bullet damage, so shocking it was to them, the violence so fast and ferocious and magical to people used to hand-to-hand combat and wounding with spear or arrow, which almost never killed instantly.

The Asmat panicked and bolted in all directions, disappearing into the jungle. "Stop shooting!" Lapré yelled. He did a quick search, found two dead, and set fire to the biggest canoes. Shortly before dusk, Lapré and his men climbed back on their boat and headed downriver.

Lapré's explanation to van Kessel about his actions: "It was raining cats and dogs, and the people acted so strange."

Lapré spent the night offshore and returned up the Ewta the next day at five-thirty a.m. Now, however, the river was blocked. Throughout the night the men from Otsjanep had cut trees, felling them across the river, so many that it took Lapré six hours to make it the few miles to Otsjanep. The village was deserted, but from the jungle they heard chanting and the beat of drums. Lapré did not pursue them.

Over the next few days Lapré visited nearby villages. Basim, just a few miles away and closely related by marriage and blood to Otsjanep, was deserted. Buepis he found "quite skittish." At the mouth of the Fajit, he made contact with a powerful chief named Betekam, who had managed the feat of marrying five wives from five different villages, thereby acquiring not just power and prestige but free passage among them. Lapré had left five dead and one injured in Otsjanep, Betekam said, and the village had been hostile because it didn't want to let go of "old customs and headhunting." The villagers, Betekam said, were afraid and did not want to return. Lapré offered a deal, to be conveyed through Betekam: he would leave them alone if they returned to their village and turned over the heads of the men from Omadesep they had taken.

There is no evidence any heads were ever turned over to Lapré, and his action did not stop headhunting in Otsjanep or anywhere else in Asmat. Lapré admitted that he was probably just driving villages deeper into the jungle and farther up rivers, away from the government. When he visited Otsjanep three months later, many of the inhabitants fled, and men hid under their houses, "waiting to see which way the cat would jump," he wrote in his patrol report. "The course of affairs is certainly regrettable, but on the other hand it has become clear to them that headhunting and cannibalism is not much appreciated by a government institution all but unknown to them, with which they had only incidental

contact. It is highly likely that the people now understand that they would do better not to resist authorities. Their attitude of intentional resistance, which found expression in the rejection of contact items and the Dutch flag . . . was all the more reproachable. . . . However regrettable it may be that there had to be casualties, this is to be preferred over the fact that the village is slowly but surely walking into the forest and nothing can be done about it. In the latter case, every grain of respect would have gone up in the air and eventually there would have been more casualties because of the headhunting raids."

The words, given the people he was writing about, are absurd. To us, to a Westerner, they make sense—a straightforward analysis of a people resisting government, who required the teaching of a lesson. But a Dutch flag? A government institution? The rule of law? To the Asmat, Lapré's raid was altogether something else, a profoundly unsettling experience, something far more than a simple imposition of rational law: the confusing appearance of superbeings, the spirits their whole lives were built around appeasing and deceiving and driving away, had come to kill them with nearly supernatural weapons. For a Catholic it would be like devils or angels appearing in the flesh to attack them for . . . for what?

And what of the spirits of the five killed by Lapré? They were out there, wandering around, causing mischief, haunting the village, making people sick, as real in death as they were in life. The Chinese crocodile hunters had killed eight. Omadesep had killed four more. Lapré now added five. Seventeen men, women, and children were dead. The world was out of balance, an open wound festering in the village each and every day, even more so because Lapré was a white man. It's hard to imagine the consternation this caused. How to explain it? How to deal with it?

10

March 1958

MAX LAPRÉ WASN'T operating in a vacuum. If the world of the Asmat and Otsjanep was in turmoil, so was the larger world around New Guinea. Within days of Lapré's raid on Otsjanep, the new US ambassador to Indonesia, William Palfrey Jones, presented his credentials to Indonesian president Sukarno at a ceremony in Jakarta. Cameras flashed as Sukarno and Jones raised champagne glasses filled with orange juice (a Muslim, Sukarno did not drink alcohol) and toasted the health of Sukarno and President Dwight D. Eisenhower. Jones reiterated his nation's position—that it had no interest in meddling in Indonesia's internal affairs and every interest in helping the country maintain its hard-won independence.

Jones's comments were more specific than they sounded. The islands of the Indonesian archipelago had

INDONESIAN PRESIDENT SUKARNO.

a deep and complex culture that had been subjugated by the
Dutch for as long as anyone alive, or their grandparents or great-
grandparents, could remember. In 1928 Sukarno had proclaimed
that a united and independent Indonesia was everything. "Prince
and pauper, patrician and coolie, Moslem and Christian—all
could be united in a passionate drive for a single goal, Sukarno
saw," wrote Jones. "This goal was liberty, or *merdeka,* a word that
became the rallying cry of the cause." On August 17, 1945, in the
waning days of the Japanese occupation, the Indonesian national-
ist movement proclaimed the Republic of Indonesia.

The Netherlands wanted its colony back, however, and moved
in with tanks and aircraft. Only after four years of war and negoti-
ations through the United Nations Commission on Indonesia did
the Dutch surrender their claim. During the negotiations, how-
ever, the Netherlands insisted on keeping West New Guinea—the
western, Dutch half of the island. Indonesia was Muslim; New
Guinea was Melanesian and animist—a separate place, so the
Dutch argument ran. Sukarno set aside the New Guinea issue,
and the agreement was signed, creating the Republic of Indonesia
in 1950, with the stipulation that further negotiations on New
Guinea would take place within a year. But with the formal birth
of the Republic—a country with 150 million inhabitants spread
across thousands of miles—the Netherlands balked, ignoring its
agreement to further discuss Indonesian claims to New Guinea,
and was supported by Britain, Australia, and the United States.
Jones's words were a careful balancing act regarding Indonesian
sovereignty, Papua, and Sukarno's own balancing act with the In-
donesian Communist Party (PKI).

When it became Sukarno's turn to speak during the ceremony,
his word choice was equally specific. Sukarno emphasized Indo-
nesia's independent foreign policy—it had no wish to take sides
with either major world bloc—and stressed the importance of
"completing Indonesia's revolution by effecting the return of West

Irian" (the Dutch colony of New Guinea). For Sukarno and Indonesia, the "return" of Papua was *the* fundamental issue; without it, in his mind, Indonesia remained divided and unfree.

Between 1954 and 1957, Indonesia submitted four draft resolutions on the issue to the UN General Assembly, but none were passed. In retribution, in 1956 the country nationalized Dutch businesses and expelled tens of thousands of Dutch still living there, deepening the antagonism between the two countries.

For the Dutch, keeping its Papuan colony was purely emotional—no valuable natural resources had yet been discovered there, and the colony cost the Netherlands far more than it earned. But the Indonesian army and Communist Party were locked in a struggle for dominance, and President Sukarno maintained power by dancing between the two—and distracting both by whipping up nationalist fervor over the occupation of West New Guinea and British Malaysia. Percy Spender, Australia's minister for external affairs, feared that Indonesia would make "hostile and aggressive neighbors." Indonesia appeared unstable, on the verge of economic collapse. Communism was spreading throughout Southeast Asia, and the PKI was growing in strength, winning 27 percent of the votes cast in local elections in 1957. Economic collapse would be the opening the PKI was hoping for, the theory went, part of the feared "falling dominoes": Vietnam, Cambodia, Thailand, Indonesia. A Communist Indonesia would be bad enough, but even worse would be a Communist foothold in New Guinea, just across the Arafura from Australia.

Rebuffed by the West when he sought Western military assistance, Sukarno made official state visits in 1956 to both Moscow and Beijing, returning with $100 million in credit from the Soviet Union and a more modest amount of aid guarantees from China. Meanwhile, the British, who still held territory on the island of Borneo, feared that the transfer of West New Guinea to Sukarno would set a precedent for the takeover of its Borneo ter-

ritory. The official US position on the issue was neutral, a balanc-
ing act to avoid strengthening the PKI and to placate Australia
and Britain.

The Netherlands knew it couldn't hold on to its colony forever,
but it hoped to do so for another ten years. "New Guinea had
been the abandoned child of the Dutch government," said Wim
van de Waal, the Dutch patrol officer who was stationed in As-
mat in 1961, who now lives in the Canary Islands. "But then it
was all they had, and because of rising internal political pressure,
they had to *do* something with it. The Dutch didn't want to talk
about it, but the government knew it had to step up development
in order to show that they were capable of leading the Papuans
toward independence." Which is why the missionary and govern-
ment presence in what had been a forgotten corner of the empire
accelerated throughout the 1950s. Jones's words to Sukarno not-
withstanding, in 1957 the US policy had became one of opposing,
"by appropriate measures, any attempt by a Communist-oriented
Indonesia to seize West New Guinea."

The Dutch set up elected regional councils throughout the is-
land, hoping to create an elite who could govern the country by
1970, when it proposed granting West New Guinea independence.
"It is essential for the Netherlands to see to it that, once the time
for independence has come, a sufficient number of qualified indig-
enous inhabitants are available to take over the greatest part of the
administration," a 1960 Dutch policy paper stated. It was a dif-
ficult task, though, given that all but a handful of the elites, found
almost exclusively in Hollandia and on Biak, were still living in
the Stone Age. How were headhunting cannibals supposed to gov-
ern themselves? It was why Max Lapré was never censored for the
killings in Otsjanep and why Dutch officials would repeatedly tell
visitors that headhunting had been vanquished even when it was
still flourishing. And given the Netherlands' three-hundred-year
occupation of Indonesia and its reluctance to give up its colony, it's

easy to grasp Lapré's need, as he sailed up the Ewta River toward Otsjanep, to teach them a lesson.

BY THE TIME Michael Rockefeller prepared to go to New Guinea in 1961, Sukarno, after feeling increasingly snubbed by the West, was buying hundreds of millions of dollars' worth of Soviet weapons and threatening to take West New Guinea by force. With John F. Kennedy's election, Washington's policy changed; Kennedy's advisers began advocating that New Guinea be given to Indonesia to appease the Communists and keep Sukarno away from the Eastern Bloc—in direct opposition to the policy of the Netherlands, Britain, and Australia.

The Dutch foreign minister, Joseph Luns, created what would become known as the Luns Plan. The Dutch would withdraw from New Guinea and terminate sovereignty in exchange for a UN administration and a "member state study commission" that would supervise the administration and organize an election to decide its final status, creating an independent country that would be politically aligned with the West and friendly to Dutch business interests. Walt Rostow, a national security adviser to Kennedy, opposed the plan. Returning West New Guinea to Sukarno, he wrote to Kennedy, was the only option to keep Indonesia from being "driven into the arms" of the Soviet Union. And he wrote that the United States should be honest with the Dutch and tell them that self-determination for a bunch of "Stone Age" Papuans would be meaningless.

Into this tangle stepped Michael Rockefeller. He wasn't just another Western college kid with a backpack; he was the son of one of the richest and most powerful and influential men in America, a man who had just a few months before run for president, whose family had once donated the land for the UN itself. The Luns Plan was scheduled to be formally presented to the UN in September 1961. The Dutch would do whatever it took to make Michael—

and his father—happy; they needed American allies wherever and however they could find them. They would provide logistical support and an anthropologist from the Netherlands New Guinea Office of Native Affairs to Michael when he finally arrived in Asmat, and that assistance would have profound effects on the story of his disappearance.

PART II

11

March 1961

"IF YOU CAN believe it, I'm finally in New Guinea," Michael Rock-efeller wrote on March 29, 1961, to his best friend, Sam Putnam. He'd flown from Boston to Tokyo, via New York, the takeoff de-layed an hour because the New York radar had gone down, giving him "heart failure as I had visions of missing the flight out." En route to Tokyo the plane was nearly empty, and he slept sprawled

DANI MEN REMEMBERING MICHAEL ROCKEFELLER AND THE HARVARD PEABODY EXPEDITION, BALIEM VALLEY, 2012.

across four seats. There are different kinds of travelers; people ease into new cultures in different ways. When I hit the ground in a foreign world, I revel in the place with a big meal. It's a ritual, bodily taking in the new place, and Michael did the same, eagerly consuming Japanese culture with a "wonderful" meal of tempura.

From Tokyo he'd flown on to Biak, an island off the north coast of New Guinea, home to a former US Army Air Corps airfield on which the Dutch maintained a squadron of aircraft to protect its colony. There he linked up with Karl Heider, a Harvard graduate student in anthropology. When Heider had arrived the day before, he disappointed the throng of Dutch officials who'd gathered, thinking they were welcoming the son of the governor of New York. The two spent a day walking around in the heat and humidity of Biak and then departed for Hollandia on a DC-3. Michael perched in the cockpit, marveling at the winding brown rivers emptying into New Guinea's north coast, when the pilot poked him in the ribs and pointed out the window—the right engine had died. Michael scrambled into his seat, Heider clutched his most valuable papers and possessions, the plane landed safely again in Biak, and they flew on to Hollandia the next day.

Michael was heading not to Asmat but to the Great Baliem Valley in the island's highlands. He was tall and slender, clean-shaven, and square-jawed like his father, with thick black-rimmed glasses. He'd grown up in the family townhouse in midtown Manhattan and on weekends at the Rockefeller estate in Westchester County, New York. As Abby had done with Nelson, so Nelson did with Michael, taking him to art dealers on Saturday afternoons, a father-and-son bonding ritual that schooled his taste. His twin sister, Mary, remembered how the two of them loved to watch their father rearrange his art. And when he was eleven, his mother finally discovered why he'd been coming home from school late: he'd spotted a painting he liked through the second-floor window of the Old Masters art gallery on Madison Avenue, rang the bell,

and its owner, Harry Yotnakparian, started letting Michael hang around as long as he didn't get in the way.

By the time he was nearing the end of his four years at Harvard, Michael was, in the words of Sam Putnam's girlfriend, "a quiet, artistic spirit." And he was torn. Though his appreciation of art had been nurtured since the day he was born, his father expected his son to be like him—to pursue a career in one of the family enterprises, banking or finance, and indulge his artistic passions on the side. Michael graduated cum laude from Harvard with a BA degree in history and economics, but he yearned for something else, a different way of being. He'd traveled widely, working on his father's ranch in Venezuela for a summer, traveling to Japan in 1957, and he'd been surrounded not just by art but by primitive art. Who's to say where wanderlust comes from, whether it's innate or whether experiences or books or even objects inspire it—but without a doubt, Michael had it.

Imagine growing up surrounded by objects that had been coveted by your father and that spoke of far-flung places. Imagine not just appreciating those same kinds of objects yourself, but wanting to go to their source to find them and bring them home. As graduation neared, Michael and Putnam schemed. They'd been best friends since prep school at Phillips Exeter, where Michael had been art director of the yearbook and Sam editor. Now they wanted to get away, to have a big adventure before Putnam attended medical school and Michael pursued what seemed an inevitable life of business—one last hurrah, as Putnam's then girlfriend put it. Putnam had dabbled in film and knew Robert Gardner. Gardner ran the Harvard Film Study Center and was fascinated by film as ethnographic record. He wanted to make a movie about an uncontacted Neolithic people, "to employ the art of film to a humane observation of a remote and seemingly alien group of people," a film, he said, "about the world outside myself that also revealed me and my inner world."

In 1959 he'd begun casting about for the right project when a distant cousin told him about an obscure tribe in New Guinea whose culture was based on ritual war. Gardner contacted Victor de Bruyn, the head of native affairs in Dutch New Guinea, who said his government might not only be interested in a film but able to help with the funding. Gardner talked to the anthropologist Margaret Mead; Robert Goldwater, director of Nelson Rockefeller's Museum of Primitive Art; and Adrian Gerbrands, deputy director of the Dutch National Museum of Ethnology, who'd recently begun doing fieldwork in Asmat. De Bruyn suggested a film about the Dani tribes living in the Grand Baliem Valley, and the Dutch government eventually contributed $5,000 toward the expedition.

In some ways, the Dani had long been more isolated than the Asmat. Although encounters with the West along the southwest coast of Asmat had been few and far between, at least the jungles and swamps were known to be inhabited. But anyone who gazed into the interior of New Guinea saw one thing: the high and jagged mountains that ran along its central spine. And if you traveled upriver from the coast, those rivers eventually narrowed and turned into whitewater at the walls of steep mountains. Up there was simply uninhabited wilderness. In the 1930s, Australian explorers and gold-hunters began discovering the highlands on the Australian side of the island. Then, in 1938, an American named Richard Archbold, on an expedition sponsored by the American Museum of Natural History, flew over the Grand Baliem Valley. He was astounded. Instead of jagged, uninhabited mountains, he found a green valley. Instead of the sparsely populated and isolated communities of the coastal people, he found a heavily populated pastoral, a world of rising tendrils of smoke and intricate, carefully terraced gardens and irrigation canals, stone walls, vine suspension bridges, and grass huts—and fifty thousand people, naked save for grass skirts and penis gourds, who thought they were the only

people on earth. The Dani living in the Grand Baliem Valley were the last great uncontacted civilization.

By 1960 there were a few Protestant missionaries, a small contingent of Dutch officials, an airfield, and not much else there. The United States and the Soviet Union were sending rockets into space, but the handful of Dutch officials in the "city" of Wamena lived without running water or electricity. Little contact had been made at the north and south ends of the valley. The Dani were not headhunters or cannibals like the Asmat, but they engaged in a cyclical war of revenge with their immediate neighbors that intrigued Gardner. He, like most observers fascinated with indigenous people, felt they might offer insight into humans in an uncorrupted state, and he wanted to observe and film them over months to glean insights into man's propensity for violence and war.

Gardner began thinking about including writers and photographers who could depict the project in other mediums. At lunch one afternoon on Martha's Vineyard at the home of the playwright Lillian Hellman, he met the writer Peter Matthiessen and invited him along to the Grand Baliem Valley. "He said I'd be paid," Matthiessen told me, "and that was really important to me." Gardner used to take smoking breaks on the steps of the Peabody Museum in Cambridge, and there he met Karl Heider. When Michael came to him, Gardner sensed a possible source of funding and offered him the opportunity to be the film's sound engineer.

It was the perfect postcollege adventure, and Michael invited Sam Putnam to join them a few months later, at the end of his first year of medical school at Harvard. Michael plunged in, learning everything he could about sound recording and asking Gardner if he could practice with the expedition's new Nagra tape recorder at the 1960 Republican National Convention, where his father hoped to be nominated for the presidency. Before he could go, however, there was the issue of the draft. Michael got a six-month gig in the US Army Reserve and was recommended for training in teletype

repair. "My first reaction was one of terror," he wrote Gardner from basic training in Fort Dix, New Jersey, " . . . and I pictured myself shipped off to Fort Leonard Wood, Oklahoma or Fort Jackson, Kentucky." Instead, he wrote a "passionate" letter to his captain, "describing my utter incompetence in the recommended field." Clearly it didn't hurt to be the son of the governor of New York, for his orders were quickly changed, and he was off to Fort Devens, just down the road from Harvard, to be trained as a "code traffic analyst." "At least my typing will get a good practicing [*sic*]." Still, he said, the army had taught him "the assets of a highly ordered day-to-day existence. I have received all sorts of useful pointers for field life in New Guinea from such things as bivouac and courses in first aid, land navigation, etc. Furthermore, I am in sterling condition."

That was in November 1960. Gardner knew about Michael's interest in art, and a few weeks later he helped Michael out further by introducing him to Adrian Gerbrands, an ethnologist living in New Guinea. Gardner said Michael had been excited by Gerbrands's work in Asmat, and "he became more and more interested in meeting you and visiting the Asmat area." Would that be possible in mid-May during a break in filming in the highlands? Gardner asked. "I can assure you that he knows how to take care of himself and would be not the slightest burden."

BY APRIL 2, Michael was in Wamena at last, and he was excited. "The flight in was spectacular," he wrote "Sambo." He flew in "over Lake Sentani, jungles, mountains, the huge impenetrable swamp of the interior, more mountains, and then finally the Baliem Valley opening up like a sudden giant, fertile cavity before me. How badly we were misled in all the pictures we saw! The Baliem is a thing of magnificent vastness, decorated with the green of the valley floor and blues of the surrounding mountains. Tones are ever changing in the shifting light. The mountains rise . . . over 10,000 feet on all sides and are constantly hidden and altered by

the clouds that gather about them. The valley floor is broken into fragments by the Baliem and its tributaries, hills and rocky rises, and the handmade barriers of the Ndani peoples. The climate is like Maine in the peak of summer. Only the sun is better."

A few days later they brought hundreds of pounds of equipment via boat and foot to the northern part of the valley, where they made camp at a small stream at the base of a wall of rock and sparse pine trees. It was a beautiful spot, slightly elevated yet protected, far enough from the Dani family compounds for the expedition to get much-needed personal space, but close enough to get involved in everything. Matthiessen and Eliot Elisofon, a photographer for *Life* magazine, soon joined them, and Matthiessen had a strong first impression of Michael. "He was very, very young and a little bit spoiled. He quoted Dad a lot."

It was a magical time. The Baliem is as beautiful as Michael described it, a place of a thousand shades of green changing as the clouds roll by, surrounded by jagged peaks in every direction. At six thousand feet, its temperatures are cool, with cold nights, no humidity, and few mosquitoes. When Michael arrived, the Dani there were untouched, the men naked except for long gourds covering their penises in stylized erections and a layer of pig grease, the women naked save for loose grass skirts and net bags slung with a child or pig from their heads and across their backs. It was, in some ways, the best of two worlds—having access to the primitive balanced with being able to retreat to a comfortable camp full of urbane colleagues. The team shared civilized meals in the cook tent—omelets and orange juice and coffee for breakfast—and drank Heineken at night as the Dani gathered around, amazed by their clothing, mirrors, and cameras. During the day the visitors fanned out into villages of family compounds to watch and record the Dani. Michael found them "emotionally expressive" and fantastic to look at. "Polik, the warrior," he wrote, "struts around with a fifteen foot spear and the most incredible headdress. His face,

often peering through hair that reaches his shoulders, is always blackened with charcoal and pig grease is kind of the epitome of Neolithic wildness."

When word came of a battle, they'd all gather on a grassy plateau no-man's-land where opposing villages assembled to shout at each other and run at each other and threaten and occasionally engage each other. The film team's whiteness granted them an immunity as the Dani grew used to their presence, allowing them in their midst even as they battled—as if a team of filmmakers were allowed to witness and record the set-piece battles of World War II with impunity. They were so close to the action that one day an arrow hit Michael in the leg, and the team was careful to keep it secret. It was a strange kind of war, however, compared to the destructive violence of the much more developed world. "They went to war with a set of rules far more civilized than ours," said Matthiessen. "One killing was fine."

Michael worked hard, recording the sounds, songs, music, and warfare as well as taking photographs, which he especially loved. He "shot wildly," he wrote, exposing eighteen rolls in a single day. Sometimes it was too much, and one night the team unloaded on Michael, criticizing him for missing important sound recordings. "Michael went away in tears," Matthiessen said. After that night, Michael grew up and worked hard, according to Matthiessen, but he was "disorganized. Messy. He forgot things."

Michael shared a tent with Heider, who got to know him well. "Mike was very quiet and very modest," Heider remembers, "though of course everyone knew who he was, who his father was. He didn't take up much space, and it was easy to be around him. And he had patience." The Dani opened up to him. While Elisofon, the professional, would pose them and stage photos, Michael would just watch quietly, shooting what he saw. In the evenings Heider was astonished to see the wealthiest member of the team darning his old army socks. But Michael was ambitious, and he

began to think seriously about his photography. In late April, he wrote his friend Sam with an idea: they should put together a book on the Dani. "It seems to me that there is a large opportunity for me and you if it can be somehow managed with medical school. The photography ought to be good enough to form the basis for a photographic essay on the Ndani culture to come out in book form. Certainly this is a wild and conceited thought and would be very difficult to do well. Let me know what you think," adding in a postscript, "Keep this confidential, for I have told no one but you and wouldn't unless it was more definite."

There are people who don't like hanging out with spiders and dirt and naked men in pig grease, but Michael Rockefeller wasn't one of them. It was especially nice to be among people who didn't care that he was a Rockefeller, who had no idea what the name even meant. In New Guinea, as the weeks passed, home began to dissolve into abstraction, to lessen its hold. Material possessions began to lose their importance. There was something liberating about the intense focus on a single project. What was important was right here—a world of sweating, naked bodies, of feasts and smoke-filled huts, of pigs and pig grease. Here, at last, he was free from social conventions. Free from being a Rockefeller.

AS APRIL GAVE way to May, Michael began planning his trip to Asmat with Putnam. In the Baliem, he was the youngest member of a group under the leadership of Gardner; now, for the first time, he would be plunging in alone with his own agenda. "Michael's father had put him on the board of his museum," said Heider, "and Michael said he wanted to do something that hadn't been done before and to bring a major collection to New York, and Asmat was the obvious choice." His goal was a short trip of two to four weeks with Sam that would serve as reconnaissance for a longer journey after the filming was finished. He was hardly a lone entity, however, plunging into the unknown without resources. Michael

was both part of a Harvard expedition that had the backing of the government and a Rockefeller—not to mention a trustee of the Museum of Primitive Art. He was treated like a VIP wherever he went outside the Baliem Valley.

Michael wrote to Robert Goldwater about his forthcoming trip and suggested the possibility of also collecting along the Sepik River of Australian New Guinea. "Collecting along the Sepik . . . needs some reflection and discussion," Goldwater wrote him back. "As you know, there have been several collecting expeditions there in the last few years, and from what we have seen brought back it does not in general seem any longer to be a very promising area."

However, Goldwater introduced Michael to Australian officials, provided a letter of recommendation, and said that he was "looking forward to your coming up with a fine group of objects." And the Dutch New Guinea Department of Native Affairs provided Michael with an anthropologist to guide and accompany him. René Wassing was thirty-four, with a tidy mustache and ropy, muscled calves. He worked across the island in Hollandia and had never been to Asmat before. The two linked up in the capital and on June 20 flew to Merauke, where they had lunch with Resident F. R. J. Eibrink Jansen, the highest government official in the area, along with the Dutch controller and the head of the regional council. In the afternoon, they loaded up on food in the local Chinese-owned shop and then departed that evening at five on the government launch *Tasman,* heading north along the coast, where Wassing noted that they encountered turbulent seas.

Early on the morning of the twenty-second, they arrived at the government post of Pirimapun, where they saw their first Asmat people and canoes, some with delicately carved bows, pulled up on the mud. There wasn't much in the settlement—a dock and a few thatch houses belonging to Wim van de Waal, a slender, blond, twenty-one-year-old Dutch patrol officer who was overseeing the

construction of an airstrip; Ken Dresser, a Canadian Protestant missionary and medical doctor; and a handful of Papuan policemen.

Van de Waal was Lapré's polar opposite. He'd finished high school late, when he was twenty, and before he could attend university he had to complete two years of military service, which he felt was a waste of time. His best friend's brother had been a patrol officer in New Guinea, a more exciting and exotic alternative to military service.

Out of three hundred candidates who applied as colonial patrol officers, sixteen were selected, and van de Waal was among them. He traveled from the Netherlands to New Guinea in late 1959. After nine months in Hollandia learning Malay and receiving instruction in colonial government, he was sent to Pirimapun in October 1960. "It was an 'exploration district,' one of the wildest areas of all of New Guinea," he said. He had almost no instructions. " 'Make contact,' I was told, 'so that little by little they will gain the trust of the government.'" And he was to make an airstrip, because only in Pirimapun was there enough dry ground. He had no equipment, not even a wheelbarrow. For a month's work, he paid his workers with an ax, a knife, and some fishing line and hooks. Once a month a supply vessel docked. He had a radio and a generator, which he turned on twice a day to report that he was still alive.

Van de Waal loved it. There wasn't much to do except "move a bit of sand" for the airstrip and wander short distances by canoe. As the postmaster, he'd send letters home postmarked with odd dates, like September 35, 1960. After a couple of months there, he had a carpenter in Merauke create a catamaran out of two dugout canoes connected by a platform topped by a thatch hut. With an outboard motor, van de Waal had freedom; he could go anywhere and could sleep on the boat. He wandered throughout his region, up and down rivers, making contact. Officially, headhunting was no more. That was what Michael was told, as were his father and sister when they arrived a year later. It was

what everyone from outside had to be told, given Papua's political situation and the Dutch need, as it readied the country for independence, to present it as capable of leading itself as a productive member of the international community a decade hence. "But there was still headhunting," van de Waal said, "and sometimes even massive raids." As there would be for years to come: in 1970 the American missionary Frank Trenkenschuh arrived in the villages of Sogopo and Ti the day after warriors had killed five men and women, and even in the early 1980s Schneebaum heard stories of headhunting raids and killings in the remoter fringes of Asmat.

Still, van de Waal traveled undefended, with only a cook and boat boy. He had a handful of Papuan police officers in Pirimapun, but he always left them behind. He had a revolver, which he never took out of its box. Why were van de Waal, Gerbrands, and men like Zegwaard, van Kessel, and von Peij able to travel and even live among a people so fierce and warlike? For the Asmat, every exchange was greased with constant payment: of tobacco, to which the Asmat had become addicted, as well as steel axes and fishhooks and fishing line. Remembering their first encounter with Australian explorers in the New Guinea highlands in the 1930s, a Koiari man said: "We didn't know where these creatures came from; we wondered if they had come from the sky, from under the ground, or from inside the water. We thought they might be *remo* [spirits], but we had never seen *remo* before. . . . We were very scared of them and thought that eventually many of them would come back and finish us all off. Yet at the same time we liked the good things they had brought with them, such as matches and knives."

The Asmat's love of Western goods was matched by their fear of the gun. Its power hung over every encounter between armed Westerners and native people. The Asmat were fierce and ruthless warriors on the battlefield, but bamboo arrows and wooden spears

were no better than toys against the firepower of modern guns. Confrontations with armed whites in New Guinea were little different from those with the conquistadors in the Americas. In a story recounted by Jared Diamond in *Guns, Germs, and Steel,* when Francisco Pizarro met the Inca emperor Atahualpa at the Peruvian highland town of Cajamarca on November 16, 1532, Pizarro's 168 men were in the middle of enemy territory surrounded by 80,000 armed Inca soldiers. The battle didn't last long: in minutes Atahualpa was captured and thousands of natives lay dead, with not a single Spanish casualty. When Englishman Charlie Savage arrived in Fiji in 1808, "he paddled his canoe up a river to the Fijian village of Kasavu, halted less than a pistol shot's length from the village fence, and fired away at the undefended inhabitants. His victims were so numerous that surviving villagers piled up the bodies to take shelter behind them. . . . Such examples of the power of guns against native peoples lacking guns could be multiplied indefinitely," writes Diamond.

Indeed, an investigation of the Strickland-Purari patrol, a government-sponsored exploration into the Australian New Guinea highlands, reported in 1935 that the "patrol had opened fire on the natives on at least nine occasions." Fifty-four men had been killed by rifle fire, "with no member of the patrol killed or seriously wounded in the skirmishes." Natives learned quickly that they were virtually powerless in the face of gunpowder.

The Asmat did their best to placate Westerners and to work around them. The whole Asmat cosmos was one of reciprocal violence, and that meant not just between men, or villages, but between men and the spirits. Other men weren't just full of vengeance; so were the spirits. If they weren't placated, they could attack a village just as forcefully as its human enemies, by making men, women, and children sick. Certainly in the early years of European contact, and probably for a long time after, the Asmat were never quite sure who these white interlopers were. Spirits or

men? To attack them wasn't just to risk a physical reprisal like
Max Lapré's, but to risk something even more frightening: a spiri-
tual reprisal.

While Zegwaard, as the lone white on the rivers in the mid-
1950s, had simply appeared in villages in the immediate after-
math of raids, as time went on the Asmat were smart enough to
hide the practices that the priests and colonial administrators dis-
approved of. As Lapré noted in his reports, the Asmat simply went
farther into the jungle to carry out their ceremonies, which were
integral to their whole place in the world. It is easy to celebrate
our shared humanity—after all, we are all human beings who love
and hope and fear and feel and dream and mourn—and to dis-
miss our differences, forgetting that those differences are powerful
and fundamental to the way we see the world, each other, and our
place within it. We both shake hands. We both smile. We both eat
together and laugh and look at the same river and the same palm
trees, and we both have to disappear into the jungle to take a piss.
But what each of us perceives, what we believe, and what's impor-
tant to us can be profoundly different. All of Asmat culture was
based on reciprocation; Lapré might have insisted on Dutch laws
and the power of the government, but after the bloody fight at the
Ewta between Omadesep and Otsjanep, Faniptas had given one of
his children to Dombai in an offer of peace. It's almost impossible
to know the power of an Asmat bisj pole or the meaning of a song
or the sacredness of a skull to an Asmat, or the importance of giv-
ing gifts of sago to the jeu and its elders. And so people like Wim
van de Waal and Michael Rockefeller were able to collect and pho-
tograph and dig into Asmat culture, to travel with the Asmat and
be deep in their midst, without ever really understanding their
world and the unseen dimensions of its reality.

VAN DE WAAL showed Michael and Wassing around his little king-
dom at Pirimapun for a few hours and introduced them to van

Kessel, who was building a house there. The priest and Michael chatted briefly, a conversation that excited Rockefeller and would determine the rest of his short life. Van Kessel, he wrote Goldwater a few days later, was the "first whiteman" to explore the southern Asmat area of the Casuarina Coast. He had deep experience in Asmat and recommended that Michael pay attention to the south. "For several reasons, I think he will prove my most valuable contact . . . and he appears to be willing to help me in my collecting for the Museum of Primitive Art. He could be particularly valuable since he has the confidence of the natives in the area and therefore probably has greater access to the good pieces than I ever would." Michael asked Goldwater to send van Kessel a letter affirming his connection to the museum. Van Kessel was exactly what Michael needed: the missionary knew how to grease the skids, he could speak Asmat, and he knew the power of the people's sacred world. Had they managed to travel together, Michael's fate might have been far different. Instead, it would be on his way to meet van Kessel that Michael vanished.

By noon Michael and Wassing were gone, arriving in Agats that evening. Michael spent the night in the comfortable house of a Dutch official. The next morning they followed the same route as I would, fifty years later, passing Warse and arriving in Atsj late that night, now traveling by native canoe and rowers. Father von Peij was away, and they slept in the post office. They paid each rower a lump of tobacco a day and one length of nylon fishing line.

In the morning, they pushed on toward Amanamkai, where Gerbrands and David Eyde, an American anthropologist from Yale, were living. There, Asmat sucked them in. Gerbrands took them to the jeu Aman, which had just been rebuilt and was in the middle of celebrations surrounding its reconstruction. "There has been something mysterious about my arrival in first the Baliem, and now the Asmat," Michael wrote in his journal. "Both have been coincident with important ceremonies." The jeu was huge,

more than a hundred feet long, with sixteen fireplaces lining its back wall, each fireplace belonging to a different family group, and each marked with a carved pole. The floor was cool to the touch, springy, covered in the peeled bark of the sago palm, and the light inside was magical—dark with shafts of sunlight and thick smoke. The jeu was packed with sweating men, a semicircle of drummers standing or sitting around the central hearth, which belonged to the group as a whole, surrounded by men dancing like cassowaries—bouncing up and down on the balls of their feet and waving their knees in and out. One man would start singing, a mournful melodic chant, and then all the men would join in. It was hypnotic, primitive, powerful, otherworldly, an alternative universe untouched by time or technology, a world romanticized and revered, yet only hinted at in the sleek, sterilized displays of Michael's father's museum. Now it was Michael's to explore and untangle and harvest.

The dancing and drumming went on for hours, all day and into the evening, when a canoe of men from Omadesep arrived, bearing the message, Wassing noted, that Otsjanep "made the region unsafe and that the situation was tense." This was "troublesome" news, because Michael and Wassing had hoped to go to Omadesep and Otsjanep and needed rowers, who appeared reluctant to make the trip. But with the help of Gerbrands and Eyde, whose Yale dissertation was about headhunting and warfare, Michael reveled in the art and the ceremony, noting that the bisj poles were "a revenge figure . . . whose placement usually preceded a headhunt in former days. The figures represented people who have been headhunted and will be avenged." It never occurred to him that he might end up sating the lust for revenge of a people he had yet to meet.

They spent the next day waiting out a heavy rain that thundered down all afternoon, Michael snapping photos from the veranda of the men's house of the intense downpour and men and canoes paddling through it. The day after that he paid the men to

reenact an attack. Michael was in ecstasy as hundreds of warriors, some naked, draped in dogs' teeth necklaces and their faces white with chalk, in "tens" of canoes, swept out of the Awor River. The canoes separated into two groups and rowed "as though possessed" toward each other, throwing lime and circling the canoe containing Michael and Wassing "like a whirlwind, paired with yelling and howling and accompanied by the blast of horns." Michael shot photos, overwhelmed by "the grace of the movements in paddling, the sheer strength and speed, the sense of numbers and the rhythm in each canoe, and the pageantry of the occasion for the Asmat."

They left two days later at three p.m. in three canoes, short on rowers because of the tensions between Omadesep and Otsjanep. Wassing, Gerbrands, Putnam, and Michael sat in the middle of the leaky canoes, naked men fore and aft. "First there was the quiet, leisurely departure down the Awor," Michael wrote. "The rowers placed little effort behind their strokes, allowing the out-flowing tide to carry the canoes easily along. Or perhaps this was only my imagination due to the beautiful ease that always seems to follow from one's having lived a particular movement for a life time." Michael wanted to save film, but he couldn't help himself, for he was "beset with one marvelous sight after the other. . . . I was able to watch the rowers for hour after hour, particularly the rear man of René's canoe. The forms never lost interest; the thrust and pull being cast against the lush tangle of plant life and towering trees along the river's bank, and lit by sunlight, rainstorm, brilliant sunset, a full moon and the blue-black night. Could one not take pictures even at the risk of being repetitive?

"I only wish I could have somehow recorded the twittering mass of sparrows that we saw perched in the trees along the ocean's shores. Hundreds and hundreds of the small birds flew madly from one tree to another, succeeding in accomplishing glory knows what. Obscure objects darted among the branches, and first one tree and then the next would bend from the weight of

a myriad flying creatures lit for an instant among its branches. The air was filled with the whir of wings and the scream of a thousand birds twittering at once." The sun set in a blaze of red-orange, and then the full moon rose, big and glowing, and they paddled on in silence, save the lap of river against canoe and the occasional voice of the lookout in the bow.

After seven hours, they arrived at a bivouac not unlike the one Amates would take me to on the mouth of the Faretsj River. Swarms of starlings surged around the boats, filling the shadowy night with chirps and the rustling of thousands of wings. The group wolfed down a cold dinner of tea, leftover rice, and herring and spent the night. Three more hours of paddling up the Faretsj in the morning brought them to Omadesep. At first Michael was disappointed—a school was there, and in session! And when he asked to see carvings, he felt "almost disgust" with items that "showed the effect of hasty craftsmanship stimulated by the white man's knives and curio interest." Michael realized that they were items "made for sale, not use." He started asking for shields and drums, and "slowly, quietly, interesting objects began to appear. First a shield, broken, but old and quite handsome. Then one drum after the other . . . with an interesting variety of carved handles. With this, disappointment vanished and I became immersed in that pent up excitement that is only contained by the realization that impetuosity would lead to disaster." He was, of course, too young, too inexperienced, too rich, to contain his excitement and its impetuosity, and he would tragically fail to heed his own words, especially the day he crossed the mouth of the Betsj River. While he paid for his new treasure "with prices varying in their degree of inadequacy," Putnam recorded the artists' names and entered them in their journal.

IN FRONT OF the school they found four bisj poles, huge twenty-foot-tall carvings from a single piece of mangrove, from which the top figure sprouted a four-foot-long lattice flag, or penis. All As-

mat carvings are beautiful and complex—drums, shields, spears, bowls, paddles—but none compare to the bisj poles. Their three-dimensional detail, their dynamic lines with limbs and faces inter-mingled with praying mantises, hornbills, and crocodiles (eaters of fruit and meat, like the Asmat themselves)—all carved freehand, with not even a sketch or line drawn, and no two the same—are things of power and haunting beauty. But removed from their sur-roundings and culture, as Michael intended, they were stripped of their meaning, of their profound significance in Asmat life, and became little more than exotic objects to be consumed by the dis-criminating patrons of the Museum of Primitive Art, who had no real understanding of their purpose.

Rockefeller and Gerbrands looked at the four poles and de-clared them marvelous. With no sense of irony, Michael wrote: "This was one kind of object that seemed to me inviolate for the encroachment of western commercialism upon Asmat art. I quickly decided to buy one made by Faniptas"—the same man who had tricked Pip and company from Otsjanep into following him to Wagin. But Gerbrands convinced him to buy them all; to have all four as a complete ceremonial set was too good a chance to pass up. (Today those poles stand in the Metropolitan Museum of Art in New York.) Then Michael had an idea. "I thought how marvelous it would be to have those poles standing before the yeu [sic] for which they had been carved." Gerbrands plunged in, and soon it was agreed: the poles would be set up before the jeu and the "entire ceremony that accompanies such an occasion would be re-enacted."

Many parts of Asmat ceremonial life are compartmentalized. Certain songs are so powerful and so special that they remain se-cret even from women and children within the village itself. As-mat reveal some things and don't reveal others. When pressed by outsiders, they will sometimes concoct stories to satisfy them.

Exactly what ceremony the men of Omadesep performed with

the bisj poles is hard to know. They stood them up in front of the
jeu, per Michael's request, and sang, drummed, and danced around
the poles. Not surprisingly, however, Michael found it "quite dis-
appointing" and hard to shoot. "There is no magic involved and no
offering or religious attention paid to the poles as such. This fact
probably accounts for the ease with which the Asmat were induced
to re-enact the ceremony. Where there is no danger of angering a
god or misapplying magic, such an occasion must be welcome by
the village."

He was right—who knows what they'd been doing—but he
also reveals here a crack in his character, a certain hubris. Rou-
tinely described as kind, gentle, hardworking, and without pre-
tense, Rockefeller was also just twenty-three years old. He was
young and rich. Used to getting what he wanted, he seemed
unconscious of his own role in distorting the local economy and
disrupting village ceremony, or of the contradictory nature of his
entire enterprise. Here was the heir to one of the largest fortunes on
earth plundering sacred objects for pennies—the most privileged
person on earth dabbling in the world of the most marginalized,
the lowest of the low on the totem pole, so to speak. Despairing of
the objects made for sale, he had nevertheless arrived in the village
to buy its objects. He was commodifying the culture and its art
with every purchase. Over the next four months, Michael would
spend prodigiously, which he suspected contributed to a certain
reticence and resentment in Gerbrands, whom he called "an elu-
sive personality closed to the world like a clamshell." It took
Michael three days to get Gerbrands to call him "Mike" instead
of just "Rockefeller," and Gerbrands grew annoyed at Michael's
constant questions and either gave abrupt answers or just said he
didn't know. But it took Sam, a pauper compared to Michael, to
explain how Gerbrands might be feeling as the twenty-three-year-
old descended out of nowhere.

"Towards the end of the trip I began to think that maybe [this]

closed, distant quality in Adri [Gerbrands's nickname] stemmed from a kind of disillusionment that came from a frustration at his ambition," Michael wrote. "During his stay in New Guinea I know that he had been continually exasperated by such things as defects in the lenses he had bought in Japan, inadequacy in his film supply, the failures of his tape recorder to arrive, and constant difficulty in obtaining the rowers for his various trips. . . . I think Sam may well have been right in pointing out that such a man as Adri might be a bit resentful when relative upstarts such as ourselves come along equipped with the best camera equipment, quantities of film, money enough to buy bisj poles and any number of objects to say nothing of our ability to pay for the putting up of 2 bisj poles ceremonies . . . and then speak of another collecting trip later outfitted with an outboard motor which he had been unable to afford."

In his description of his purchase later that afternoon can be seen the first glimpses of a burgeoning obsession. A man named Givin brought Michael a spear, which he immediately bought. "This was an old, beautiful one of a kind I had never expected to get. Somehow I had been led to believe from Bob that I would only be at the end of a long line of collectors that had already ravaged the Asmat. Yet now I wonder whether this is the case. I have seen too many beautiful things even in my short stay to feel discouraged by a conviction that the art has gone. Now . . . I am almost confident, at least excited. In any event this one purchase set off a chain reaction among the people. Spear after spear appeared from the dark corners of the houses about the village. I bought four marvelous ones."

In any treasure hunt there comes a moment, if your journey is a success, where imagination and reality coalesce. The journey is born from imagination, from envisioning a strange place, finding the trail, tracking it down. Michael had imagined himself deep in an exotic culture, surrounding himself in it like a thick coat,

and now here he was. His dream was becoming a reality. When that moment comes, that realization that you've done it, the more the quest becomes the only thing that matters—and the deeper I went into Asmat myself and read Michael's journals the more I understood that, identified with it. Hunting art and chasing a story, they are the same. Rain, heat, cold, danger—out there in the wild everything becomes subordinate to the task, and the closer you get to the treasure the more you're willing to do to get it. There is nothing more intoxicating; it makes you feel powerful, invulnerable.

Michael wanted Asmat art, but not just any art. He wanted the authentic, objects that were touchstones to a world that was pure, that touched a distant past and a version of ourselves that was gone. But the purer the object, the more authentic it was, and the more power it had, the more trading in those objects put him on the threshold of an alternative universe. He had no understanding that by trading in bisj poles he was trading in the souls of men, souls that could make you sick, that could kill you. Michael was working with a bottomless supply of money—the one thing that limits most people, that checks them, that forces them to use friendship and reciprocity and patience with others. And there is a profound difference between people who are friends and people who want your money. Had Michael had less money, he would have had to move more slowly, would have had to settle in villages for longer, to trade, to make connections, to become known. Instead, he averaged a day or two in every village; he arrived, bought, and moved on.

OMADESEP AND OTSJANEP lie on parallel rivers—the Faretsj and the Ewta—that are connected, like the top of a horseshoe, by a navigable swamp. Officially, headhunting may have been over, but it was clear to Gerbrands, Wassing, and Michael that tensions between the two villages were high. In the tangled knot of Asmat

allegiances, they found a man named Tatsji, who, "because he had relatives in Otsjanep, was inviolable" and so could serve as escort, wrote Wassing. And suddenly a lot of others wanted to go too; at eleven on the morning of June 30, a fleet of canoes set out up the Faretsj to Otsjanep. Faniptas went too, though it's unclear whether Michael or Wassing knew who he was, beyond being a carver, or whether they knew that after the disastrous trip to Wagin and the ensuing violence three years before he had given a daughter to Dombai in Otsjanep in reciprocation, to make peace. "It was a marvelous paddle upstream," Michael wrote. "A large number of dugout canoes from Omadesep loaded with warriors accompanied us, using the occasion of our trip and the protection it provided to negotiate a peace treaty with Otsjanep, the much feared, powerful enemy and traditional rival."

The river twisted and turned and narrowed, and they paddled past overhanging or fallen trees under a burning sun. The river grew ever narrower and then turned into little more than a creek through the marsh and tough, man-high plants. Near the head of the Ewta, as it emerged from the swamp, they passed the village of Warkai, which was abandoned. That was always in Asmat a sign that a village had either been recently attacked or had been the attackers; with the increasing government presence, villages often hid deep in the bush to carry out the butchering and eating of their victims.

As they entered Otsjanep territory, the paddlers became wary; "every tree and river bend," noted Wassing, "was watched carefully." They came upon a group of houses on thirty-foot-long poles, a temporary refuge of safety that had recently been built by Otsjanep—yet another indication that war and headhunting were alive and well. Tatsji let out a long, melodious yell, explaining who they were, where they came from, why they had come, and that there were no government, police, or missionaries with them. All was still. Silent. The rowers chanted in unison this time,

all of them, the same announcement of their arrival. Then, from all around them in the jungle, horns echoed. Men and women streamed out of the bush, singing. The tension evaporated as men jumped into canoes and paddled out to meet them. They hugged. They shook hands. And they began frantically trading—sago and bulbs of taro for tobacco and fruit.

As wild and untouched as the Dani in the Baliem had been, this was different. Though the Dani fought each other, deaths in warfare were uncommon, and the Dani were farmers, their sweet potatoes giving them a sense of time, a sense of being settled— and most important of all, an abundant and reliable food supply. The Asmat Michael was with were pure hunter-gatherers, canni- bals, with a culture far stranger than that of the Dani, and Michael could feel it. "Now this is wild and somehow more remote coun- try," he wrote, "than what I have ever seen before." A group of men from another village that had never seen whites were there. They had never seen fishhooks or the nylon line that Gerbrands gave them, and they sang throughout the night, in Michael's words, in celebration of meeting the whites. But was it in celebration? Or something else, something more complicated, a way of grap- pling with a profoundly unsettling experience, an encounter with strange, otherworldly superbeings who might be their ancestors in corporeal form?

Michael continued on in the morning away from the tempo- rary refuge high up the river to the permanent village, the row- ers from Otsjanep concerned that their women, left behind at the temporary refuge, might be attacked by Omadesep. When they finally reached the main village of Otsjanep, it was the largest they'd seen, with five huge men's houses. Men and boys swarmed around them, a gridlock of dozens of canoes and hundreds of swimming men. Michael grabbed his Nikon and shot like mad. They found seventeen bisj poles still in the jeus of Otsjanep, with details they'd never seen before—the flag of one of them featured

two praying mantises facing each other. The ceremony that the Omadesep poles—which Michael had bought—were carved for had been completed: the souls inside them had been dispatched on to Safan, and instead of being dumped in the sago grounds to rot, the poles had been taken by the village's teacher. But these poles in Otsjanep were still in the jeus, were not yet disposed of, not yet thrown into the jungle, which hinted that they still embodied the souls of men whose deaths had not yet been revenged, reciprocated. They were a promise, a pledge, to right that balance, to—in our crude terms—avenge their deaths. Michael and Wassing also appeared to have had no knowledge of Max Lapré's raid three and a half years before, though Michael noted that the poles seemed to have been carved for a feast that had taken place in 1959—just a year after Lapré's raid.

If that seems as though it would have been a long time before, it wasn't. The Asmat had no watches or clocks, and they forgot nothing. The village of Otsjanep, as Michael could see, was a place apart, a city by Asmat standards, a place with its own customs and styles of carving unique in all of Asmat.

In exchange for tobacco, the village erected a bamboo scaffold in front of one of the men's houses facing the river, where they mounted the poles—a custom particular to Otsjanep. Men drummed and sang, and Michael offered to buy seven of the poles, for one lump of tobacco and one ax each, plus a length of fishing line and a hook for each rower. The men from Otsjanep agreed. Michael gave them a partial down payment, and the men said they'd bring the poles to a rendezvous spot on the east bank of the Betsj River in three or four days, and then transport them on to Agats, where Michael would pay them with more axes, knives, and tobacco. He also bought twelve shields.

Michael, Wassing, Putnam, and Gerbrands left Otsjanep on July 3 to visit a few other villages, and the canoes had to cross the mouth of the Betsj. What Michael wrote in his journal is

remarkable, given what would happen to him in four months: "On our way to Biwar we had to cross the estuary of the Betsj River which at this point is several miles wide. Strong monsoon winds sometimes sweep the heavy swell from the Arafura Sea far into the estuary, making the crossing a rather hazardous undertaking in an Asmat dugout canoe. . . . Though there was kind of a swell when we arrived at the estuary our Asmat paddlers, after having measured the sky and waves with expert eyes, decided that the crossing could be made."

Three days later, they arrived at the rendezvous spot, where they camped and waited for two days. The men from Otsjanep—and the bisj poles—never appeared. The paddlers from Amanamkai told them that the men from Otsjanep might have been afraid to leave their women and children behind. That's one explanation. But they had already done just that when they'd left their temporary safety camp to escort Michael to the main village. Another reason may have been this: the deaths represented by the poles were unreciprocated, the poles were still active, still inhabited by Osom, Faratsjam, Akon, Samut, and Ipi, killed by Max Lapré. And if they were, the men of Otsjanep would not have parted with the poles for all the money or tobacco in the world.

12

· · · · · · · · · · ·

March 2012

FIFTY YEARS AFTER Michael Rockefeller shot photos of the men danc-
ing around the bisj poles in Omadesep, I stood in the same place.
The Faretsj River lay five feet down a bank of mud. Perpendicular
to the river, the men's house stretched a hundred feet, a massive
structure of poles and *gabagaba*—the stems of sago palm—fronted

MEN IN OMADESEP CELEBRATING THE CONSTRUCTION OF THEIR NEW JEU.

by a long veranda reached by notched logs. Across the river was a wall of lush jungle—nipa palm and coconut palm and tangled green vines. Next to the jeu was a maze of poles sticking out of the muddy ground—the foundation for a new men's house. I was lucky. We'd arrived in Omadesep just as the men were beginning to celebrate its construction, and Amates said the festivities would begin soon.

By now, I had been navigating the rivers and villages with Amates and Wilem for almost a week. It felt dreamlike. We had traveled in the darkness and at dawn and late afternoon—whenever the tides dictated. We had motored through crushing downpours—the water cold and fresh, the drops hard and big—and in the blazing sun. I hadn't felt hot water on my skin since arriving in Agats over three weeks before. I hadn't seen a chair or a cushion save the sofa in Amates's sister's house in Atsj. We ate three meals a day of rice and ramen, supplemented by very small bits of crab, shrimp, fish, and sago, and there was no oil, no fat, no alcohol, and little sugar except what Filo put in my instant coffee. My weight was dropping fast.

In the village of Betjew we slept on the floor of the school, a school with one teacher for eighty students, only half of whom came to class on any given day. "They go fishing or to the jungle to collect sago," he said, "and I cannot keep them." We paused for a night again in Atsj, where men gathered on the porch as rain cascaded down and drummed and sang and chanted through the night until dawn. "They sang about a man and a woman," Amates said, in his usual frustratingly incomplete explanation. "The man was killed by people from Baiyun. It is a love story."

In Amates's village of Biwar Laut, we spent a day and a night. Years before it had broken off from Omadesep, Amates said, telling the story. "Some women from Omadesep were fishing when five boats came to the Faretsj and some of the men fucked the women," Amates explained as we turned upriver from the Ara-

fura toward the village. "The women's husbands found out and attacked Biwar and killed Biwiripitsj. Biwar attacked Omadesep and killed Escame. My grandfather told me this story." Egrets flew overhead. Some men in a canoe called out Amates's nickname— "Ates!"—when they saw us. At the dock, a crowd materialized and Amates's sister appeared, a gaunt woman in a T-shirt. Seeing Amates, she exploded in screaming and wailing. At an old wooden house, we found his father, small and thin but muscled still, with close-cropped white hair. He, too, sobbed and wailed and rubbed Amates.

As we settled on the porch of his sister's house, Wilem walked up bearing crabs as big as my hands, wrapped in wet palm leaves. He threw them on the fire, and in walked a woman in a stained, ripped sundress, with a pierced septum and strings in her ears. She, too, exploded in wailing and sobbing and clutching, and then slumped to the floor, holding her head in her hands, weeping and rocking. Rising, she stumbled, as if drunk, out the door, the emotion so high she could barely walk, and she stumbled screaming along the boardwalk for fifteen minutes. "My mother's aunt," explained Amates.

Leaving Biwar, we traveled through a cut in the jungle that was barely five feet wide and so shallow we had to pole. I couldn't see the sun or sky at all. The mud banks glistened and teemed with white-bodied crabs with orange legs and mud puppies, primitive tadpolelike creatures with huge heads, long tails, and only a pair of front legs. We ducked beneath overhanging trees and vines and past mangrove roots that looked like the fingers of ancient giants. Butterflies danced over us, and after an hour we broke into the Suretsj River, which was a mile or more wide.

We spent a night in Owus, Wilem's village on the Bow River, where he introduced me to his wife and their three children and then quickly disappeared. It rained all afternoon and evening, and we sat swatting mosquitoes and flies by candlelight. "You know,"

Amates said, "Wilem has two families and two wives here." Which was as it had always been in Asmat, even though they now considered themselves Catholic.

After leaving Owus, we'd encountered a sixty-foot-long dugout manned by a Bugis trader, filled with supplies. We flagged him down, loaded up on clove cigarettes and tobacco, and motored on. On another river, we hailed some fishermen and bought a three-foot-long catfish, which Filo later cleaved into chunks and fried in oil. It was the most protein I'd had in days.

Even as we went deeper, there was that wall that I couldn't pass through, an unsettled feeling that didn't go away and which I'd never felt anywhere else in the world. Slowly it began to sink in. The thing I couldn't quite shake, couldn't quite figure out, couldn't put my finger on, was cannibalism.

Headhunting and cannibalism and the rituals associated with them—all of Asmat culture, to put it simply—had only begun changing little more than a generation earlier. Amates's father and the parents of possibly every single person over the age of forty had eaten human flesh. And not eaten it like we eat steak today—purchased in some air-conditioned megastore all wrapped in plastic—but with active participation in the butchering of bodies, the cutting off of heads, the evisceration of the skulls and chests and bowels of men, women, and children. Think of the blood. The gore. The dismembered limbs and hands. Maybe it was just in my imagination, my own American squeamishness about the human body and death, but what had been ordinary for the Asmat—just a few years before!—was utterly inconceivable to me. Living in huts, hunting and gathering your food, believing in spirits and magic, warfare—these are all just different varieties of what we all do every day. We used to be naked; now we wear clothes. We used to live in palm huts; now we live in wooden houses. We used to believe in exotic magic and spirits; now we believe in Jesus and the Holy Ghost. Big deal. These are all differences of degree, not

kind. But what the Asmat had done regularly had crossed a line uncommon in human history, even in traditional hunting-and-gathering cultures. The most horrific, most monstrous thing we could think of had been central to their everyday life. And to me that fact hung over every moment in Asmat. It was the elephant in the room—even now, forty years after the practice had finally been stopped by missionaries and the government.

If I asked anyone about cannibalism, they would acknowledge it. Sure, we used to eat people, but now we don't. They didn't want to talk about it. They are Catholics now, though many still have multiple wives and all believe in an active spirit world and ceremonies that their Catholic God has no part of. Under the influence of the Church, they have been schooled to believe that what they did in the past was wrong, and they feel shame about it, at least in conversations with Westerners. What they think of it in private among themselves is hard to know. Many of their songs recall it, after all, and their whole ceremonial life has been based on it; it is clearly still part of their consciousness.

The longer I stayed in Asmat, the more I felt that disconnection—between what had been and what appeared to be now, between what they talked about openly and what they thought about in private, and between the Western fascination (my own included) with the idea of cannibalism and the actuality. As Michael Rockefeller wandered through Asmat, the headhunting and the killing and eating were still widely practiced. Every piece of art was rooted in it, and every Asmat he met in the remoter villages had consumed human flesh. And every piece that he collected, even now displayed in the Metropolitan Museum of Art in New York, refers to it—the very poles that stand in the Michael C. Rockefeller Wing of the Met were created to avenge deaths, and they had the blood of the murdered rubbed into them. Yet he had never seen headhunting or cannibalism. Few Westerners ever had, besides Zegwaard, and it's questionable whether

even he actually saw any humans being slaughtered or consumed. I wondered: What would have happened if they had? If I had? What if it had been going on in their sight? Would they have seen the "art" any differently? What would I do, how would I feel, if that butchering and those feasts were going on around me?

In his field notes, journals, and letters, Michael repeatedly makes reference to the connection between headhunting and the art he was collecting. Yet he remains disassociated from it, never confronting it; it's an academic, historical association. That was the wall I was feeling. I wanted to know what it was like, what it felt like, what they felt and thought about decapitating someone's child or wife and butchering the body with their hands and rough tools. They did it, they knew all about it, everyone in Asmat did—the whole museum in Agats was built on it—and yet no one spoke about it. Tobias Schneebaum romanticized the Amazonian Indians he lived with until the day they raided another village, brutally murdering their victims with clubs. Schneebaum went with them, he watched it all, he pushed a spear into the chest of a man already dead, and it horrified him. And then he participated in the consumption of one victim's heart, raw, bloody. It affected him so deeply that he fled soon after. My guess was that so, too, would Michael have done, and so, too, would I. Somewhere, somehow, there was some fundamental and profound cultural difference between me and the Asmat around me, as there had been between Michael and the men he was photographing, writing about, collecting from. The idea fascinated us because we never had to see the thing itself. But it was what separated me from the Asmat every hour I was with them.

BY THE TIME we got to Omadesep, we were traveling farther from Agats into narrower and more remote rivers. Atsj, Ayam, Becew, all had stores, docks, trash from Western consumer goods, a few generators that roared on in the evening. Omadesep had nothing, not even a store, and what really struck me was its lack of trash.

There wasn't any. It was a place with only a few manufactured products—pots and pans, a few machetes, fishing line—and nothing else that didn't come from the sea or the jungle.

Under a flat white sky, and in humidity you could swim through, I heard screams, wild howls, a rhythmic clacking sound. Amates grabbed me and led me to the end of a rickety dock crowded with barefoot children, some naked, others in the ubiquitous tattered and stained T-shirts and gym shorts. Coming down the river were twelve canoes packed together in a mass, just a foot apart, ten to twelve men in each canoe. Though all were wearing shorts, they were decorated for battle, draped in dogs' teeth bandoliers and carrying spears embellished with cockatoo feathers, their bodies smeared with chalk Xs and bands around their legs and arms. They had black grease across their faces, and their eyes were encircled in red, like the enraged King Cockatoo, and they wore cuscus fur hats sprouting cockatoo feathers. They were born on the water, born standing in their tippy canoes, and they clapped their paddles against the sides of the canoes. "Huh, huh, huh, huh," they grunted, a guttural yell interspersed with high-pitched ululating cut by a single, deep voice singing a few lines of a groaning, melodic dirge, before the grunts and paddle-beating started again. They jumped up and down and horns blew, like the foghorns I'd heard as a kid at my grandparents' in Newport, Rhode Island, and clouds of white smoke engulfed them—lime—as they rowed to the shore. From out of the scrum emerged ten or fifteen men carrying an eight-foot-long cylinder, the top trunk of a sago palm, wrapped in a fancy dress of green sago leaves; sago is female and so wears a skirt, for sago comes out of the inside of the tree as a child comes out of a woman. They hoisted the dressed sago log up into the jeu.

Inside the jeu it was dark, but shafts of sunlight pierced the palm walls and roof. Five men sat cross-legged on the springy floor, their backs to the central fireplace hearth, each with a long, narrow, carved drum across his knees. Here, the center of the jeu,

was also the center of the Asmat cosmos. It was where the world
of the living and the world of the dead met, where both were pres-
ent. The men were dressed as animals that eat fruit, headhunters.
Tucked into rattan armbands were long, sharp daggers of casso-
wary thigh bone—the same daggers used to pin the heads of vic-
tims to the floor in the origin tale of Biwiripitsj and Desoipitsj.
They drummed in unison, chanting; one man started the song
and the others soon joined in, and it ebbed and flowed in between
moments of silence with no apparent direction—each man just
knowing his part. "Ohhhhhhh," a voice would sing, a long, drawn-
out, deep voice, followed by speaking, then more long "ohhhhh-
hhhhs." "He is singing the name of a man killed by Omadesep
in Biwar Laut a long time ago," Amates said. Thousands of flies
buzzed. The men smoked. Sang. Drummed. Chanted. On and on
it went, for hours, as others filtered in and out, the crowd gather-
ing until there were fifty sitting around the sago log, which was
white and glistening and covered with flies.

At some signal that I never understood, a man with an ax began
slicing the log lengthwise, pivoting the ax head at each cut, sepa-
rating an inch-thick layer of sago, which peeled away like the layers
of heart of palm. Again and again he sliced, each time the stalk
becoming narrower, until it was the diameter of a fishing pole. The
end of the log bulged into a head that was repeatedly shaved into
small chunks. Men took their drums to the fire, heating the heads
made from the skins of iguana, to tighten them, rubbed their
palms over the drum heads, constantly adjusting the small knobs
of beeswax, stuck to the drum heads like gobs of chewing gum,
that tuned them. I lost track of time in the dark and the smoke and
the heat and the pulsating drumming and chanting, each chant
a story of death and headhunting and battles that stretched back
years, generations, according to Amates, and recalled the ancestors
and their spirits.

During a smoking break, I asked Amates to ask about the trip

to Wagin in 1957. Max Lapré's reports mentioned it as the reason for his actions, but offered few details. Again the long explanation from Amates. We all smoked. The men nodded. Looked at me. They remembered. All of it, as if it were yesterday, and I heard the names Pip, Dombai, Su, Kokai, Wawar, and Pakai. And then one man, Everisus Birojipts, started talking. He was bare-chested and unadorned, and though clearly older, his chest was firm, broad, strongly muscled. He had short hair and a scruffy beard. He had been a boy and had accompanied his father on the journey, and he grew animated as the story unfolded. The quest for dogs' teeth. The rain and the fighting in Baiyun and Basim and Emene. His fear.

Over the past two decades, I'd reported hundreds of stories from all over the world, but this one felt different. Michael's disappearance had been so long shrouded in rumor, and took place in a land so distant, that it had taken on the quality of an impenetrable myth. His own family had so long publicly clung to the notion that he'd drowned; they'd found no way to investigate what happened, and it was easier to give yourself to the mystery, to accept that he'd been swallowed up in this unreachable green and watery fantasy than to untangle it. Here, beyond a certain point, the Rockefellers had been powerless. It didn't matter how many searchers they might employ, how many attorneys they might set to the task, it mattered little what laws or courts might say, or how many powerful people they might know—all the tools of the rich and privileged had been useless here. The Asmat didn't care about any of them, were immune to all of them.

But whatever happened to Michael had been real. Asmat was real—and here, strange as it seems, the spirits had been real too, and I began to think of him as having been lost to this spirit world. Something had happened here that had roots deep in Asmat culture, and I was starting to see that every day I spent in Asmat the story was coalescing into a touchable narrative. The more I understood about Asmat culture, the more I began to think of the mys-

tery of Michael's disappearance in an Asmat way, as if he were one of those spirits who'd never been pushed on to Safan. The Asmat had closed every loop through their rituals—and through violence—but Michael was still floating around out there. Perhaps my journey, both in Asmat itself and through the archives, wouldn't just solve the mystery but lay his spirit to rest once and for all.

In Birojipts's telling, the six men from Otsjanep attacked the men from Omadesep first, though I doubted that, since they were in the minority by far. But at the Ewta there was no doubt: "There were a lot of men from Otsjanep waiting for us, and we were exhausted and resting and sitting and Otsjanep people came and killed us with arrows. My father, all the people behind me, were dead," he said, "and only a few came back to Omadesep. So many were killed."

By late afternoon, the jeu was filled, a hundred men crowding the floor. Other men appeared, bearing ten-foot-long pieces of green, freshly cut sago palm leaves that they hung like curtains around the central section of the jeu, always a sign that spirits were present, since they inhabited the leaves of the sago. When the sago log was gone, the layers were broken into small pieces and distributed. "We must go," Amates said to me. "We can stand by the edge." In an instant, the men divided into two groups, one on each side of the jeu. Wild yelling and screaming erupted, they started pitching the chunks at each other as hard as they could, and around the hearth the old men with their drums hit the deck. The throwers yelped. They howled. It sounded like barking dogs and squealing pigs, and the chunks flew, hard, a snowball fight of sago. When it was over, the drummers drummed and the singers sang and the men danced as though possessed, the crazy cassowary dance of moving up and down on the balls of their feet while frenetically pumping their knees in and out. The jeu shook and the floor moved up and down and clouds of dust enveloped it like fog from the stamping feet and one man pulled his track pants down, lost in ecstasy.

That night, twenty men appeared in the house we were stay-
ing in. It was still hot. Stifling. Without power, candles flickered,
stuck onto the wooden floor. We passed out tobacco, and I lis-
tened and watched. Smoke filled the room. Pale white lizards crept
along the walls. Outside, the crickets buzzed. In bits and pieces,
one man and then another, whose names I didn't know, told me
about Lapré coming to arrest the men after the raid, and as always
in these villages time shifted and there was no way to separate
generations—the village was one, and things that happened to
their fathers happened to them. "We were afraid," they said, and
in those moments I felt the clash of cultures, their confusion over
what was happening and why, who Lapré had been, the guns and
the sudden violence they unleashed. I felt their anxiety over the
aliens who might be superbeings, who might be their very ances-
tors, with guns and boats in their midst.

THE NEXT MORNING we left Omadesep for Otsjanep, as Michael Rock-
efeller had done, though the river was too low and we had to take
the sea route. The entrance to the Ewta was so narrow that I never
would have noticed it from offshore. It was a tunnel through thick,
monotonous green mangroves hanging over the river from the
banks, dangling vines. We motored slowly, and I imagined Max
Lapré here, his heart beating against his chest, armed and ready for
a confrontation, looking for warriors hidden in these very trees and
brush, and I imagined the Asmat watching him come, these strange
men in their big, loud boats and their guns. A constant stream of
canoes slipped past us, heading to the sea, some with women and
children, some with men standing, their paddles dipping and strok-
ing in perfect time with each other. Their ragged T-shirts and shorts
made them look like street people, and I wished they were naked,
though I also wondered if that was just my own hope for an exotic
experience with naked savages. The river twisted and turned, and
after half an hour the trees cleared and thatch houses appeared on

the left bank. The place felt wilder than anywhere I'd been before. There was no dock, just muddy banks lined with canoes, which we climbed over, picking our way across the logs and poles over the mud. Men stared, Amates and Wilem talked, and we were led to a two-room wooden house, its walls black with soot.

This was Pirien, a village adjacent to Otsjanep that resulted from a violent split between the five jeus soon after Michael disappeared. We were barely inside the house when men started appearing. One. Two. Five. Soon I counted forty squeezed into the sweltering, furniture-less room, crowds of young boys peering in through the windows. We sat on the floor, a sea of faces and sweating bodies and flies, staring, waiting. Amates brought out the tobacco, passed pouches of it and rolling papers to the elders, who emptied the pouches and divided it up, passing mounds of the brown weed around the room. Soon we were enveloped in a cloud of smoke. Amates talked, the men nodded. Some introduced themselves. There was Ber, son of Dombai, former head of the jeu Pirien. Tapep was the son of Pep, who had been chief in the 1960s and who had married Osom's widow, one of the men killed by Lapré. I wasn't sure why they were here, what had brought them. They didn't ask me anything, but they seemed to want to see me, and they wanted the tobacco I'd brought, though I was never quite sure what Amates was saying that I didn't understand.

I asked them how the village had split. There was a lot of discussion, and Amates relayed the story: Dombai was the head of Pirien jeu, and he had three wives. One morning at five a.m., the head of Otsjanep jeu asked Dombai to go into the jungle and collect sago, while Dombai's three wives went in a canoe to fish. Dombai was suspicious, so he asked men to follow his wives. Eventually Dombai's spies saw the women fucking—that's the word Amates used—three men from the Otsjanep jeu, including the head of the jeu.

When the three women returned to Otsjanep, well, there

was trouble. Dombai confronted them. The women threw open their skirts and said, yes, we fucked them, and many other men from Otsjanep too. The men made a fire and burned the women's clothes, and that was that.

Not a problem, Dombai said. Not a problem.

But Dombai remembered. One year later, the men from Pirien jeu attacked and killed Bifack, Por, Fin, and Ajim in retribution and moved their women and children half a mile downriver to a new place, and the Pirien jeu became the village of Pirien. What happened to one man in the jeu happened to them all. There was no separation. No individuality. No I. Collective guilt ran deep in a place where men took certain other men as lovers/brothers and also sometimes shared each other's wives, where everyone was related and the bisj pole carvings were a tangle of men standing on and connected to other men.

There was a lot of crying. The children were sad. The men from Otsjanep wanted peace. So they gave a daughter to Pirien, and then the men from the two sides drank each other's urine, an act of submission and bonding.

When I asked about Lapré's raid, they grew quiet, and Amates suggested we take a break and head upriver to Otsjanep itself. The river twisted and wound, and after half a mile the trees cleared and we entered the village. On the left bank, there were no plank houses at all, nothing but thatch huts and mud, smoke, and a few banana trees and coconut palms, crowds of people sitting on porches, watching our arrival. Some of the women had no shirts, their breasts dangling long and flat against their bellies. We pulled the boat up to the banks, climbed over canoes and over branches and log walkways, Amates talking to the watching crowd. Children gathered, pressing close. The clearing behind the houses stretched for a few hundred yards, and near here, somewhere, had stood the original village that Lapré attacked and that Michael visited.

The vibe here felt strange. Dark. Oppressive, as if there were

something hanging over the village. That wall again, though now it was almost visible to the naked eye. No one moved. If I'd been a cat, my fur would have been standing up. I looked at people and they looked back, but there was no recognition, no welcome, nothing that drew me to them. No one shook my hand. No one invited us into their house. I felt like I had no traction here. I asked Amates to ask if anyone knew about Lapré and his raid, or even had been an eyewitness to it. Amates spoke, but it was like he was speaking in a foreign language. Faces were blank, emotionless. A few people said a few words. "They don't remember anything," Amates said. "They don't know anything about this." As always, I couldn't tell if Amates was being straight with me, telling me everything he knew, or if there were things he was filtering, things he was keeping from me.

I'm not sure what I had been thinking, imagining that I could drop into a village and have its people simply open up to me, a complete stranger, a white no less. Had I made the same mistakes as Lapré, or Michael? Showing up with the wrong people, with the wrong motivations? I wanted something, it was true. Not just whatever they were willing to show me, but their deepest secrets, their account of the events that had preceded the possible murder and cannibalization of one of my clan, one of my tribe, my countryman. I had imagined they'd want to tell me, to share it with me, that they'd rush to show me his skull or thigh bone and celebrate the brutality, the violence, that was a part of who they were. I imagined they'd be proud of it. Why did I think they'd be so eager? In America people's egos get the best of them: they like to talk about what they've done, they're open to journalistic flattery and the idea of being affirmed by seeing their names in a magazine story. And we were talking about events that took place fifty years ago, that involved their fathers and grandfathers, not themselves. I imagined those events would be less immediate, less dangerous. But the people of Otsjanep were as blank and silent as stones.

Getting nowhere, feeling unwelcome, we climbed back in the

boat and returned to the wooden house downriver in Pirien. It was late afternoon. A huge black pig rooted in the mud under the house, now empty of visitors. Dogs yelped and fought. Children played on the boardwalks, but I couldn't see any adults anywhere. I couldn't keep the flies off my face, my eyes, my nostrils. They were starting to make me feel crazy.

"They are very afraid," Amates said, apropos of nothing.

"Afraid?" I said. "Of what?"

"There was a tourist who died here," he said. "An American tourist named . . ." and the name he said was garbled. I couldn't understand it. This was news to me. In all I'd read, I'd never heard of an American tourist dying in Asmat.

"When?" I said. "What was his name?"

Amates's English was slow, the words hard to comprehend no matter what he said. He said the name again, and then again, more slowly, and it was a hard name for an Asmat to pronounce, but this time it was unmistakable: "Michael Rockefeller."

I couldn't believe it. I had never mentioned Michael's name to Amates, not once. All I'd said was that I was a journalist writing about Asmat and that I was interested in its history and the story of the trip to Wagin and Max Lapré's raid.

"Michael Rockefeller?" I said, feigning ignorance.

"Yes, Michael Rockefeller," Amates said. "He was an American. He was here in Otsjanep. They are very, very afraid. They do not want to talk about this."

"How did his name come up?" I asked.

"They told me," he said. "Today, when we were talking, they are afraid you are here to ask about Michael Rockefeller. And they are afraid. Very afraid."

"Why?"

"Otsjanep killed him. Everyone knows it. My grandfather even told me this when I was a little boy."

13

September 1961

"WHAT TIME IS it and where am I? It is nighttime with the crickets going berserk all around me and I'm back in Hollandia," wrote Michael in September 1961. "I arrived exhausted today and found that tomorrow at 8:40 a.m. René and I will fly to Merauke in order to make a 6:00 p.m. boat to the Asmat. I am now surrounded by my little reality for the next ten weeks: a chaos of cameras and recording equipment cluttering up everything including my mind."

Immediately after returning from his first Asmat voyage in July, Michael wrote Goldwater a long letter. "I think I can report with some confi-

BISJ POLES COLLECTED BY MICHAEL ROCKEFELLER FROM OMADESEP AND OTSJANEP IN THE METROPOLITAN MUSEUM OF ART.

dence that my first trip to the Asmat has met with success." He
was elated with the objects he'd collected. Though he and Gold-
water had been told that Asmat was "already well acculturated,"
that was only partially true around Agats and "for anyone taking
a very rapid, relatively short trip . . . by motor boat," he wrote.
"However there remain 2 parts of the Asmat which are as yet very
little known: the extreme Northwest and the entire Casuarinas
Coast, which has only just begun to be patrolled and is known
well only by the missionary, Father van Kessel." He wrote that
while it was true that "headhunting has ceased"—a strange thing
to say given the simmering tensions he'd seen between Omadesep
and Otsjanep and the art he was hoping to find, which was based
entirely on headhunting—"Western ideas have made remarkably
little dent on the Asmat mind." The art and ceremonies associ-
ated with it, he wrote, were healthy in nearly every village. His
biggest coup, he said, was acquiring the bisj poles from Otsjanep,
which he'd negotiated for but which hadn't been delivered. "These
have resulted from the well known bise [*sic*] ceremony . . . the
poles from Ochenep [*sic*] have carved patterns all over the figures'
arms and legs. This is apparently a style typical of the Casuarinen
[*sic*] Coast area. Dr. Gerbrands tells me that there are none like
these in Europe. Here once again we were able to induce the vil-
lagers to put on part of the bise [*sic*] ceremony for us. 12 poles
were involved, they were placed, not standing but leaning on a
constructed wooden framework out over the water of the river—
before all 3 men's houses of the village." Again there's that strange
disassociation, almost a denial. If the culture was intact, if West-
ern ideas had made no dent in the Asmat mind, then by definition
that meant headhunting—and the eating of human flesh that was
part of it—was alive and well. Which, of course, it was. In fact,
that very month, Sanpai, one of the warriors from Atsj who'd ac-
companied Lapré in 1958, had been invited to a feast in Otsjanep.
But the villagers were just up to their old tricks. "He arrived in

Otsjanep and was immediately stabbed/shot with an arrow, murdered and eaten," wrote von Peij. Which meant that the deep, vibrant spirit world was alive too, and yet it always feels, reading his letters and journals, as if Michael was trying to shy away from it.

Instead, he was thinking of the things he was getting and what he could do with them and how he could acquire more good stuff. The opportunity to purchase the poles, he said, was "unique" for the United States, and he was off to a great start. He'd also decided to forget Australian New Guinea and concentrate on the Asmat.

Goldwater wrote van Kessel, as Michael had requested. "Mr. Rockefeller is, as you know, the son of the founder of the Museum of Primitive Art, and he is himself a valuable member of our Board of Trustees. You will have been able to appreciate his real enthusiasm, scientific background, and artistic understanding. We at the Museum are looking forward eagerly to the collections he will be able to bring back to the Museum, because we know they will be well chosen and documented. But Mr. Rockefeller is young, and new in the field. Any instruction and assistance you can give him will be greatly appreciated by our Board and our Staff, and eventually by the public who will admire these works and so gain in insight and understanding. May I add my sincere personal thanks for your friendly cooperation."

Michael wrote van Kessel to say he was particularly interested in Otsjanep "for its lack of acculturation in spite of some less auspicious after effects of Mr. Gaisseau's visit." This sentence, the only one of its kind in his letters and journals, is remarkable, and eerily prescient; it is the only passage that indicates he was aware, if even dimly, of the turbulence there, the turbulence that he himself would fall into. Gaisseau was a French filmmaker who led an expedition across New Guinea in 1959, a trip that began in Otsjanep and resulted in the film *The Sky Above, the Mud Below.* Upon arrival in the village, just a year after Lapré's raid, the crew found a large number of bisj poles—probably some of the

same poles Michael had seen and tried to buy. Although Gaisseau was able to get the village to perform for his cameras—he filmed them in repeated takes drumming and singing and paddling their canoes—his Dutch police escort became aware of an increasing agitation in the men and began fearing for his life, so much so that he forced the crew to abandon Otsjanep after just a few days of filming there. Michael also asked van Kessel if he knew of any other villages in the area "with equally as talented sculptors less influenced by Western ideas."

Van Kessel said he'd happily assist Michael. He recommended that Michael go to northwest Asmat first, then come south and meet him in Basim, where they could take off together. He mentioned three villages, but wrote, "I will not exclude Otsjanep."

If Rockefeller's initial interest in working on Gardner's film had been a lark, a last hurrah before turning to more adult pursuits, that wasn't true any longer. His field notes from his first trip and the letters he wrote reveal a deepening seriousness regarding his collecting. His photographs show an intuitive grasp of light and shadow and form. His field notes are illustrated with hundreds of drawings illuminating stylistic details of Asmat symbology. For his second expedition he laid out "objectives; themes of investigation; criterion for stylistic variation." He wanted to explore the "extent of communication between areas and trace the distribution of different kinds of objects." He was a Rockefeller, a family that took achievement and hard work seriously; they were philanthropists and connoisseurs, ambitious enough to run for the presidency of the United States three times. Michael wanted to produce books, mount the biggest exhibition of Asmat art ever, and wow his father and family so much that he wouldn't have to start his career as some Rockefeller Plaza leasing agent.

As the Harvard team finished its work in August and celebrated in Hollandia, Michael received disturbing news from home: his father was divorcing his mother to marry a Philadelphia

socialite and campaign aide named Margareta "Happy" Murphy, news that wouldn't be announced to the public for another two months. Michael immediately flew back to New York. He'd been living in primitive conditions for five months. He hadn't seen his family and friends, hadn't eaten a meal that might not make him sick, hadn't seen a television, in almost half a year. No matter. Where others might have savored the comforts of home or gotten sucked into the domestic family drama playing out, Michael did something else. He briefly saw his family and Sam Putnam, met with Goldwater at the museum, and then turned around and returned to New Guinea.

After a few days in Hollandia, he and Wassing flew to Merauke, where they hustled to catch a boat to Agats that same day. It felt good to be back. It doesn't matter where you go in the world: when you get to a place for the second time, it feels different. You know your way around. You know the best place to find a boat and how much to pay. You know where to grab a meal. You've returned, and people regard you differently.

Darkness falls quickly near the equator, and as he sat happily on the floor of his wooden room without furniture, electricity, or running water, Michael finally got caught up with his journal, to the flickering light of a kerosene lamp. "The key to my fascination with the Asmat is the woodcarving. The sculpture which the people here produce is some of the most extraordinary work in the primitive world. And equally as remarkable as the art is the fact that the culture which produces it is still intact; some remote areas are still headhunting; and only five years ago almost the whole area was headhunting."

It's one of the only times he acknowledges the headhunting directly, in contradiction to his letter to Goldwater. He felt enthralled, excited, in his element. He felt that he was starting to put his finger on it all, to find the treasure. The world was rich and exotic and full of life, and a lot of people were scared by it, but he

savored it, felt confident traveling out to its farthest corners and deepest crevices. "Nights here are really the most fun. Something like teeth grinding in the Baliem: a rhythm created by the patter of mice feet over the walls and ceiling with crickets and frogs burping in counterpoint. The roosters here are affected by a curious neurosis which causes them to begin crowing at midnight. Last night we had an earthquake rock us to sleep."

Michael wanted to find a motorboat to explore faster and farther, but all he could find was the standard Asmat canoe, which had little room to carry barter goods or the art he was hoping to collect and which also required rowers, who had to be fed and paid and would only go to certain places. There was a single government vessel in town, but the patrol officer hardly wanted to be Michael Rockefeller's chauffer for two months. The conundrum of Asmat is transportation: you can be right there in Agats and yet feel a million miles away from the rivers and villages because you can't move without a boat.

By coincidence, patrol officer Wim van de Waal, fifty miles south in Pirimapun, had been restless. Though he'd never before gone so far out of his district, he yearned for a few more white faces and conversation, and he'd taken his catamaran all the way up the coast to Agats, where, by 1961, twenty-five or so Western government officers and missionaries were living. The catamaran was great on the rivers, but not so great on the Arafura. Van de Waal was methodical and careful, and through trial and error he evolved a way to pilot the boat into the waves at the right angle so as to not get swamped. "The sideboards were only ten or fifteen centimeters above the water, and I just experimented over the months I used it," he said. "If it was rough, you couldn't be in the ocean, especially if the tide was coming out." But he'd never had any problems, so he thought, *What the hell, why not go all the way to Agats?*

There he ran into Michael, and they shared a warm beer, two young men in the throes of a big adventure who couldn't have

been more different. Van de Waal said, "He was stuck, flabber-
gasted that he, Michael Rockefeller, couldn't get a vessel."

"How'd you get here if you're from Pirimapun?" asked Michael.

"I came in my own catamaran," said van de Waal.

Van de Waal showed it to Michael the next morning. The min-
ute Michael saw it he wanted it, the boat of his dreams, a Tom
Sawyer–ish vessel forty feet long, carrying a perfect thatched house
across its twin hulls. It was big enough and stable enough to carry
plenty of goods to trade and some of what they could collect. And
he and Wassing could sleep in it rather than in the smoky, loud jeus.

"Will you sell it to me?" Michael said.

Van de Waal dithered. He wasn't against selling his boat, but he
needed it for a few days, and he needed to make sure he could get
himself and a carpenter back to Pirimapun some other way, to make
a new one. "He was a nice guy," van de Waal said, "but you could
tell he was used to getting whatever he wanted, and he was pushing
very hard." Van de Waal talked to the patrol officer in Agats, who
immediately agreed to take van de Waal back to Pirimapun on the
Tasman when he was ready. "He was so happy, because Michael was
bugging him for transportation. 'My God,' he said, 'I've just gotten
rid of a problem.'" The deal was done: van de Waal agreed to sell
Michael his boat for 400 Dutch New Guinea guilders, about $200.

"Mike was keen to do everything big and quick," van de Waal
said. He wanted to have a forty-five-horsepower outboard flown
in from Hollandia on a PBY Catalina airplane, but van de Waal
said no. It was too powerful, too big and heavy—van de Waal
himself only used a ten-horsepower motor. Michael settled on a
fifteen-horsepower Johnson, bought for $1,000 in Hollandia. At
the local Chinese general store, he bought forty axes and $300
worth of tobacco, fishing hooks and line, and cloth—a wealth of
barter goods. By the time he disappeared, he'd spent more than
$7,000—equivalent to $53,000 today—in one of the remotest
places on earth. One thing he didn't buy, however, was a radio.

"He should have had one," van de Waal said. "I feel he really underestimated the dangers. Not of attacks from the Asmat, but of nature. The mouths of the rivers, and the volume of water, is so huge, and Wassing was just a bureaucrat."

On October 7, Michael wrote van Kessel. He now had a catamaran, he said, and he and Wassing were going to explore the Casuarina Coast for a couple of weeks with van Kessel, then settle in a village for two to three weeks to film the carvers at work. He hoped the priest could suggest a good village and help make all the arrangements. "Both Rene Wassing and I very much look forward to [our rendezvous in] November," he wrote, the last message van Kessel would receive from him.

On October 10, he and Wassing and Simon and Leo, two teenagers from the adjacent village of Sjuru, set out from Agats in the catamaran. Here Michael made his gravest mistake. As long as he was with native rowers—men who knew the weather and the water, the tides and currents, the rhythms of the villages and their alliances and antipathies—he was safe. Although Simon and Leo were Asmat, they were only teenagers in a culture that venerated headhunting prowess and age. Even if they had known the waters, they would have found it difficult to challenge Wassing and Rockefeller, their elders and the holders of the purse strings. And in the villages they were nothing—they had no standing whatsoever. In his own boat Michael was free to come and go as he pleased, but he would arrive and depart like an alien, bound to no one and nothing, save his trade goods. And that made him vulnerable in every way—to the winds, to the tides and waves, to the Asmat themselves.

They made a quick swing south first, to the village of Per, which interested Michael because it was a small village with its own style of art, dominated by one carver, named Chinasapitch. Michael arrived in the village to find that the carver had just finished a beautiful canoe prow, which he refused to sell. Finally Chinasapitch agreed to make not just a bow ornament for Michael

but an entire canoe. It was a great beginning, and Michael was psyched. He was out in the world and making things happen. That evening he reveled in it all. "The evening was crystal clear, and the sun set before the open mouth of the Por River. Then the new moon appeared and the outlines of the family houses, canoe river poles were cast against a violet and rose sky and sea."

They visited Gerbrands and David Eyde in Amanamkai, where they were greeted like returning heroes. The chief was wild with excitement, and the villagers swarmed out to meet them in canoes, jumping in the mud and pulling the catamaran up the river to the village. "The Asmat has a special shout which is chanted at once by many men and used as a form of welcome. All the village lined the river bank and we heard this again and again as we made slow progress upstream."

Over the next three weeks, he and Wassing turned north and visited thirteen villages. Michael collected everywhere and in quantity, loading up on drums, sago bowls, bamboo horns, spears, paddles, shields, and even decorated ancestor skulls. He made intricate drawings of designs and stylistic differences between villages and artists, and he filmed and photographed carvers at work. He felt energized, constantly excited, increasingly comfortable and confident as a collector and explorer, now one of the world's foremost authorities on Asmat art. While his father, the ambitious and famous governor, had acquired the primitive objects he coveted from dealers, Michael was here, traveling the rivers among headhunters and cannibals.

"The only difference between Mark Twain and us is that his characters used poles all the time while we use an outboard engine most of the time and poles part of the time," he wrote. "We have been known to get out and push after propelling ourselves naively onto a mud bank at half tide. The boat has been christened 'Chinasapitch,' the name of the most brilliant single artist we have come across thus far. Occasionally it is called 'Fofo,' the name of a hornbill which we obtained in the village of Amanamkai."

AT THE END of the first week of November, they returned to Agats, Michael in high spirits. He'd collected hundreds of objects. As he cataloged, organized, and began arranging the transport of it back to New York, Agats felt easy and familiar. He knew its nooks, crannies, and rhythms, where to get tobacco and fishhooks or a warm beer in the evenings. He savored lounging under his mosquito net in the morning and, as he put it, "making use of the Sisters' major contribution to modern Agats: a lunch delivery service. At 1:00 every day you get a stack of seven pots, each containing some unusual goody."

He was intellectually fired up. "The Asmat is like a huge puzzle with the variations in ceremony and art style forming the pieces. My trips are enabling me to comprehend . . . the nature of this puzzle. I think now that with my trip, with all the anthropological work that will have been done here, and after a careful study of the large collections of Asmat things now in three Dutch museums, it would be possible to organize a mammoth exhibition which would do justice to the art of these people: to show the artist functions in Asmat society[,] to explain the function of the art in the culture, and to indicate by means of the arrangement of the objects the nature of style variation throughout the entire area. Nothing approaching this has ever been granted a single primitive people. You can imagine what fun I am having dreaming these wild dreams and creating earth-shattering hypotheses about the nature of Asmat art."

And yet there is something missing in those journals, in those efforts to decipher Asmat art. He wants to know how the artists work and what the symbols depict, how they vary from one village to another, and how to explain the function of the art in the culture. Absent, though, is an emotional need to know the Asmat as people, to connect, to answer the question of why he, Michael Rockefeller, was interested in their art, and what it might mean to him, beyond the academic questions. His notes feel clinical. There's no deeply personal need, no burning pathos. It's clear he likes to be in the

wild, but he also seems oblivious to parts of that experience. There's not a single account of friendship with any individual Asmat. He needs and wants the objects, good and beautiful and old Asmat artifacts, but less so the Asmat themselves. It's like he sees the art as the thing itself rather than as the product of something larger. He keeps denying that headhunting and cannibalism still exist.

Maybe he was just too young, not yet mature enough to understand why he was there, incapable of personalizing his experience rather than simply intellectualizing it. If we had him with us today, if he'd lived, maybe he would have been able to articulate what he was seeking, what had driven him. There had to have been a reason. To seek anonymity, to escape the safety of his family, to make the world understand a culture so different from his own—any of these would surely have been beautiful and understandable.

IT WAS A pivotal moment in Asmat history. Throughout the 1950s, even as an ever-increasing number of missionaries and government officials arrived, Asmat culture remained largely unaffected by their presence. When Omadesep and Otsjanep set off toward Wagin at the end of 1957, there were no more than thirty whites in ten thousand square miles of swamp and river, most of them in Agats, and the world still belonged to the Asmat. Now, just three and a half years later, the balance was shifting. There were police posts in Pirimapun, Agats, Atsj, and Ajam; missionaries in Agats, Atsj, Basim, and Pirimapun; and non-Asmat Papuan catechists in many other villages, not to mention Adrian Gerbrands and David Eyde in Amanamkai. Westerners weren't just on the periphery of Asmat lives, weren't just strange ghosts passing through, but had become a huge cultural force that was constantly pushing for change. Asmat society and culture were still there, still pure in many ways, but in turmoil—everywhere the Asmat turned were these powerful men, coveting their drums, shields, spears, skulls, bisj poles, which those men paid for with things the Asmat now

wanted, needed, couldn't get anywhere else. The whites were fascinated by their ceremonies, yet constantly interfered with them, and these powerful men backed up their actions, the Asmat knew, with the threat of violence, guns, against which they could not compete. Whenever conflicts heated up between villages, there was some priest or policeman or government official jumping in, thwarting the very things that had defined them as men, that gave them prestige with each other and their women.

One day in Atsj, Father von Peij got wind that two boys had been killed and eaten by Amanamkai. He ran outside and saw sixty canoes gathering, about to row to Amanamkai. He jumped in his boat and went with them, putting himself between the gathering canoes of warriors. He was petrified, afraid for his life, but he repeatedly tried to push them apart. The warriors yelled and screamed and shot arrows and hurled spears around him, but not at him—he was the white Lord, the Tuan, and they knew the power he represented and the repercussions if they killed him. "They were so angry and I was so scared, but I had to do it." Those kinds of disruptive incidents were now happening all over central Asmat near Agats and increasingly at its peripheries in the south and northwest.

Nor, of course, was the turmoil and change uniform. Some villages and some people embraced change faster than others. The closer to Agats a village was, and the bigger the river on which it lay, the more contact it had with whites and the government.

It was this place undergoing profound change and unrest through which Michael and Wassing were now traveling, and Michael was about to get swept up in all of it. His father had opened the door for him that day in 1957 when he launched the Museum of Primitive Art. The epic battle between Otsjanep and Omadesep— never again would so many men be killed in one clash—had unleashed Lapré, whose killings of Osom and his fellow villagers had never been reciprocated. And at the very moment when Michael was ranging over Asmat's rivers, alone, with no Asmat es-

cort except the two teenagers, Joseph Luns was trying to persuade the UN General Assembly to approve his plan for retaining Dutch New Guinea, a weird, exotic island that most of the world barely knew existed.

ON WEDNESDAY, NOVEMBER 15, at five p.m., Michael had tea at the parsonage with a group of missionaries, including Zegwaard and von Peij. Outside it was quiet, peaceful, Agats a tiny oasis of civilization on the edge of a fierce, roiling, and wild place. They sipped their tea and sat in chairs in a cozy wooden house and discussed their travel plans. Both von Peij and Michael were heading south on Friday. There were two routes past the mouth of the Betsj River—the shorter route over the Arafura and a longer one weaving in and out of rivers and small cuts. "I'm leaving for Atsj on Friday at five a.m.," von Peij told Michael, "via the Mbajir River between the Siretsj and the Betsj, when the tide will be high, and I'll be in Atsj by one. Don't take the sea route; come with me on the rivers. It's November, and the sea is rough."

"I can't," Michael said. "I have to go to Per first, but I'll see you in Atsj and Amanamkai." Three of the seven bisj poles from Otsjanep that he'd bought in the summer had been delivered to Amanamkai.

In remembering that conversation, von Peij was speaking about Michael at length for the first time in fifty years. He lived in a small room in an apartment for retired priests and nuns in Tilburg, Netherlands, decorated with a few Asmat carvings. He was a tidy, precise man in a green sweater vest and white shirt. "It was fifty years ago," he said, and he was tired of carrying the burden his whole life. "Why not speak about it now?"

The two men parted, agreeing to meet in a few days in Atsj. From there, Michael would proceed to Basim to meet van Kessel and begin exploring southern Asmat and the villages of the Casuarina Coast.

14

February 2012

I'D BEEN OUT on the rivers for nine days. My legs were covered with red welts, I was shedding pounds like I'd been on some crazy crash diet, and I was frustrated with Amates's English skills. I needed to go deeper, but Wilem and Amates were fighting over money and we were running out of tobacco and fuel, so, like Michael, we headed back to Agats.

We floated down the Ewta with the tide in the early morning, and I felt a lifting. The bubbling water was the color of strong tea. The breeze swept the flies away. We were leaving not just a place

ASMAT PADDLING A DUGOUT CANOE IN THE EARLY 1960S.

but a consciousness—one in which the "I" was different for the Asmat than for me. It was group, tribe, family, tied together in ways difficult to grasp. For me, an American, "I" is the biggest, most important unit. For us, freedom is everything. The right to do as we please, unbound by clan or village or parents—to move two thousand miles at will, to make a call home or send an email or say hi via Skype. We can reinvent ourselves, change churches or religions, divorce, remarry, decide to celebrate Christmas or Kwanzaa or both. But these men in Otsjanep are bound to each other. To their village and its surrounding jungle, to the river and the sea. Most will never see anything else, know anything else. And I kept wondering if I was as guilty as Michael, also filled with a Western conceit that I could just walk into a place and not only get it but also dominate it. Could I make the Asmat spill their secrets? Would they ever? Should they?

They are also bound to a spirit world, a place where powers I couldn't see exist. The powers and spirits are like the edges of a black hole for scientists: a phenomenon they can never see directly, only measure its effects. It is a place of the imagination. It isn't on any maps; no satellites or GPS can ever pinpoint it. It is a metaphysical place, as real to the Asmat as the dock or the moon or the river. They are part of it, it is part of them, and it is as powerful as any "real" thing, maybe infinitely more so, because what can be more powerful than your imagination? Their Catholicism is an overlay that eliminated headhunting and cannibalism and turned the act of carving a bisj pole into homage to the ancestors, whose deaths no longer need to be physically avenged. But that old spirit world is sprinkled everywhere still. As the bubbling water swept by and women in canoes, their fishing nets piled in the center, floated past, I wondered how to enter that world. Where was the doorway?

IF AGATS HAD felt like the end of the world when I'd stepped off the plane, now it felt like Paris. My cell phone worked. The hotel

still had little power and only a bucket of cold water in which to bathe, but at least I had a bed and a chair. A friend back in the United States worked the phones and came up with Hennah Joku, a former journalist whose father was from Indonesian Papua and whose mother was from Papua New Guinea. She spoke perfect English and happened to be just over the mountains in Jayapura. She said she'd fly in to help translate as soon as possible—which meant days.

Van Kessel, von Peij, and others had lived in Basim, Atsj, and Amanamkai for decades, but stepping off the boat, I always felt like I was the first white man who'd ever come to the village. In Agats I was the only Westerner, and people stared at me, even though the Catholic bishop who lived there from 1961 to 2001, Alphonse Sowada, had been an American.

Then, one evening, I spotted a ghost in a baseball cap and slacks—Vince Cole. Pastor Vince was the last American missionary in Asmat. He'd lived in the twin villages of Sawa-Erma for thirty-seven years, and now he had come to Agats for a couple of days of meetings. He invited me for a drink, which sounded wonderful, since there was no alcohol in Asmat and I hadn't had a drink in a month. "We'll drink mass wine," he said.

At eight that night, I threaded my way carefully in the dark along the crooked boardwalks (often missing boards) to the wooden house where Vince was staying. He welcomed me inside, in bare feet and chino slacks, bearing a bottle of wine. He was sixty-seven years old but looked ten years younger. He was big, strong, with long gray eyebrows and a prominent space between his two front teeth. The wine was warm and sweet. A single bare lightbulb lit the room, which was simply furnished with a basic sofa and a couple of chairs.

Vince was a dinosaur, and I liked him. The son of working-class parents in Detroit, he'd studied Islam and Urdu at McGill University in Montreal and become a Maryknoll priest. He'd orig-

inally planned to go to Pakistan, but that fell through, and in 1967 he ended up in Jakarta, where he first met Zegwaard and Sowada. He liked their approach. "They weren't evangelical," he said, tilting his glass back, "and we saw eye to eye—that it was our role to defend people's rights, and Asmat was the place to be if you had that bent."

For Vince, the biggest issue facing the Asmat was the encroachment of Indonesians flooding Papua and Asmat itself. They controlled everything, and had brought in consumer goods, even prostitution and HIV. If a village had a store, it was run by an Indonesian; Indonesian traders plied the most remote stretches of river in floating shops. Parangs and fishing hooks were one thing, instant ramen another. "The people invite them to come, to open stores, to log," he said. "They have never been beyond one or two villages, and they don't understand what's waiting for them around the next corner. They cut down their own trees; they cut themselves off at their own knees." And Asmat was potentially rich in coal, oil, and gold. It was an old story, the same in Asmat as in the Amazon or so many other places in the world—native people who were innocent about the world, who had few defenses against its encroachments. "They are easily influenced by the outside, too easily. I don't even like to be here in Agats, but people from the villages jump at the chance to come here, to see the bright lights."

Between Asmat and the highlands, in the foothills before the great wall of mountains rising in central New Guinea, Indonesia was establishing a new *Kabupaten*—an administrative district—rumored to be thick with coal and other minerals. Government officials had recently asked for Vince's help in talking to the tribes and acquiring the mineral rights under their land, and he'd said sure, if it could be done through a process of long-range planning to handle the payment in a way that would benefit the villages. "But they just wanted to get it done, so they literally arrived one day and dumped $200,000 in cash on the village. Guys flooded

downriver and bought tobacco and used outboard motors for double what they were worth and the money was gone."

Toward the foothills at Momogo a road was even being built through the highlands to connect with Jayapura on the other side of the mountains. Maps showed projected road systems winding throughout West Papua, all the way to Agats, which was hard to imagine given the miles of swamp and mud and tides. But roads had been built in tougher places in the world. In villages far upstream, where some Asmat had been interacting with the road crews, Vince had recently found leprosy. His urgent appeals to the government health workers in Agats went unanswered; they were too busy, it was too far. Alcohol had been banned in Asmat, but you could buy it if you tried hard enough, and the source was reported to be the Indonesian army itself.

Despite Pastor Vince's many years here, there was much he still didn't understand. "There are so many taboos." When he arrived in Sawa, he had the thesis of an Australian professor who had spent time in the village. "I read his paper on ancestor feasts, and when I finally saw one, I was asking all of these questions, and the answers I got were totally different from what the professor had written. Finally, I said to them, 'This professor says it's all different from what you're telling me.' And they said, 'Well, he was persistent and we didn't want to make him angry, so we just made stuff up.' So now we have an agreement. If there are things they don't want me to know, they just say so, and they don't make things up.

"Everything is secret and related to the spirit world, and it can have ill effects on their life. There are certain songs and stories that only they are privy to, and if they told outsiders they'd be putting themselves at physical risk of sickness or death."

Asmat ceremonies can last for months, and they start on no set schedule. "Just the other day the men in Sawa-Erma announced they were having a feast," Vince noted. "I asked them, 'Why? Why now?' And they said, 'Because a man was in the jungle and he met some

ancestors, spirits, and they told him now was the time.' They wait for some message, an ancestor or an animal, you just don't know."

Once, he said, the villagers were having a *jipae* mask feast. The making of the masks, which are intricate, full-body costumes, is kept secret from women and children. Vince asked the men if he could take photos of the masks being made in the jeu. He was surprised when the men said, "Sure," as long as he didn't show them to the women and children. He felt a little weird about it, but took a roll of photos and then weeks later had them developed. And they were all blank. Nothing was there.

He paused.

Then he began another story, about a crocodile that had run amok and started eating people near Sawa-Erma. "People thought the croc was an evil spirit. The victims were from every village but one, where a guy lived who they thought was the crocodile. One day a man was walking with his bow and arrow, and he saw the croc and shot an arrow up in the air, and it came down into the croc's eye, and the croc ran itself into the mud bank, where people killed it with axes and spears and feasted on it for three days. And the same day the croc died so did the guy who was presumed to be it."

We both said nothing. Stillness and the hum of crickets, the barks of lizards. And in the stillness it was hard not to wonder, to feel, to imagine the power of this coincidence—or was it? In a place where everyone believed, it was hard not to become a believer yourself. And that is how unshakable belief works: if you know something is taboo and you do it anyway and get sick, who's to say it isn't real? It took Western Europe a thousand years to go from the medieval world to the Enlightenment and the Age of Reason, and still people struggle with the supernatural. Asmat, by contrast, was a pre–Stone Age culture just fifty years ago.

"When I first came to Agats, you could walk from one end of town to the other in ten minutes and you knew everyone. The changes seem fast to me; I can't imagine how they see it. . . . I wish

I could crawl into their heads and feel what they feel. And how much they're picking and choosing to share, how much they're embarrassed to tell—it's hard to know. There are just whole areas that you can't go, where they can't let you in, and you have to project, and you don't know if it's your own projection based on your own background. At six months, I could have written a book, but now I wouldn't know where to start.

"They don't distinguish between what they see in a dream and what they see in real life," Vince pointed out. "A dream has the same validity as something they see with their eyes." Yet the Asmat aren't completely beholden to the spirits; they adapt and interpret according to their needs. "Upriver from Sawa-Erma they have this piece of wood they whirl around, a bullroarer, and the sound it makes is the voice of the spirits. One day I was at a feast, and they swung it around to see if everything was going to go well and they'd be able to hunt a wild boar. They swung it and all got long faces. 'What's wrong?' I said. 'Doesn't look good for wild pig?' Well, they just took the bullroarer and shaved it down—changing its shape changed the sound it made—and swung it around again and they were all happy: the day was auspicious for hunting."

I'd been thinking a lot about Eden and Genesis, since Asmat felt biblical to me sometimes, a strange sort of Eden before whites came, and I asked Vince about it. "It's a myth," he said. "It's not a fact, but something you strive for. Harmony. Peace. For everything that was expressed in Genesis before man destroyed that possibility. The whole Bible is driving you into a deeper meaning about what it means to be human, and God is the unknowable. It's not about the answers but about the questions."

We gulped the bottle down and listened to the crickets and a pack of barking dogs. I had a strange sensation. Vince was a priest whose lineage descended from Zegwaard and van Kessel and von Peij, and he had met them all, the men who had been the earliest, most important agents of change in Asmat. Zegwaard, he said,

had been crazy tough. Once, when Vince went to see him in his office in Jakarta, Zegwaard was throwing a guy out the door: "I was walking up the stairs, and I heard this commotion and a door flies open, and he had this guy by the bum's rush—one hand on his belt and the other on his shirt—and he literally heaved the guy out of his office." And Vince had known Schneebaum, called him Toby. They had traveled together, he said, to places that had never seen a white man before. "He was open. He'd talk about anything, and he wore his homosexuality well. It's just what he was, and he had so many insights and drew so well, it used to amaze me." Yet here Vince was saying that the most important thing was getting the Asmat to appreciate their own culture in the face of a world that was hurtling toward them with ever-greater speed. "For me, they have to believe that what they have is valuable and not be afraid to acknowledge it. Christianity can do a lot of damage, and the religion doesn't make any sense if they lose that."

Vince didn't know anything about Michael Rockefeller's disappearance—he'd come to Asmat in the 1970s, and Sawa-Erma was relatively far away from Otsjanep, in central Asmat. "But that village was always considered to be badasses," he said. "Same as Sawa-Erma, which was why I was attracted to it, because people said I couldn't do anything with it. They were fierce in war. Why? What made them individualistic, not listen to officials and priests? I still don't know."

15

November 1961

IT WAS JUST getting light on Friday, November 17, when Father von Peij left Agats. Michael Rockefeller and René Wassing followed soon after. The catamaran was fully loaded. Fuel. Boxes of axes and fishing hooks and nylon line. Cloth. Bricks of loose-leaf tobacco. Rice and chocolate bars and a sixteen-millimeter film camera, Michael's Nikon cameras, notebooks and field journals, a small portable typewriter—everything they'd need for another month, this time along the Casuarina Coast of southern Asmat. They slid down the wide silvery-blue Asawets, past the canoes and huts of Sjuru, and into the swampy netherworld where the spirits dwelled.

MICHAEL ROCKEFELLER PADDLING AN ASMAT CANOE, SHORTLY BEFORE HE DISAPPEARED.

It always felt good to get back to Agats, and it always felt good to leave. Michael

couldn't wait to see Otsjanep and the coastal Asmat again, which had had little contact with the West and which he could explore with van Kessel, someone who seemed to know the villages and people well. With Michael and Wassing were the Asmat teenagers from Sjuru, Simon and Leo, and they operated the engine as Michael let his mind wander, wondering if the southern Asmat would recognize the designs of their northern cousins, wondering how big an exhibit he might be able to organize. He loved to visualize showing everything he'd collected to his father and Goldwater. Their amazement. Their curiosity. His father wanting to know everything, admiring his daring.

Von Peij made Atsj by noon on Friday, and Michael and Wassing arrived in Per around the same time, to check on Chinasapitch's progress on the canoe he was carving. It was magnificent—hollowed from a single tree trunk forty-eight feet long, painted with red and white stripes, tied with sago tassels along its sides. Today the canoe rests on display in the Metropolitan Museum of Art in New York.

They spent the night and left the next morning, Saturday, November 18. Before them stretched the mouth of the Betsj, which Michael already knew was a treacherous place, especially in the months of November and December, when strong prevailing winds and currents blow out of the southwest. Not only did the outflowing tides of the three-mile-wide Betsj hit those winds and waves, but across the mouth lay a series of mud banks. When the Arafura was calm, the winds were light, and the tide was slack, it could be as still as a swimming pool. But at full bore it was a turbulent place of stacked, confused waves and crosscurrents; Michael had already seen how dangerous it could be and how careful the Asmat had been navigating the mouth of the Betsj. He'd heard von Peij say he was scared of it. Yet he disregarded von Peij's admonition to take the inland route, and neither Simon nor Leo advised him otherwise.

The trouble with seas and waves and wind is that it can take an experienced eye to read them, to see what lies ahead. The sun was shining, and the sky was dotted with big white puffs; he and Wassing saw no storm clouds that would have made them nervous. They started across. Wassing took the throttle. The waves were small at first, and rolling in from abeam; the catamaran rose and fell in a gentle sway. As they motored farther out, the wind freshened. It felt good. Cool and bracing.

Things in boats happen quickly. Once you get into trouble, it's hard to get out of it unless you know what you're doing and act decisively. One minute the water was gentle and easy, the next the boat was bucking hard. Spray flew over the starboard hull every time the boat slammed into the troughs, which were becoming deeper, more irregular, as the waves grew bigger, tilting the boat hard, throwing it around. The craft was losing momentum and control and the engine was screaming as the prop flew out of the water, then surged forward as the stern dipped and the prop bit again. The catamaran made noises it wasn't supposed to. It creaked and groaned, wood rubbing and nails moving in their holes. Michael and Wassing tried to turn more into the waves, but that just slammed them harder; the boat felt like it would break apart. Sideways to the short walls of water, though, the flat boat felt like it would capsize. Still, they weren't really scared. The shore was right there, the two sides of the Betsj's yawning mouth.

But things grew wilder, more uncontrolled, the boat shuddering, water pouring into the canoe hulls, which made the catamaran only ride lower, become more sluggish. Their only option was to turn inland, upriver, to run with the waves, against the outgoing tide. Wassing swung the boat, a wave picked it up, and they tipped forward, bow down, like a surfboard taking off, and flew forward on the power of the wave. They were moving so fast that Wassing throttled back, but the wave passed and the stern sank, plunging into a trough just as another wave swept over them.

Silence. The motor was dead, soaked. Wassing, Michael, Simon, and Leo all took turns pulling the cord, yanking and yanking, but nothing. They were still in the river mouth, shore a half-mile away, the outflowing Betsj pushing them to sea. The boys wanted to jump in and swim to shore. Come, they said. We need to go. If we get swept out to sea, no one will find us. No, Michael said, we can't leave my cameras, my notes, all the barter goods. And I can't swim well, added Wassing. They weren't afraid; they were just dealing with a problem they had to solve.

The boys were born on the rivers; Asmat are amphibians. The solution was obvious. Simon and Leo jumped in and started swimming. Wassing and Michael watched, staring, their fates dependent on the two boys. Though they focused on the waves as long as they could, hoping, they didn't see the boys reach shore.

Their catamaran continued to fill with water. Michael and Wassing gathered what they could and placed it on the roof of the little cabin, and then they climbed up too. But losing power is the worst thing that can happen to a boat in rough seas. It becomes flotsam, a piece of driftwood tossed at the mercy of the currents and waves and wind. It wasn't long until a wave flipped over the waterlogged boat. They salvaged what they could, some food, some water and fuel, Michael's backpack, and scrambled on top of the overturned hulls. Everything else was gone. Every minute was wet. Under a shining sun and blue sky, within sight of land, even as the seas calmed and they drifted away from the turbulent river mouth, they were in a nightmare. All they could do was hope that the boys had reached shore and would summon help.

Which they had. It was midafternoon when Simon and Leo waded through the mud onto shore. They headed north, a slow, arduous trek through the mud, but it was a mud and a landscape they knew, and they reached Agats at ten-thirty p.m. By one a.m. on the nineteenth, the radio was buzzing. Immediately, Dutch authorities in Agats scrambled the government vessel, the *Eendracht,*

which headed downriver to look for Wassing and Michael. But the boat had been inspected the day before, and the spare barrel of fuel put on the dock. In the haste to launch in the dark, the barrel was left behind. When the *Eendracht* was ten miles from the catamaran's last estimated position, it ran out of gas. And it had no operating radio.

Michael and Wassing, meanwhile, spent a long, cool night on the overturned hull. The stars were huge overhead. Lightning flickered on the far horizon. Save for the slapping of water on the hulls, it was silent, the sea calm. They pried a couple of boards from the floor of the deck and tried to paddle, but got nowhere. They told stories. They tried to sleep, Michael with the motor's empty fuel tank strapped around his waist. They talked about what they'd do when they got rescued. They watched the moon rise and set. They slept some. They had no idea that just ten miles away bobbed a rescue vessel without fuel. They saw the purple shadows of first light at four a.m. and the sun rise at five. They didn't know where they were, but the tides and currents had carried them south, out to sea and back in toward the coast, and they could still see land, a dim, low shadow to the northeast. Wassing thought they were three miles off the coast, though they were probably farther away. Where were the boys? Had they made it to shore, but just gone back to Sjuru and abandoned them?

"Let's try to paddle again," said Michael at five-thirty. They tried, but the upside-down boat was too big, too heavy and waterlogged, to make way under the power of two men and their narrow boards.

"I think we should swim to shore," said Michael.

No way, said Wassing. I wouldn't dare swim. I'll never make it, I'll be exhausted. And you should never leave the boat, it's the number one nautical rule—so long as it's afloat, it'll keep us alive and can be seen by rescuers. Don't go, he said. We'll be found, I'm sure of it.

No, I can do it, Michael said. The water is warm. All I have to do is keep swimming. We could be out here forever and never be found. And it's high tide now. We're as close as we're going to be right this minute.

He'd made up his mind. Maybe it was his youth. Maybe it was because he was a Rockefeller and he thought he could do anything, had no experience with the idea that things couldn't always be done. Wassing couldn't persuade him otherwise. "If you can make it, I don't do it," he said. "I don't take responsibility for you."

Michael had the one fuel tank already strapped to his waist; he found the spare gerry can stuck under one of the hulls, emptied it, sealed it again, and then added it to his webbed belt. He slipped off his pants and shoes and lowered himself into the water. It was eight a.m. on November 19. He was swimming against the out-flowing tide at first, but by four p.m., when he was the most tired, it would reverse and start carrying him in. The sea felt warm, almost hot. He hugged a fuel can and said, "I think I can make it." Wassing watched Michael swim away until he became a dim form, three dots, and then disappeared from sight.

November 1961

THE DAY AFTER Michael and Wassing departed Agats, heading south, so too did the men of Otsjanep. Slowly, haltingly, they were being pulled into the modern world. The airstrip at the government post of Pirimapun was finished, and the post was expanding. Van Kessel built a house there, though he still lived most of the time in Basim. A Canadian missionary, Ken Dresser, who was both an airplane pilot and a medical doctor, had moved to the post with his wife and young child and small Cessna. Add a dozen or so native Papuan police officers and Pirimapun was now a thriving little town.

Van de Waal had let it be known in the surrounding villages that he would happily purchase building supplies—rattan, jungle wood, and gabagaba, the stems of sago palms that served as the

BER, SON OF DOMBAI AND THE HEADMAN OF PIRIEN.

principal building material—from villagers who brought it in. Sometimes he put out the word when he needed something specific, but it was difficult to arrange a delivery for a certain date because the Asmat didn't have any calendars and could only count to five, the number of fingers on one hand, before jumping to "many" or "much." Their only real-time anchors were the tides and the next full moon. Which meant that often they just brought material when they felt like it, and van de Waal would set aside what they brought for when he needed it. Payment wasn't money, of course, but tobacco and fishing supplies and axes. Sometimes when he didn't need anything, villagers would sit for days in front of his house, hoping he'd change his mind.

SO IT WAS that, on the evening of November 18, eight canoes of men from Otsjanep filled their boats with gabagaba and headed to Pirimapun along the same route they'd taken almost exactly four years before on their way to Wagin and the Digul. Among them were some of Otsjanep's most elite men. There was Ajim, a short, powerfully built man with an equally short temper and a head of greased ringlets; he had killed so many, had taken so many heads, that he was regarded as the most powerful man in Otsjanep. Whites thought he was an unreliable troublemaker. He wore six-inch-wide rattan bracelets on his left wrist and biceps as armor against the snap of the bowstring. There were Fin and Pep and Dombai, Fom and Bese and Jane. Most of the men had multiple wives and skulls to their names, and every one of them was related in some way to the men who'd been killed by Lapré.

They paddled down the Ewta at slack tide, around five p.m., then turned south along the coast, staying well offshore on the Arafura. They were traveling at night because the sea was calmer then, and they still remembered what had happened in 1957, fearing the villages they passed along the coast. They were carrying

what they always carried—spears and bows and arrows—and a lump of smoldering coals burned in the stern of each canoe.

It was an uneventful trip. They made Pirimapun on the morning of the nineteenth, and van de Waal bought their gabagaba. They lounged around the post, snoozed, and peeked at the weird cargo there, and left that evening for the nighttime journey back up the coast to the mouth of the Ewta, where they'd arrive at dawn as the tide was still coming in.

November 1961

THE MORNING AFTER Simon and Leo arrived in Agats, Dutch officials began organizing a search-and-rescue effort in earnest. At nine a.m. on Sunday, November 19, the Dutch Resident of Merauke, F. R. J. Eibrink Jansen, telephoned P. J. Platteel, the governor of Netherlands New Guinea, with the news, as last reported by Leo and Simon: René Wassing and Michael Rockefeller were drifting at sea. This wasn't just a couple of missionaries or tourists, but

DUTCH PATROL OFFICER WIM VAN DE WAAL SHOWING NELSON
ROCKEFELLER AND MARY, MICHAEL'S TWIN SISTER, AROUND
PIRIMAPUN A FEW DAYS AFTER MICHAEL'S DISAPPEARANCE.

Michael Rockefeller. If that wasn't bad enough, the very next day Joseph Luns, the Dutch minister of foreign affairs, would address the UN General Assembly in New York to present his plan for the future of the Dutch colony.

Telexes flew at the highest levels of the government, between Interior Minister Theo Bot and the Dutch ambassadors to Australia and the United States. The US State Department telexed Nelson Rockefeller that his son was lost at sea.

On the island of Biak, three hundred miles to the north, the Dutch Royal Air Force kept a squadron of twelve Lockheed P-2 Neptunes. The plane was the first designed specifically for maritime patrol, reconnaissance, and antisubmarine warfare, and the squadron was stationed at Biak to patrol the waters of New Guinea to scout possible Indonesian incursions into the Dutch colony. Dutch colonial administrators in the outback, like van de Waal, might be living in wood huts with nothing but a radio, but the Indonesian military threat was taken seriously, and the squadron on Biak was modern and sophisticated. The Neptunes had a range of four thousand miles and radar so sensitive it could pick out a floating coconut.

Rudolf Idzerda commanded the squadron. At thirty-eight, the former fighter pilot had already survived two emergency bailouts by parachute—once when his Sea Fury was shot down by Japan during World War II, and once when his plane was tangled in a hurricane off the coast of Florida during training in the United States. He would go on to become a rear admiral. Late on the morning of November 19, the squadron got the call, and Idzerda's Neptune was the first plane up, at 1:30 p.m.

Von Peij, waiting for Michael to come by Atsj and Amanamkai, heard the sound of an airplane circling out to sea around 4:00 p.m.

Farther down the coast, and also waiting for Michael, van Kessel heard and saw the airplanes too.

After three hours, Idzerda's navigator picked up a radar contact,

and Idzerda soon spotted the half-sunken, overturned catamaran, at 4:10 p.m. It had drifted sixteen miles southwest of where the boys had left it. René Wassing spotted the plane and couldn't believe his luck; he thought the Neptune had simply stumbled upon him on a routine patrol. Idzerda opened the bomb bay doors and flew a hundred feet overhead. A crewman pushed an emergency raft out of the Neptune. It hit the water near Wassing and inflated.

As soon as Idzerda located the boat he radioed his coordinates to base, and as darkness fell he dropped flares that lit the night sky like a football stadium. Believing that Michael was still on the craft, he had no idea that he'd swum away from the boat. In Pirimapun, van de Waal received a radio call, and he and Ken Dresser jumped in Dresser's aluminum skiff and headed out. It was dark and the sea was quiet, and Idzerda overhead vectored them toward Wassing. But Idzerda was running low on fuel and had to return to Biak. In the dark, van de Waal and Dresser couldn't see anything, and they returned too.

That night, a few hours by canoe north of Pirimapun, a Dutch missionary named Ben van Oers was visiting small villages along the coast. He was asleep in the men's house when he was jolted awake by horrendous screaming. He rushed out of the jeu to find two canoes full of men pulling up to the muddy banks. They were hysterical. Shaking. As if they'd just escaped death. "Fire has fallen from the heavens," they told him. "A lot of fire on the sea near Pirimapun." *Maybe the Indonesians have finally invaded,* van Oers thought. He jumped in a canoe with a handful of rowers and headed toward Pirimapun, arriving just as dawn broke. Ken Dresser was pumping fuel into his small plane, and he saw the patrol boat *Tasman* heading out to sea.

Wim van de Waal was in it, and at 9:07 a.m. he spotted the rubber raft. It was upside down, and Wassing lay on its floor, sunken into the raft because the floor was just a sheet of rubber with no rigidity. He was sunburned and dehydrated, but otherwise

fine. Van de Waal hauled him aboard. "Mike is gone," Wassing said. "He swam away. I tried to persuade him not to, but I couldn't stop him."

IT WAS SUNDAY morning in New York, ten hours behind New Guinea. The governor had announced the dissolution of his marriage and his affair with Happy Murphy only days before, though he and Mary had now been separated for two months. And now he was there, in the family home in Pocantico Hills, New York, on a Sunday. The children—Rodman, Ann, Steven, and Mary, Michael's twin sister—hovered around their mother, "wary and watching. Why had he come?" Mary wondered. "Why had he called us all to meet?"

He held a yellow cablegram in his hands. "I have troubling news," he said. He'd just finished talking to the US State Department. "They received word from the Dutch government in New Guinea; they don't know the specifics yet, but Michael is missing."

A few hours later, Nelson, his daughter Mary, Eliot Elisofon (the *Life* photographer who had covered part of the Harvard Peabody Expedition in the Baliem with Michael), Robert Gardner, and a few trusted aides and local New York reporters boarded a flight to San Francisco. At what was then called New York International Airport, just before boarding the plane, Nelson received a radio telephone call from Hollandia. Static crackled on the line, and he could only hear a small portion of the message: Michael's boat had had problems, and he'd swum away from it.

At every step of the way, photographers and journalists surrounded the governor and Mary, a crowd of hundreds pushing in around them, a crowd that grew at every stop.

"I'm headed out there," he told reporters in New York. "I hope they'll find him before we get there, but at least we'll be there when they do find him, so if there's anything I can do, I will."

In San Francisco he received a telegram from President Ken-

nedy. "I am extremely sorry to hear about your son," wrote the president. "Everyone connected with the Government is most anxious to be of every possible assistance. I hope you will call upon us for whatever assistance the Defense Department or any other agency can render."

"If the boy has met trouble, I should be there," Nelson told reporters. "If he is safe it will be a joyous reunion."

"Mr. Rockefeller told reporters he had full confidence in Michael's resourcefulness and stamina," wrote Homer Biggart in the *New York Times* when the news exploded across the world's newspapers. "He kept telling his aides that his son was able to swim long distances and was capable of surmounting any hardships onshore.

" 'Keep your fingers crossed,' the governor said again and again, raising his crossed fingers and smiling wanly."

Of the people in Governor Rockefeller's party, only Gardner had been to Asmat before. "He emphasized," wrote the *Times,* "that while the Asmat people on the coast had practiced headhunting until about ten years ago, the region was now 'safe.' The natives have taken to wearing clothes and are eager to trade with white men, he said."

From San Francisco they flew on to Honolulu, where the governor chartered a Pan American Boeing 707 for $38,000 to fly on to Biak, via a refueling stop on Wake Island. The chartered flight left at 1:30 a.m. and offered no respite; reporters packed the plane. Though she'd gotten used to the publicity surrounding the family since Nelson had become governor, Mary felt overwhelmed and angry. "We found ourselves within a new group of strange, staring faces . . . and the sounds of conversation we heard upon entering turned to expectant silence that spread up and down the aisle as we found our seats in the front of the large cabin.

"I didn't dare ask Father why we had to charter such a large plane or why he felt it necessary to play host to this swelling group of press.

"I think I must have displaced the anger I felt then at Father onto the press. I found myself in a way over my head, in a situation without context, holding on for dear life to Father's strength and ability to control our family's destiny and to grasp a victory out from under any shadow of defeat. Sitting beside him, I reached for his hand, for I could feel my own sense of self shrinking, and our fairy-tale mission beginning to fade and break apart. Where was Michael in this press corps' vision? It was too unsafe to reach for the answer."

November 1961

IF THE OUTSIDE world had barely come to southwest New Guinea, now it was descending with a force and intensity that the villagers had never seen, had never known existed, could never have imagined.

As Nelson Rockefeller and his press pool hurtled toward the

NELSON ROCKEFELLER (*CENTER*) AND RENÉ WASSING (*LEFT*) EXAMINING THE GASOLINE CAN PICKED UP BY THE DUTCH NAVY THAT MAY HAVE BEEN MICHAEL'S.

island, the portal that Nelson opened that cold day in 1957 was thrown wide as reporters from around the world rushed to New Guinea to join them. All this just as the Netherlands' minister of foreign affairs, Joseph Luns, was making his case in New York to the UN General Assembly. Jan Herman van Roijen, the Dutch ambassador to the United States, sent a series of cables to the Ministry of Foreign Affairs, which forwarded them to Governor Platteel in Hollandia. "In con-

nection with the enormous publicity to be expected, I need not point out to you—also with an eye to the still not unfavorable course of the review of the Dutch proposals in the UN—it is of supreme importance to provide Rockefeller and the accompanying reporters the most assistance possible from the Royal Navy accommodations and facilities." He urged that everything the military and the civilian government could do should be done, on sea and on land. "It should be prevented that Nelson Rockefeller and the reporters accompanying him get the impression that any reasonable option would have been neglected to find the missing person."

In a second, breathtaking cable the same day, Theo Bot, the Dutch minister of the interior, wrote to van Roijen, Luns, and Platteel. Michael's disappearance was manna from heaven, the perfect opportunity, and they mustn't let it go to waste. "As a consequence of the tragic disappearance of Rockefeller junior, the international press . . . gives more attention to Dutch New Guinea than the opening of the New Guinea counsel and the Dutch proposals in the UN could generate," he wrote. "We should turn this to our advantage as much as possible with an eye to the success of the Dutch proposals in the UN. In particular I'm thinking of: one: as much as possible a unified response of the members of the New Guinea counsel with regard to the future of Dutch New Guinea. Two: self-control and loyalty (Dutch) officials toward foreign guests so that a repetition of Hastings' experiences [Hastings was a critical Australian reporter] will be prevented. Three: Emphasize modern development of Dutch New Guinea as opposed to picturesque primitivity of south coast and interior. Four: to highlight the idea of 'nation in the making' and real practical possibilities with regard to the future of Dutch New Guinea on condition that the UN will give the opportunity to do so by means of sending a committee etc. as proposed by the Netherlands. Of course I will gladly leave the manner of implementation of the above to your insight."

It was a stunning moment of geopolitical maneuvering. The

world's eyes were now on New Guinea, including Nelson Rock-
efeller's, and it was the Netherlands' chance to show that its colony
wasn't just some backwater full of headhunters, as President Ken-
nedy's advisers were arguing, but a nation in the making, with a
well-oiled government that could make things happen. For Dutch
officials, the search for Michael had become part of a larger strat-
egy: to leave no canoe unturned and no patch of ocean unexam-
ined, and to have Nelson Rockefeller return home, if not singing
the praises of the Luns Plan directly, at least saying how great the
Dutch in New Guinea were. And the same for the international
press—whether Michael turned up dead or alive.

AS THE GOVERNOR and Mary winged their way across the Pacific, the
search ratcheted into higher gear. On Monday, November 20, a
Dutch DeHavilland Beaver and the Neptunes continued combing
the sea and coast. A PBY Catalina flying boat was brought in from
Lae, in Australian New Guinea. Ken Dresser and missionary pilot
Betty Greene swept the coast in their Cessnas. The Dutch patrol
boats *Tasman, Eendracht,* and *Snellius* scoured the seas. Asmat in
canoes were asked to search the rivers. In Biak a Dutch marine
tied gerry cans to his waist, jumped in a swimming pool, "and
showed that the person involved could make good speed in swim-
ming," though "if unconscious head goes front forward in the wa-
ter." As a test, the navy dropped gerry cans into the water; they
were successfully spotted by the radar of a Neptune. The Dutch
attaché for New Guinea affairs at its embassy in Canberra, Austra-
lia, cabled that he was overwhelmed, that Michael's disappearance
had stopped all other business and reporters had taken over his
telephone, that he was scrambling to issue journalism visas and
landing permits to chartered airlines to carry them in.

NELSON AND MARY paused briefly in Biak, where they were met by
the commander of Dutch forces, L. E. H. Reeser, and told of the

search activities to date, including the tests with the gerry cans. After thirty minutes, they boarded a DC-3 to Hollandia, just as Michael had done eight months before, and then met briefly there with more officials. "My daughter Mary and I are very satisfied that the government is doing everything in its power and we are very grateful," Nelson said before continuing on to Merauke, southwest of Asmat proper.

It is a truism that you can't really understand a place, can't grasp it, until you arrive there. You can picture it, or imagine it, but it's an abstraction. Whatever they imagined Michael had been doing and seeing and feeling in Asmat over the months he'd been gone, the reality of the place began to hit them when they flew over Asmat, staring at the flat swamp through binoculars, and then landed in Merauke. The vastness. The heat and humidity. The utter primitiveness. Merauke might have been the administrative center of the southwest coast of the Dutch colony, but it was "a flat, ugly little settlement," in the words of Peter Hastings, the Australian reporter who'd been covering Indonesia and New Guinea for years, had met Michael in the Baliem Valley, and had even gone to the movies one night with him in Hollandia. He described Merauke as "comprising a few bitumen roads . . . a hotel of sorts . . . a great sullen river and a dirt road that in the dry season is passable to the Australian border."

Into this backwater town on the afternoon of November 23 descended a hundred journalists, Nelson Rockefeller and his daughter, and their entourage. It was a mad, sad scrum. Asmat, huge and inaccessible, lay 150 miles north and was not a place the Dutch wanted them to go anyway. Though the governor and Mary had flown ten thousand miles around the world, they weren't much closer to the action than if they'd stayed in New York.

The journalists were in the same position. They were in New Guinea, but there was nothing to see, to do, to report on, except what was in front of them. And what was in front of them were

the Rockefellers, a grieving, exhausted, and overwhelmed father and sister on the edge of one of the wildest swamps on earth. "The story we had all arrived to report was ostensibly the search for Michael," wrote Hastings, "but in reality turned out to be however distasteful or harrowing or intrusive, a watching brief on the private and public agony of Governor Rockefeller and his daughter, Michael's twin sister, Mrs. Mary Strawbridge."

Jan Broekhuijse, an anthropologist with the Dutch Department of Native Affairs who had been assigned to Gardner's film project, was flown in and met the governor in Merauke. "He was," remembered Broekhuijse, "a hurt, broken man."

It was like a public whipping, a public exposure, one of the world's most powerful men rendered impotent by geography and culture. "For the first time in my life," wrote Mary, "I noticed lines of worry creasing Father's brow and observed moments when he stared off into space."

Eliot Elisofon spent a day in a Catalina searching. The plane dropped off drums of aviation fuel in Pirimapun, from which the search was being conducted, and for eight hours he alternated thirty minutes on and thirty off, standing at the Catalina's side window blister, gazing down, looking for anything Michael-related. Asmat filled him with dread. "The coastline here is dismal. Filthy swamps seem to merge with the edge of the sea in a mud flat, deep enough to submerge half the height of giant tropical trees that have been swept out to sea by the numerous rivers that interlace this southern coast like the blood vessels of a plastic man. We have seen giant manta rays, hammerhead sharks, snakes, porpoises and thousands of birds. Our search is not just the water's edge, we cannot call it the beach since there is none, but also adjacent sea. Even if he made shore the mud is terribly difficult to get through and his excellent physical condition would be no further help in trying to cross the flats. I have been told that a man falling down into the mud cannot get up without help and Mike certainly didn't have any."

The search droned on. The governor held press conferences and attended a church service. René Wassing was trotted out to tell the story of his last hours with Michael, whose "restless nature made it impossible to endure our drifting around," he said.

Wassing's nervousness, Mary wrote, "mirrored my own deep anxiety and challenged the place where I clung to hope. I remember Rene's eyes going from one Dutch official to the other as he spoke. I sensed he felt responsible to them and could not be completely present with Father and me concerning what had happened to Michael."

On November 23, the commander of the US Pacific Fleet had cabled the admiral of Dutch New Guinea: "I can provide patrol planes, a converted carrier with helicopters, and surface units. . . . Please do not hesitate to inform me of any support which might assist you, and I will be pleased to provide it to the utmost of my capabilities. Please pass this to Governor Nelson Rockefeller."

The admiral responded: "I am considering your kind offer."

Indonesia objected—and played its card. "The Indonesian minister of Foreign Affairs has suggested Friday that Holland is trying to use the disappearance of Michael Rockefeller as a way to cause the rift between Indonesia and the United States," reported Reuters. "When asked for comment on reports that a spokesperson of the Dutch ministry of defense had said that the American seventh fleet was prepared to offer a carrier for the search, the spokesman of the Indonesian Ministry of Foreign Affairs said that he could not understand why an aircraft carrier was needed for that purpose. 'We understand what a father feels at the loss of his son . . . ; from a human perspective we understand how everyone is prepared to help in the search. We do not understand why that would require an aircraft carrier.'"

The spokesman said that if it was true that the United States was sending an aircraft carrier, it showed that the Dutch colonial authorities were not capable of performing their own duties.

The politics of it all was too hot. On November 24, the Dutch rejected the offer. "After consultations with Governor Nelson Rockefeller we have come to the conclusion that at the moment sufficient means including Australian aircraft and helicopters are available to continue a close search of the area; consequently additional forces will not be required. Your kind words and speedy offer have been a great help for us in our difficult and sad task."

Though the Rockefellers expressed hope, Dutch officials were increasingly convinced that Michael had drowned before ever making it to shore—or at least that's what they wanted to believe. The Associated Press reported that officials in Hollandia had "abandoned all hope," and the *New York Times* quoted Theo Bot, Holland's minister of the interior: "There is no longer any hope of finding Michael Rockefeller alive. Our people on the spot consider the situation hopeless." The likelihood that he could be alive at sea by this time, of course, was nil, but the Rockefellers clung to the idea that he might have made it to shore. "I'm a realist," the governor said. "If Michael reached the interior of the coast it may be a long time before we hear of it."

Eibrink Jansen, the resident in Merauke, backed him up: "If Michael reached shore there is a good chance of survival. The natives, although uncivilized, are very kind and will always help you. It's quite possible they took him to a hut."

The governor refused to abandon Merauke. He wanted to stay longer, to keep the search going, and he praised his hosts "for having inspired so much loyalty and affection among the Papuans," reported the *Times,* "that the natives were enlisting for the search." Which, of course, was just what the Dutch wanted him to say, and Platteel (who had been instructed by Bot to turn Michael's disappearance to the Dutch advantage) cabled Bot in The Hague. "Rockefeller enthusiastic about rescue action and help from government. During press conference he emphasized repeatedly his deep admiration and gratitude for government and officials. The

person involved is highly impressed by the cooperative attitude of the population which has answered a call from administrative officials to help in droves. He sees this as evidence of a very good relationship between the Papuans and the Dutch officials. Speech Rockefeller recorded by television and reporters. Correspondents complimented me with public praise from Rockefeller about New Guinea government and personally addressed to the governor about unlimited and unconditional assistance."

Nelson Rockefeller's continued presence paid off. Also on November 24, two Australian army Bell 47 G2-A helicopters were flown in from Australia by a C-130A Hercules and assembled with floats in Merauke. Using fuel cached in Pirimapun, they fanned out to individual villages and rivers, flying a search grid ninety miles along the coast and six miles inland. Like all outsiders plopped into Asmat, Captain Dick Knight, one of the pilots, saw nothing but "a torrid, hostile wilderness. . . . It was certainly a forbidding area in which to fly, particularly at the 'low and slow' pace necessary to conduct any sort of reasonable search peering down into the forest. Each aircraft carried . . . a 7.62mm Self Loading Rifle; and each pilot had a 9mm pistol."

A third helicopter from a Dutch frigate joined the Australians. And then something: on the same day, November 24, a red Johnson gasoline can for an outboard engine was picked up far to the south by the patrol ship *Snellius,* and a Catalina and Neptune were immediately directed to the area. The tank was shown to Wassing; that could be one of them, he said, but he couldn't be sure.

The search had new life. Mary and Nelson flew with Eibrink Jansen by Catalina for a few hours to Pirimapun, where van de Waal showed them around in a starched white uniform, Nelson looking like he was at a country club in a white V-neck T-shirt, white shorts, white socks, and white bucks. Van de Waal took Nelson to the gabagaba hut in which he lived. "Is *this* yours?" Nel-

son asked van de Waal incredulously. They stood on the dock and looked to sea. What else could they do?

They landed briefly in the Catalina on the river next to the village of Amanamkai, shook a few hands, then flew back to Merauke. They waited. Held press conferences. Hoped. But Asmat was unyielding, impenetrable. Helicopters, airplanes, ships, phalanxes of Dutch officials and reporters, and ultimately even the great square-jawed governor, the man who brought primitive art to New York, were defeated.

On the morning of November 28, nine days after Michael had swum away from the raft, Nelson flew to Hollandia, then Biak, and on to Tokyo and home.

19

November 1961

IF THERE IS a moment that captures the search for Michael, it's Eliot Elisofon's description of his hours in the Catalina. He isn't really *in* Asmat at all, but above it, encased in an aluminum tube, gazing at what to him appears to be a deadly and forbidding land. It's not hard to read his letter and wonder how anyone could live at all in the world he describes. It doesn't seem habitable: the sea is full of sharks; the shore is mud so deep a man falls in it and can't get up. But no reporters ever went anywhere in Asmat, not even to Agats. Nelson and Mary never spent a single night there.

THE AUSTRALIAN ARMY HELICOPTER UNLOADED FROM A C-130A
IN NEW GUINEA TO SEARCH FOR MICHAEL ROCKEFELLER.

To the Dutch officials in Merauke, Hollandia, and Amsterdam, and to the Rockefellers and the reporters covering the tragedy, Michael vanished into a great mire, an environment so hostile and remote that they threw up their hands and surrendered. He was simply gone. They looked at the mud and swamp and jungle and projected their own disconnection: no one could survive in that. Never mind that the Asmat had been living in the mud for generations. They walked in it. Rolled in it. Covered their bodies with it. And all that ocean and all those sharks. Never mind that the Asmat had been swimming in it and boating in it for as long as there had been Asmat. Michael must have been gobbled up by sharks or grown tired and drowned, and that's what the official cause of death became: Michael Rockefeller was taken by sharks or drowned. It was neat and tidy, and it fit the way Westerners looked at the world. And it worked for the Dutch government, which wanted the outside world to believe New Guinea was full of eager future citizens of the world, not Stone Age headhunters who practiced cannibalism.

There were, however, huge reasons to doubt either possibility. First, sharks rarely attack humans. While it's possible that Michael could have been a victim, I never heard a story about shark deaths in Asmat; the animal rarely shows up in their carvings or symbols. He'd had two gasoline tanks tied to a rope that was tied to his waist, and none of that rope was found—not even a knot or tail end on the Johnson fuel can that was recovered 150 miles away. The Neptunes had been searching the very next morning after he'd swum away, and they never spotted anything—not a chunk of human flesh left behind, not the cans.

He could have just grown tired and drowned, except that he was tied to the floating gas tanks, which tests showed the Neptune radars could pick up with ease. As carrion, he might then have been bitten by sharks, but again, he wouldn't have been consumed whole. More important, none of this would have happened

quickly, and the radar of the Neptunes should have spotted him, or pieces of him, and his flotation aids.

In the end, the chance that he was attacked and consumed by sharks so completely that neither he nor the rope or belt or other gas tank was found is low.

ON THE GROUND, everything looked different. The day Michael disappeared, both van Kessel and von Peij were waiting for him, von Peij in Atsj and van Kessel farther south in Basim. On November 19 both heard the sound of engines, rare in Asmat, and looked skyward to see the circling Neptunes, and both were alerted by radio the next morning that Rockefeller was missing. Van Kessel immediately sent his assistant, Gabriel, an Asmat who'd been baptized and had been with him for years, by canoe north along the coast to the Ewta and Otsjanep—the farthest point north in his district—to warn the villagers and ask them to keep a lookout. Gabriel saw nothing out of the ordinary, only two young men at the mouth of the Ewta.

Van Kessel followed him, traveling up the Ewta at four p.m. on November 20. Otsjanep lay only three miles inland, and villagers traveled up and down the Ewta constantly, fishing at its mouth. But as the sun sank low that afternoon and the green of the prehistoric-looking nipa palms and the blue of the sky and the silvery brown of the river deepened, van Kessel saw no one. The usually bustling river was deserted. He camped for the night in a bivouac at the mouth of the Faretsj.

Throughout Asmat, Dutch officials were cranking up the search, and Asmat from the villages were fanning out, prowling the shore and rivers. Van Kessel linked up with the *Tasman,* on which the Dutch police commissioner, known as the HPB, was sweeping along the coast. Gabriel, meanwhile, spent the entire day on the Ewta and along the beach south to the Fajit, on which lay Basim. Although many villagers were searching, he saw no one from Otsjanep.

It's hard to know exactly how this frenzy of searching appeared to the Asmat, but it was something they'd never seen before. So many steel ships. So many airplanes. So many white men. That the missing man was a Rockefeller, the son of one of the richest and most powerful men in the world, meant nothing. They knew only that he was a white man, a Tuan, who was gone.

As the days passed and the search intensified, the helicopters arrived. No one in Asmat had ever seen one before. Some had seen airplanes high in the sky; a few in Pirimapun and Agats and Amanamkai had seen Catalinas land on the water, but most had never seen these strange spirit canoes up close. Equipped with floats and Australian army pilots, the helos came out of nowhere, out of the sky, and landed on the rivers beside villages, their rotors thundering and blowing eighty-knot gusts of wind that made clouds of water and sticks and debris. The villagers fled into the jungle in terror, screaming. Considering the Asmat reticence and wariness with outsiders, it's little wonder that the helicopter pilots found nothing, heard nothing. On November 27, Nelson's last day in Merauke, van Kessel's assistant, Gabriel, flew on a helo to Otsjanep and, as always, the village emptied at the sight of the machine. Gabriel pushed into the underbrush beyond the village, and finally Ajim and Fin appeared. They said they knew nothing of Michael, but Gabriel noticed, again, that no one from the village was helping in the search.

In Atsj, von Peij watched as ship after ship and one helicopter after another came and went.

And then Asmat became quiet. The helicopters were shipped home. The Neptunes stopped circling. The *Tasman* and *Eendracht* returned to their regular patrols. In Atsj, von Peij waited a week to let the villagers go to the jungle to collect sago before he went on his rounds. His first stop was Jow, where everything seemed back to normal.

The next day he traveled the long way to Omadesep, via the inland creeks and cuts by canoe. The day was hot, but he felt glad

to be out of Atsj, glad to have the Rockefeller search behind him, glad to be back to his regular routine. He arrived in Omadesep around noon.

"There are some men who want to meet you," his catechist said. "They have a message for you."

"Let them come," he said.

20

December 1961

IN BASIM, van Kessel started hearing strange, conflicting rumors. That something unsettling had been spotted on the sea. That the village of Warkai, just up the river from Otsjanep, was saying a white man had been killed and eaten by Otsjanep. Everyone seemed to know something. On December 3, van Kessel sent Gabriel back to Otsjanep. He sat and smoked, talked, listened. There have been rumors, he told the men in each jeu, that a man from the village named Bere told Omadesep of a white man having

AJIM (*NAKED*), PHOTOGRAPHED BY FATHER VAN KESSEL IN BASIM SHORTLY AFTER MICHAEL ROCKEFELLER'S DISAPPEARANCE.

been killed. "We saw a fierce giant snake in the sea!" said Wotim, but that was all. They denied knowing anything else. But Bere went on a rampage, running through the village, yelling, screaming, telling everyone he hadn't said a thing, and then he ran off into the jungle. Van Kessel sent a canoe from Basim to Otsjanep and brought Bere and three other men back to Basim to question them. He did so one by one in his house on December 5.

"I just made it all up," said Bere.

"I didn't see a snake," Wotim said. "Just a piece of wood."

"There was a giant crocodile in the sea," said Aitur.

"I saw something with a face, but it was just a tree trunk," said Ekob.

Van Kessel asked them why Aitur didn't kill the crocodile. "We didn't have any weapons with us," he said.

He called in Wotim again, but Wotim ran into the jungle.

On December 8, he sent Gabriel to Otsjanep yet again, this time with a large supply of tobacco. They gathered in the Otsjanep jeu and sat and smoked. "Men of Otsjanep," Gabriel told them, "some of you have already been questioned, and you know that the Tuans are searching for a Tuan from America. They know the corpse washed ashore in the neighborhood and that you must have found it and didn't know what to do with it, because the government could suspect you of wrongdoing. Hand me his shorts, so I can show it to the Tuans and they won't have to search any longer."

It was a tactical speech designed to get them to admit they had the body, not mentioning any murder or the suspicion of one. But no one knew anything. Pep had a new dagger made from human bone, though, and he offered his old one to Gabriel. Ajim wasn't there. And Gabriel felt they were behaving strangely. He "saw they were acting; people exaggerated their amazement and they gave cautious answers," van Kessel wrote in his report. "Behind his back they were whispering and they were really nervous."

Van Kessel wasn't sure, but he began to think that Michael

Rockefeller had made it to shore and been killed by the men of Otsjanep.

ON DECEMBER 9, von Peij arrived in Omadesep, which lay at the far southern end of his parish. The sun had dropped by the time he settled into the house of his catechist—a spare, native-style room on stilts with gabagaba walls, a palm-frond roof, a table, a bed, and a cupboard. He felt unsettled; he wasn't ready to hear any news. A gas lamp glowed, and on the walls nearest the light, pale bug-eyed lizards with stubby tails and suction cup toes were poised, waiting for insects attracted by the light. Though only a few inches long, they emitted a loud barking sound. Outside, crickets buzzed and a pair of dogs squealed, fighting over scraps of fish skin.

Von Peij was waiting when in walked four men. Bere and Bumes were from Otsjanep; Mbuji and Tatsji—one of the men who had escorted Michael, Wassing, and Gerbrands in the canoes from Omadesep to Otsjanep back in June, who had relatives in Otsjanep—were from Omadesep. They wore shorts, since they were visiting a priest, but they were adorned with the usual bipane shell or carved pig's bone in their septums.

"Okay," von Peij said, "tell me your story."

Bit by bit, it spilled out. On Friday, November 17, Otsjanep had heard that van de Waal wanted building materials in Pirima-pun, which they delivered on Saturday. The fifty men departed for home late Sunday afternoon, and on Monday morning they paused at the mouth of the Ewta, safe in their own territory. It was a good time to have a smoke and a bite of sago. Something moved in the water. They saw a crocodile, an *ew,* in the Asmat language. No. It wasn't a crocodile, but a Tuan. He was swimming on his back. He turned and waved. One of them said: "People of Otsjanep, you're always talking about headhunting Tuans. Well, here's your chance." An argument ensued. Dombai, the leader of the Pirien jeu, didn't think he should be killed. Ajim and Fin thought other-

wise. While they tried to lift him into a canoe, Pep stabbed him with a spear. It wasn't fatal. They rowed him to the coast, to the Jawor River, where they killed him and made a big fire.

"Was he wearing glasses?" asked von Peij. "What kind of clothes was he wearing?"

Their answer burned in his memory, a detail he'd never forget: the white man was wearing shorts, but shorts they'd never seen before and that you couldn't buy in the shops of Agats—shorts that ended high up on his legs and had no pockets. Underpants.

Von Peij listened. Nodded his head. "Where is his head?"

"Fin-tsjem aotepetsj ara," they said. "It hangs in the house of Fin. And it looked so small, like the head of a child."

"What about his thigh bones?" said von Peij, who knew that thigh bones were used as daggers. "And his tibia?" These were used as the points of fishing spears.

Pep had one thigh bone, Ajim the other. Jane one tibia, Wasan the other. As had Michael's left upper arm, Kakar his right. Akaiagap his right forearm, Akaisimit his left. Bese, Erem, and Fom each took a rib. Ainapor had his shorts, those strange shorts that had no legs and no pockets. Dombai or Bese had his glasses.

"Why did they kill him?" von Peij said.

The killings in Otsjanep almost four years earlier, they said.

Von Peij was overwhelmed. The details, especially the description of Michael's underwear, were too concrete not to be credible. He'd been in Asmat almost six years, spoke the language fluently, was as intimate with the Asmat and their culture as any European had ever been. He felt burdened. But he feigned disbelief. Said little.

The next morning he returned to Jow and sent his cook to the jeu. A few hours later, the cook returned. The same story was now making the rounds of Jow; everyone knew everything.

Von Peij moved on to Biwar Laut, Amates's village. A crowd of men were gathered there. They were excited. They wanted tobacco. *"Nda kapak to,"* they said. "We have to smoke!"

"If you want tobacco," von Peij said, "then you have to do something for me. Bring a letter immediately to Agats."

"To the HPB [the government official]?" Their enthusiasm dampened. They didn't want to go. Not to Agats. Not to any government officials. They were afraid.

"Okay," von Peij said, "then I'm not giving you any tobacco. And the letter isn't for the government, but to a priest who's just passing through for one day. That's why you have to go now." The tide was going out, the water dropping fast. In order to make the journey, they had to go immediately.

They agreed. Von Peij scratched a note: "Without having the intention of doing so, I stumbled across information and I feel compelled to report this. Michael Rockefeller has been picked up and killed by Otsjanep. Jow, Biwar, and Omadesep are all clearly aware of it."

He sealed the note in an envelope addressed to Father de Brouwer, the head priest in Agats, but inside of that was a message addressed to the government controller in Agats, Cor Nijoff.

Von Peij returned to Atsj the next day.

On December 12, van Kessel arrived in Agats to talk to Nijoff, who showed him von Peij's "small note that was absolutely clear." Van Kessel immediately traveled to Atsj to talk to his colleague.

ON DECEMBER 15, back in Basim, van Kessel wrote a long report to Nijoff. "After my conversation with Father von Peij, the one percent of doubt I had has been taken by the very detailed data which matched with my data and inspections.

"IT IS CERTAIN THAT MICHAEL ROCKEFELLER WAS MURDERED AND EATEN BY OTSJANEP," he wrote in all caps. "This was revenge for the shooting four years ago . . . and in all the villages until Sjeru [sic] people only talk about this heroic act of Otsjanep and it is known everywhere." Van Kessel spelled it all out. Names. Who had which body parts. That Tatsji, who

had free passage between Omadesep and Otsjanep, had arrived in the village as they were singing bisj songs and had seen Pep's new thigh bone dagger. And that Otsjanep was in a turbulent mood, "ready to receive" anyone from the government who might come to investigate. In rough water and high winds, Gabriel took the note that night to Nijoff, who was now in Pirimapun. Gabriel's canoe capsized three times and he arrived sick and exhausted; he would almost die of pneumonia.

Five days later, on December 20, Ajim, Fin, and several other men from Otsjanep arrived in Basim, where a relative had died. They steered clear of van Kessel's house, but he sent them a message: he would pay three steel axes for Michael's head and two for his femur. The two warriors from Otsjanep refused. "THEY DID NOT DENY THE MURDER," van Kessel wrote, "though they also said, 'Tatsji is talking nonsense.'" The priest found the two men and took a photo of them, "so one would later (if necessary) recognize the main culprits."

Van Kessel's long report found its mark. On December 21, six days after sending it to Nijoff, P. J. Platteel, the governor of Dutch New Guinea, cabled Theo Bot, the minister of the interior. The cable is marked "secret" and "destroy." It was in fact partly destroyed, and only part of it remains in the archives, but it carries a handwritten note: "Remainder not distributed.

"Resident Merauke [Eibrink Jansen] received through controller Agats [Nijoff] a letter from Father van Kessel in which it is stated that the latter assumes beyond any doubt that Rockefeller was murdered by the inhabitants of Ocanep [*sic*] village and eaten. His information, which was obtained by contact persons in other villages, would allegedly agree with similar information obtained through Father van Pey [*sic*]. According to this information, on the morning in question a number of canoes would have found Rockefeller at sea and allegedly he had already been run through with a spear when he was hauled aboard. Once

ashore he would have been slaughtered and eaten. Skull, bones and clothing are said to reside with person known by name. Resident also reports that rumors are making the rounds in Merauke about these things already and that it is improbable that the case remains outside the press. In my opinion some reservations need to be made. No evidence has been found yet and therefore there is no certainty yet. In this connection it doesn't seem germane to me to give information to the press or Rockefeller Senior at this time. If any questions arise then we could respond to these by stating that the rumor has reached us too and that it will be investigated. This will gain us some time and would enable us in case of confirmation to pick a more favorable moment for publication. Resident Merauke is still considering which action would be most proper to get definitive closure."

21

March 2012

AMATES, WILEM, FILO, Manu, and I piled into the longboat at six a.m. and headed back to Otsjanep. Although I'd read all of van Kessel's and von Peij's reports before my first visit and had spoken at length to von Peij, I had wanted to take things slow.

Finally I'd told everything to Amates and Wilem, and neither was surprised in the least. "Otsjanep killed him; every Asmat

MEN FROM OTSJANEP AND PIRIEN GATHER TO TALK IN PIRIEN DURING MY FIRST TRIP TO THE VILLAGE. THE MAN IN THE CENTER IS BER, SON OF DOMBAI; TO HIS RIGHT IS TAPEP, SON OF PEP.

knows this," Amates had said. "We will find out everything, don't you worry, Mister Carl."

This time we were returning to just Otsjanep and Pirien, where I wanted to spend a few days and finally question the men directly about Michael Rockefeller. With us was Hennah Joku, a small, quiet woman who'd grown up in Papua New Guinea and on Lake Sentani, outside of Jayapura, in Indonesian Papua, where her father had been an early leader in the Papuan independence movement. I'd been waiting for her for five days in Agats, and she'd finally arrived. Her English and Indonesian were perfect; I hoped she'd help fill in the spaces that I couldn't understand when Amates was translating.

We slid into the mud banks of Pirien just after noon. The village felt hot and still. There was no dock here; we clambered over three canoes and up onto sagging, rotting logs that formed a precarious path over the mud. At the house we'd stayed in before there was shouting.

"Tsk, tsk, tsk," said Wilem, shaking his head.

Amates looked grim. "We cannot stay here," he said.

Though the house was vacant, it was next door to a family whose outhouse we had used, for which Amates had given them money. The patriarch wouldn't let us stay. "People were angry at him," Amates said. "Jealous. Come."

We walked along Pirien's main boardwalk, raised five feet over the swamp. We descended a notched log, then walked twenty feet along a single two-by-four two feet over the black mud to a three-room house with a small veranda. Amates said a few words and *whoosh!* the family inside gathered their nipa palm sleeping mats and little piles of clothing and disappeared into the back kitchen area, a twenty-by-twenty thatched room with a mud hearth. Its floor was made of sticks an inch in diameter, placed two inches apart. Blackened pots hung from the eaves, which were filled with faded cloth and palm net bags, bows and arrows, and fishing nets.

The rooms themselves were empty, the walls black with soot and dirt. We sat on the floor, and Filo cooked lunch on his portable one-burner stove—white rice and freeze-dried ramen, with a few canned sardines mixed in. By now I had a clearer sense of who was who. We were in the house of one of Dombai's sons, the man van Kessel said had Michael's glasses. Dombai had eventually married four wives and produced fourteen children, and he'd died from being gored by a wild boar. Kokai, the man we'd met in Basim who told me the story of Lapré's raid, was related to him somehow. Pep, Fin, and Ajim were all dead, but the sons of Pep and Ajim were here, alive and well.

"Come, we go to Otsjanep," said Amates when we were done eating.

We tiptoed over the walkways again—well, I tiptoed, while Amates and Wilem and the Asmat scampered over the narrowest logs and boards with babies on their backs like they were walking on a three-foot-wide sidewalk. We jumped in the longboat and sped upriver a half-mile. The jungle cleared and Otsjanep appeared. We tied up at a low dock and climbed onto the right bank. Boardwalks ran over the swamp, and houses—thatch and palm and wood, with corrugated roofs—dotted a broad clearing. It was quiet and smelled of smoke and dampness. There were people everywhere, on every porch, in every doorway. Watching. A crowd of men and boys gathered, following us. A child saw me and started screaming, shaking violently, inconsolable, and then dived into a water-filled ditch, desperate to escape and hide.

Amates laughed. "She is afraid of you. She thinks you're a ghost."

The boardwalk ended, and we navigated across logs in the mud to a dilapidated and abandoned wooden house with a large covered porch. We sat down on the floor, our backs to its front door, and men began gathering. Five. Ten. Thirty. Soon there were fifty sitting around us. Waiting. In the front sat Tapep, son of Pep, now the head of Otsjanep.

Amates took two pouches of loose-leaf tobacco and pushed them into the circle. Wilem took another one and did the same. Tapep and the older men reached for the pouches, took fingerfuls of the brown leaves, divided them up, passed them around.

Out of nowhere, with no warning, with no apparent signal, a man yelled and started singing in the Asmat way—a long, mournful chant—and others joined in. "Yeh! Yeh," they shouted in unison, all forty men in one voice, perfect harmony. It was powerful. Haunting. Beautiful.

Amates began talking. And talking. Sometimes in Indonesian, sometimes in Asmat. When he was done, there was a moment of silence, and then I heard a different kind of screaming. Hysterical wailing. The beat of a drum from across the village. Men turned their heads, spoke, began to stand and leave and stream toward the direction of the wails.

"Someone has died," Amates said, rising. "A woman. We must go. We will come back this afternoon."

Which we did. The same men gathered. We distributed tobacco again, and Amates gave his speech again, and with Hennah's help, I did my best to capture what I could of what was said.

"We are all the same, Americans and Asmat. We Asmat have a proud history. We have nothing to be ashamed of. We do things different now, after the Bible came, but our past is who we are and we should talk about it. People in America are interested in Asmat. They want to know about us. Everyone in America already knows about what happened to Michael Rockefeller, so there's nothing to be afraid of. It was a long time ago. Mister Carl has come a long way and he wants to know these old stories." Then Amates said, "And we know Pep killed Michael Rockefeller."

A stir went through the group. They fidgeted. Pep's son, Tapep, spoke. "What happened here then was a long time ago. It is past. No one here remembers."

An old man wearing a T-shirt that said SNIPER! on the front

spoke. "Everyone in Otsjanep is young, and they are surprised at this story. I have heard it, but I was just a little boy, and I am afraid."

I watched Tapep. He swallowed, looked at me, looked at Amates. He and the men started talking in Asmat, a quiet argument. "They're worried," said Amates. "Scared."

"I heard these stories from my father," said a man wearing a T-shirt in green and brown camouflage. And the next thing I knew he was talking about "the white man, Pastor Zegwaard," bringing the Bible to Asmat. "This is all I can remember," he said.

Silence. No one said anything more. We sat and stared at each other, and I had no idea if they were telling the truth or not. Was I imagining their skittishness? Was I imagining that they were deflecting the conversation on purpose to Zegwaard?

"Let's go," said Amates. "That is enough for the day."

THAT NIGHT WE sat on the floor around the flickering lights of two tin cans filled with kerosene, a column of black smoke rising into the darkness. Shadows danced across the dirty walls. Rain poured down, the way it does only in Asmat, a shattering, pummeling onslaught. A few men from Pirien sat there too, the women and children, at least a dozen of them, out in the kitchen. We smoked. We looked at each other. It all felt untouchable to me.

"Do you think they were telling the truth today?" I asked Amates.

"Two men said, 'We know this story, but we are afraid to talk,'" Hennah said.

"What?" I said. "When did they say that? Why didn't you translate it?"

She shrugged.

"Yes," Amates said. "They know, but they are just afraid."

"They are afraid of America," Wilem said. "Of the American army. Tomorrow some men are going to Basim for tobacco and sugar. Amates and I should go with them, to talk with them alone."

In the darkness and dancing light, Amates and Wilem whis-
pered, kneeling close to me. "Manu has been hearing things.
People are afraid to be seen talking, so we will go out tomorrow
night and talk to people."

Then Amates said, "The glasses are here. Dombai's son says he
has seen them. They are in his family. His father was killed when
he was a small boy, by a bite from a pig." He paused. "If I was
teaching these people, I would go crazy! They answer a question
with a question. They say nothing!"

I don't know what time it was when I fell asleep in a corner on
the floor. I was jarred awake by chanting and drumming. It was
close by. I got up, tiptoed past ten bodies on the floor—Dombai's
son and his family, all squished together on palm mats, babies and
children in the pile—and went outside. The rain had long since
stopped, and there was no moon. It was pitch-black. Warm. Still.
The chanting and drumming were right there, right in front of the
house on the boardwalk, but I couldn't see anything. When light-
ning flashed on the horizon, there they were, a circle of a dozen
men thirty feet away. Over the drumming, staccato and deep, a
voice would begin and others would join in, the sound seeming to
come up from the very center of the earth. I sat down transfixed.
Why was this happening here, in front of my house? I wanted to
go over to them, but wasn't sure if I should. As the sound went
through me I looked at the sky, the Milky Way thick overhead, a
trillion stars. I don't know how long I sat and listened. An hour.
Two. It went on and on, with the occasional pause, the flash of
a match lighting a face, a red glowing; a laugh here, a low voice
there, and then the drums beat again and the voices rang on even
as I tried to go back to sleep.

AMATES AND WILEM disappeared at four a.m., and I spent the day
sitting on the porch and walking through the village. Children
ran wildly, everywhere. They climbed palm trees and swam in

the river and rolled in the mud. Gangs of them walked hold-
ing hands and covered in white, dried mud. A few chickens and
huge black pigs scrunched through the swamp. The flies were
incessant, swarming onto my hands, legs, arms, eyes, and mouth.
In the afternoon everyone just went to sleep. The whole village
ceased to move.

When Amates returned late that morning, he was angry. Frus-
trated. "They say nothing," he said. "They say they know but are
too afraid to say. They say, 'Maybe tomorrow.' But we'll go to
Otsjanep again in a little while. The man we went to Basim with
is afraid the other elders will get mad. It's a problem with our own
history. We don't have a problem talking about it, he said, but the
elders don't want to."

Around noon, an old man walked into the house. He whis-
pered to Amates, who took him into the other room. They sat
on the floor, smoked and whispered. It was such a big, deep se-
cret, this thing that had happened so long ago and that every-
one knew about but no one wanted to speak of. And the reasons
were so complex. The young felt connected to a past that carried
deep shame; they feared the wrath of the Indonesian government,
the American government, and probably the Catholic Church and
God himself. If they had killed Michael, it had been an act of tre-
mendous defiance, something they'd never done before and knew
wouldn't go over well with their white overlords. But I suspected
there was more to it than that, more than concerns about legal
consequences or Christian wrath. If Michael had been killed by
Otsjanep, it wasn't as simple a matter as revenge in the Western
sense. It was spiritual, sacred, a rebalancing, and there were prob-
ably elements that went so deep they couldn't be shared without
repercussions from the spirit world itself. Balance in Asmat was
a precarious thing because it was based on opposites: if they had
killed Michael, then they would be waiting, waiting for the re-
sponse, a response literal and metaphysical.

When Amates and the man emerged, Amates said we'd go back to Otsjanep in a bit. To the man's house. There he would tell us what he remembered.

THE HOUSE WAS a timeless place, all sticks and thatch and open fireplaces. Smoke curled from the hearth, and the floor was bark, covered with sweet-smelling palm fronds. We could not pass unnoticed. Walking from the boat to the house, we picked people up, the crowd grew, and by the time I was sitting on the palm floor there were twenty of us. And more coming all the time. The man looked nervous. He was tall, skinny, with a hole in his ear and one in his septum, and tight curls of gray. "He says okay, he will tell the story, but we must go, there are too many people," Amates said.

We moved to the front veranda of the abandoned house again, and again there was a huge crowd. We passed out the tobacco. Everyone rolled cigarettes, and we waited. Pep's son Tapep arrived. The man who said he'd tell us the story rose and went into the house with a few others. I heard low voices. He walked out and kept walking and he was gone.

Tapep took over. "We know this story about Michael Rockefeller," he said. "He was in a boat, and he was coming to visit Otsjanep, and his boat turned over, and he disappeared. That's all we know, and if we knew anything else we'd be afraid to say."

"Why are you afraid?" I asked.

"We are not afraid," he said. "We do not know the story." We were getting nowhere. Or maybe somewhere; he'd said more than he'd said yesterday.

"We must go," said Amates again, a refrain I was getting used to. We got up to leave, and another old man came up to me. Stuck out his hand. I took it to shake it, to say "thank you" in Asmat, and he looked me in the eye and wouldn't let go of my hand. Held it. Held my eyes. Was it my imagination? Or was he trying to tell me something?

THAT NIGHT WE were sitting around candles stuck to the floor when Manu said, "I spoke to a man who said they took the spear that hit Michael Rockefeller and threw it into a deep pool. They were scared of it."

Amates and Wilem talked. "We will go out and see if we can find people to talk," Amates said. "In the dark. Without you."

An hour later, Amates returned; Wilem was still out there somewhere. "Fin and Pep took his skull and hid it. They took it to a small creek up the Ewta and hid it in a tree. A man named Saket told me this. They are afraid to talk about it, in case there's retaliation from other people in the village."

Over four days we got no further. What was being told to us just to fill the void, to sate my insistent curiosity, and what was real? I had no idea. What the man Saket had told Amates, though, was interesting, for it corresponded with von Peij's report that the head had been moved from Fin's house to a tree farther upriver, deep in the jungle. "This head wasn't an Asmat head," Amates said. "It was too much, the people were too afraid."

I wasn't sure what to do next. There seemed no reason to stay longer. The next day no one came to the house; we were left alone, and the calling of further meetings felt pointless. Amates kept saying Dombai's family had the glasses. I told him I'd pay $100 for them, which seemed like a lot of money, but nothing turned up. There was nothing left to do but return to Agats. As we departed, six men stood on the banks and watched us go, saying nothing, not even waving good-bye.

BACK AT MY hotel in Agats, I fell into conversation with Amates, who seemed sure he could find Michael's glasses. Bones were everywhere in Asmat; anyone could produce a skull or a thighbone and I'd have no way of knowing who it belonged to without DNA from the Rockefellers themselves. The glasses would be irrefutable proof that Michael had made it to shore and been killed. Amates

wanted to go back to Pirien by himself, talk to Dombai's sons, and see what he could come up with. I should offer $1,000 for them, he said. It seemed like a lot of money, and it made me uncomfortable. But I was exhausted, had lost ten pounds, wanted a hot shower and a break; if the glasses were real, it seemed well worth it—if the glasses were real. I gave Amates $300 for travel money and headed up to the Baliem Valley to scope out Michael's old stomping grounds for a few days, then took a break in Bali.

Two days after my arrival, I received a text from Amates. Kokai, the older man from Pirien we'd met in Basim, who had witnessed Lapré's raid and was somehow related to Dombai, had the glasses, Amates said. If I could get him another couple hundred, he'd return again to Pirien, pick up the glasses and Kokai, and bring them both back to Agats for me, arriving Friday. It seemed too good to be true. But I had to see it through. In a frantic day of running around Denpasar, Bali, I wired Amates $200 through the Indonesian post office system (the only way to send money to Agats), and texted Ainum, my old taxi driver in Timika, to get me a ticket on the Thursday flight into Agats. At one a.m. I jumped on the overnight flight to Timika. Ainum was there with someone else's ticket in hand, and three hours later I was inbound to Asmat again.

I fidgeted all day Thursday and Friday morning. Finally, my telephone rang Friday afternoon. It was Amates; he'd just gotten a cell signal. "I am on the boat and near Agats, and Kokai is with me and we have the glasses and he will tell you everything!"

Thirty minutes later, Amates walked into my hotel. Alone. "Where's Kokai?" I said.

"Home. He's tired. I'll bring him back here at six-thirty."

"The glasses?"

"I have them!"

I had purposefully avoided showing him a photo of Michael wearing his glasses. Although almost no one in Asmat wore them,

and Michael's were distinctive 1960s-era glasses with big black frames and thick lenses, I hadn't wanted to give Amates an opportunity to find something similar.

"What do they look like?" I said.

"They are big!" he said. "Thick."

My heart hammered. I couldn't believe it. Proof. The first concrete evidence of Michael's fate, evidence that would tie him to the village.

That evening Amates arrived. Kokai was with him, as well as another older man named Beatus Usain and one of Amates's brothers. If Kokai had looked wild in Basim, here in Agats he looked as feral as a wild bat. His clothes were filthy, and he smelled like sweat and smoke and damp. A bag of dangling cockatoo feathers hung on his chest.

I broke out the packages of Lampion, the tobacco they loved, and passed them around. We rolled cigarettes, smoked, gazed at each other. "So," I said, "tell me the story. How was Michael Rockefeller killed?"

Kokai looked at me, stone-faced. Started talking in his gravelly voice. "The American tourist came to Otsjanep, and he was there three days. He promised to build a big post here, and said he'd go to Agats and come back. On his way back here, his boat overturned and he was never seen again. Zegwaard came with the Bible, and we are Catholics now. I remember meeting him; he patted me on the head and said I should go to school."

It was the same boilerplate story they'd told before. Nothing new, and always immediately segueing into the Bible. Amates exploded. "They said they'd tell me the story," he said, "so tell it, not this!" The past was the past, nothing bad would happen, Asmat were now friends with America, and on and on, but Kokai just sat there staring at me, sweating, swallowing, saying nothing.

Finally, I asked about the glasses. Kokai reached into a bag and brought out a bundle wrapped in dirty cloth. I opened it.

A pair of 1990s-style plastic wraparound sunglasses.

"No!" I said. "These are not the glasses. These are modern. They are not his glasses."

The tension in the room was so high it might have been a horror movie. We all drew long drafts off our cigarettes. Rain pounded on the tin roof. The room was stifling, sweat soaking all of us.

The old man next to Kokai, Beatus Usain, spoke. "I am a teacher," he said. "Kokai is the catechist in Pirien. We are Catholics now." He paused, waited, wanted to make sure I understood that. He had short hair, a strong cleft chin, and cheekbones so high they might have been stuffed with rolls of pennies. He was bold and handsome. "Pep and Fin were at the mouth of the Ewta River. 'Look,' said Pep, 'a crocodile.'" He paused again, so Amates could translate, the first time that had ever happened. "But it wasn't a crocodile, it was a man. He was swimming on his back. He saw them and stood up and yelled, 'Help me Tuan! Help me Tuan!' Pep drove his spear into his side. They took him to the Kali Jawor."

"Who told you this story?" I said.

"Pep was my uncle," he said. "He looked just like me."

I asked who was with them, about Ajim and the head, but he would say no more. Kokai didn't move, didn't speak, sitting like a statue, smoking. They wanted to leave.

I thanked them, said maybe we could talk more tomorrow, and they were gone.

I didn't know what to make of it all. The glasses had been a bold attempt at making a fast buck. Maybe even they'd come from Amates, not Kokai, but I didn't think so; Amates seemed as surprised and pissed off as I. Kokai had nothing, none of the Asmat did; they were dirt poor. I had offered a lot of money. Either Kokai didn't have the real glasses, or they were so sacred—or he was so frightened—that no amount of money would make him part with them. As for the story, it wasn't much, but it corresponded with the original reports of van Kessel and von Peij in its most essential elements.

I was still pondering it all when Amates returned early the next morning. He was full of additional small details. They'd killed Michael and eaten him at the Kali Jawor, he said, and planted some of the bones under a clump of bamboo. The head they'd placed in a hollow of a tree, far up the Ewta. We should give Kokai a necklace of dogs' teeth and a stone ax, he said; that might make him talk more.

"Wouldn't he rather have money?" I said.

"No," Amates said. "Let's go to the Kali Jawor and look. I went there when we went to find Kokai, and there is bamboo at the end of the river."

I felt that I was at risk of embarking on a never-ending wild-goose chase. Gasoline for the boat cost $10 a gallon, plus the boat itself and Wilem and Amates, and food and tobacco for all of us; going back to the Kali Jawor would cost me hundreds more.

And there was this: fifty years. There was no way we'd find bones in the Asmat mud under fifty years of bamboo growth and rains and tides. A necklace of dogs' teeth cost hundreds of dollars, a stone ax the same—I could see it going on forever, and I had no idea if the information I was getting was accurate or what they were making up to keep the profitable business of Michael Rockefeller going. My visa was running out, my money was gone. I felt like I was getting lost in a jungle—a jungle of information and myth and story.

It was time to go home.

22

January, February, and March 1962

IN PUBLIC, OFFICIALS moved quickly to put the case of Michael Rockefeller to rest. On December 20, 1961, one month after Michael disappeared, the Dutch New Guinea court of justice announced its intention to register his death. The next day Platteel sent his secret cable to Bot, informing him of van Kessel's and von Peij's reports that Michael had made it to shore and been killed.

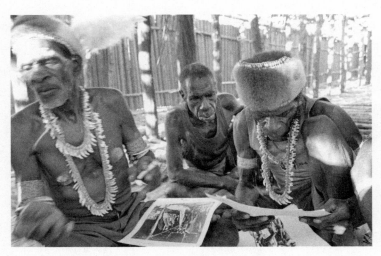

SAUER (*LEFT*), SON OF SAMUT, KILLED BY MAX LAPRÉ, AND THE HEAD OF THE JISAR JEU, LOOKS AT PHOTOS TAKEN BY MICHAEL ROCKEFELLER IN THE UNFINISHED JEU, PIRIEN VILLAGE.

Nevertheless, that very same day Platteel officially ended the public search for Michael, cabling Nelson Rockefeller: "The entire area has been extensively searched by various parties in close cooperation with local inhabitants, even any rumors were thoroughly investigated. . . . After having examined all reports I regretfully have to inform you my decision to end the unsuccessful search as I feel that not anything more can be done."

Nelson Rockefeller immediately called a press conference announcing Platteel's decision and making public his response. "All of us in the family will be eternally grateful to you for . . . the complete and exhaustive search undertaken by your government. You went way beyond the call of duty in your efforts and we will always find comfort in knowing that nothing was left undone."

Behind the scenes, though, a new search for Michael was just beginning, albeit reluctantly. The reports that van Kessel sent to the government, which made their way to Herman Tillemans, the Church's apostolic vicar (then the highest Catholic official in Dutch New Guinea), were the last thing anyone wanted to hear. Van Kessel and von Peij named fifteen men as having body parts belonging to Michael, with another thirty-five present at the scene—the political structure of the largest village in southern Asmat, all of its most important men. If they had killed Michael Rockefeller and the Rockefellers knew, well, something would have to be done. But what?

At the height of colonialism, in places like the Belgian Congo or British India or even Dutch New Guinea, the response to the killing of a white might have been simple—an armed raid, villages burned, men dragged away to uncertain and extrajudicial fates. A swift, merciless, and violent reprisal—a lesson taught, as Max Lapré might have said—would have been in order.

But times had changed, even since Lapré's raid in 1958, just four years before. The Netherlands was still trying to convince the United States and the United Nations that Dutch New Guinea

was an orderly place with a functioning government and that the Netherlands itself was an able and enlightened manager. And Michael Rockefeller was no ordinary white man. If he had been killed—and eaten, as described by van Kessel and von Peij—it wasn't a simple case of one or two guilty men who'd committed a cut-and-dry immoral anomaly and who could be identified and arrested, but a whole village doing what it considered just, carrying on its culture, a culture under intense outside pressure to change at a time when those very cultural elements were being celebrated by people like Nelson Rockefeller and his new museum.

Arrest the fifteen men named? Arrest all fifty who'd been present? What if they resisted, as they surely would? What if the whole village tried to defend them? How many police and soldiers might be necessary? How many people might die, mowed down by men armed with modern weapons? And if the government did manage to arrest anyone, what then? Subject an illiterate group of naked Stone Age warriors to a moral standard and administrative process that were totally incomprehensible to them, all while the Dutch insisted they didn't even practice headhunting and cannibalism any longer? Perhaps most important, how were they to deal with the motive? How to admit that the whole thing had been set in motion by Dutch administrative officials themselves, by a Dutch patrol officer's wanton killing of five people?

It was an impossible tangle. Arresting the men involved risked vicious bloodshed and alienation of the entire village (if not all of Asmat), both from the government and the Church, while the Netherlands was still making its case in the UN. It risked exposing the Luns Plan as absurd. It risked alienating the United States, whose support the Netherlands needed if it had any hope of maintaining control of its colony.

Van Kessel had been pushing for a trip home to Holland, and the Church wanted him out fast. Though he had been living among the Asmat for years and spoke their language, he was

considered a rogue, a man who had never followed his superiors. The Church wanted to replace him as soon as possible with Anton van de Wouw. Tillemans, his superior, wrote van Kessel. "From the Resident I got approval to see what you have written about Mr. Rockefeller. You have to admit it is a little bit extraordinary that you did not also submit this to me. However, I hope you are extremely cautious, so you or Father van de Wouw will not get into trouble because of this, and therefore the mission will not fall from grace with the population."

At the end of January 1962, Tillemans quizzed van Kessel closely about details of his report and then sent a series of letters to both von Peij and van Kessel. When I met von Peij in Tilburg in 2012, he said he'd remained silent about the case out of loyalty to his superiors. "I wrote my bishop and he forbade me to talk, to tell the story. The government felt ashamed, and the bishop [Tillemans] agreed, so the government was always silent, and I said nothing. But I have no doubt. I was in Asmat for six years and then in Merauke until 1991, and I am certain."

The original letters from the time, on apostolic vicar letterhead, back him up. "In the matter of Mr. M. Rockefeller I urgently request you to be extremely cautious," Tillemans wrote again to von Peij and van Kessel. "The notes I received from van Kessel show it is a public secret. Still nothing is published about it in the newspapers. I would regret it if the first messages to enter the world came from the side of the mission. So I want to ask both of you not to bring into publicity what you know and that which you are convinced of what happened. Just leave the scoop of talking to someone else. In time it will be revealed."

On behalf of the Dutch New Guinea resident, Eibrink Jansen, Tillemans requested a report from Alphonse Sowada, an American Crozier father who would, in 1969, become bishop of the newly created Catholic diocese of Agats. "What is most puzzling to me," Sowada wrote, "is the belief that the Asmat should kill and con-

sume Michael Rockefeller. To my knowledge, the Asmat people in their past history have never killed, much less consumed the flesh of an individual of white extraction. Why should they start at this late date when they have had ample opportunity to do so in the past? To this day, even with intensive Western contact in a few of the Asmat villages, the prevalent belief among the Asmat is that the white man is an ancient ancestor newly arrived to many benefits to the people. On a number of occasions I have been called a Mbji, namely a creature from the spirit world. For me, then, it seems quite improbable at this early stage in their development that the Asmat people would wish to kill, and further, possess the courage to kill a white man."

Sowada, however, was newly arrived; he had been in Asmat for only six months. He had never been to southern Asmat, neither Otsjanep nor Omadesep, while von Peij and van Kessel spoke the language fluently and had been on the ground in those villages for years. And both priests were convinced that Michael had been killed—and eaten—by the men from Otsjanep.

Von Peij, more conservative than van Kessel, was afraid for his own safety; he wanted a response from the government and wrote to Tillemans on February 3. "I received your letter in relation to this and will follow your advice [about keeping quiet]. I can understand they want to keep this hidden from the outside world. However, nobody can convince me that this was not what happened." If the government acts "as if it never happened, they are committing a crime. This is my honest conviction. In Ndanim, a good village where people are very satisfied with their dumb catechist, the . . . catechist shot a dog, which had just bitten his chicken to death. And then the villagers told him: 'Man, watch out a little, that Tuan from America was killed in Otsjanep and nobody did anything in response. . . .' So, unrelated to the outside world, something has to be done in Asmat. I'm somewhat afraid that what happened to Rockefeller might happen to me or a catechist too if one does simply neglect these killings."

Zegwaard agreed with von Peij. "Everywhere it's assumed that Rockefeller Junior was killed by the people of Otsjanep," Zegwaard wrote Eibrink Jansen on February 14. "The fact that this hasn't had any consequences, that there hasn't been any reprisal whatsoever, makes them feel free and able to act with arbitrariness in all kinds of circumstances without being punished for it."

Van Kessel wanted to contact Michael's family and even go to America to tell them in person what he knew. Tillemans, 150 miles away in Merauke, was adamant. "I want to ask you to make clear to Father van Kessel," Tillemans wrote to van Kessel's boss, the provincial superior, on February 28, 1962, "that there has to be absolute discretion regarding the case of Rockefeller. Bringing these sadistic colored stories into the world is in nobody's interest. He can prove nothing. . . . Leave it to the Governor [Platteel], who is completely informed about all this and who knows more than van Kessel can possibly expect. Or more than what he thinks is passed on by me.

"I reject his plan to go to America and will not give my approval. Also, correspondence with Mr. Rockefeller, tempting or not, must be forbidden. This case is way too precarious for him to get involved in.

"The governor and Resident of Merauke are worried about irresponsible behavior of priest van Kessel. I hope he will spare the mission unpleasantries. He asks for clemency with the village that would have committed the murder. Father Van Pey [sic] calls for immediate measures against that village etcetera etcetera. Let him have faith in the people who bear the responsibility for this. It is not up to Father van Kessel."

Three days later, Tillemans sent another letter to the provincial superior. "I rely on you to forbid van Kessel to go to America, whatever the circumstances might be and to forbid him to correspond with the family Rockefeller too."

Tillemans's letters read like the defense of pedophiles in the

Church, or like Penn State's reaction to accusations against its football coach Jerry Sandusky. *How could such a thing be possible? There's no proof. The rumors could damage our reputation. Better to say nothing.* Protecting itself was, of course, standard Church operating procedure, as revealed in a December 2011 report by the Dutch Conference of Bishops and the Conference of Dutch Religious Orders, detailing the abuse of more than twenty thousand children by Dutch priests and lay workers between 1945 and 2010. The Church rarely investigated these allegations, and when it did, the most common punishment was a quiet transfer. In New Guinea, by the end of January, van Kessel was shipped back to Holland, replaced by van de Wouw.

For all of its public denials, however, the Dutch government took van Kessel's and von Peij's reports seriously. Although the government had informed the Rockefellers that every stone had been peered under and the case had been closed, Eibrink Jansen decided to dispatch Dutch patrol officer Wim van de Waal to Otsjanep to investigate, along with nine armed Papuan police. On March 4, Father van de Wouw sent Gabriel (van Kessel's former assistant, who was now working for him) to Otsjanep with the pretext of building a house there for van de Wouw, but really in hopes that he might hear something further about the murder and to prepare the villagers for the coming of van de Waal and the police.

On March 23, Father van de Wouw wrote Tillemans that "Gab did not pick up anything in Ocenep [*sic*] that would point to the murder of M.R., nor the opposite," and that van de Waal and the police would arrive the following week.

Tillemans responded, cautioning van de Wouw: "If you get new information on the case of Rockefeller then be careful, because the topic is like a cabinet of glass. Of course, as long as there is no proof one keeps saying that one didn't know anything, and rightly so. If you find any proof don't mention this to anybody! Please, everything via me. So no messages to other priests or KvK [Kees van

Kessel] in the Netherlands. Keep silent in Agats too. I really ask you to keep this case strictly confidential in separate letters with a double envelope and the word 'Secret' on the inner envelope."

The word was about to get out, however. On January 13, 1962, a Dutch priest working in Asmat, W. Hekman, wrote his parents back home in Arnhem a note full of salacious details. Michael Rockefeller, he told them, had been speared and eaten by villagers from Otsjanep, in revenge for the men shot to death by police a few years before. The names of the men who still had his bones were known. An American woman had been eaten too (this wasn't true). And no one could go to the village or else they, too, would be killed and eaten. The parents leaked the letter, which exploded across the Associated Press wires during the third week of March. On March 27, Jan Herman van Roijen, the Dutch ambassador to the United States, cabled his foreign ministry. "Press reports from the Netherlands mention a message which a Dutch missionary allegedly sent to his family . . . that Michael Rockefeller did indeed reach the New Guinea coast, but was eaten there by the natives and that his skull and bones would have been preserved. For the benefit of the office of Governor Rockefeller, who contacted this embassy in this connection, it would be appreciated if I could be informed about the source and the value of these reports."

Joseph Luns, the foreign minister himself, replied to van Roijen the following day. "Similar rumors also circulated previously in a small circle in Dutch New Guinea," wrote Luns. "These rumors were contradicted as being completely unfounded by . . . the Apostolic Vicar of Merauke [Tillemans]. Any rumor in that regard has been investigated thoroughly by the resident of New Guinea, F. R. J. Eibrink Jansen, and the content of them have been called entirely incorrect." It was classic government denial. In reality, the apostolic vicar, Tillemans, had shown no interest in investigating the case, had relied on the opinion of men who hadn't been anywhere near the events, and had done everything he could to si-

lence von Peij and van Kessel, the only two men who were on the ground and had been in Asmat longer than any other white there. As for the thorough government investigation, Eibrink Jansen believed the reports were serious enough that he was sending van de Waal and a gang of policemen to Otsjanep the very week the news hit the newspapers, an investigation that hadn't even begun yet.

Nevertheless, the denials did the trick: the next day newspapers around the world reported that there was no truth to the rumors.

Meanwhile, van de Waal built a police post in Otsjanep and settled in. Slowly, he began ingratiating himself into the village, giving gifts of soap to the children, tobacco to the men, helping the men build wooden walkways over the mud and swamp. "It must have been strange for the people there," he told me, sitting around his dining room table on the Spanish island of Tenerife, where he'd lived since 1968.

At seventy-three, van de Waal looked fit and strong, with a salt-and-pepper goatee and deep blue eyes. He was a man comfortable in his own skin, and comfortable in foreign places—he had been married to a Spanish woman for decades—with a quiet self-confidence and sure-footedness that would have served him well in a place like Asmat. He hadn't said a word about the case in fifty years. But the case, and his time in Asmat—a young man's exotic interlude—had always remained with him. He showed me meticulously organized loose-leaf binders filled with original documents, including a bill of sale that he'd gotten from René Wassing for the catamaran, as well as photos of him and the Asmat and of Nelson and Mary in Pirimapun. "The Asmat in Otsjanep didn't understand why I was there," he said. "It was a complicated village, and they feel like talking about these things brings them bad luck, so I had to do everything little by little and smoked with them and gave them gifts, and eventually we started talking about old murders and headhunting and who had been killed, and when I'd tell them a story they'd say, 'Yes, that's correct.'"

He concentrated on the Pirien jeu, which he considered to be the most moderate, telling them that they were free to speak, that there'd be no recrimination if they did so. Finally he asked who killed Michael Rockefeller. "The answer," van de Wouw wrote Tillemans in early May 1962, "fell right out of their mouths."

"So far the information does not exactly match with what is in the report of Father van Kessel. Because Ajim would have been the one who stabbed M.R. to death on the shore (report K.V.K. [Kees van Kessel]: Pep stabbed him to death, from out of the proa, with a fishing spear). Also, the distribution of the head and bones is not the same as in the report. The shorts would have been buried in the mud at Kali Jawor. M.R. was then eaten and Ajim would have sucked out the brains.

"At the first arrival of the A.A. (van de Waal) and the H.P.B. in Otanep [sic] . . . Ajim would have collected all the corpora delicti, chopped them up in pieces and threw them away behind his house.

"Supposedly the information above was already sent to the Resident via the H.P.B. in Agats. However, I may repeat that the investigation has not yet come to an end.

"But A.A. is of the opinion that the Resident will not intervene before any real evidence can be handed over (possibly: shorts, skull or teeth). Without a doubt this case will have serious consequences for Lapré, because when asked, the involved men from Otanep [sic] will say it is a murder out of revenge for the folks that were shot dead by Lapré at the time.

"At last, I have to add to all this that I have tremendous respect for the peaceful way of acting of our young A.A. The case can surely be entrusted to him.

"Priest van Kessel was truly convinced of Ajim being the main instigator of this and lots of prior murders and that the inhabitants of Otanep [sic] would not accept the arrest of this unsavory character (also in appearance, comparable to Pep and a few different leaders). This also became clear in the investigation by A.A."

Van de Wouw also reported that Otsjanep was brazenly carrying on its headhunting traditions, and that in the beginning of May a woman and a young girl from Warkai, a small village between Otsjanep and Omadesep, had been killed by men from Otsjanep, with two additional people injured.

At the end of three months in Otsjanep, van de Waal asked the men to hand over Michael's remains. "I needed proof, not just names," he said. They took him into the jungle, dug in the muck, and produced a skull and bones, the skull bearing no lower jaw and a hole in the right temple, the hallmarks of remains that had been headhunted and opened to consume the brains. "There are so many bones in Asmat, and I wanted to ask about the glasses," he told me, "but that was too dangerous." Van de Waal radioed Eibrink Jansen in Merauke. "I had a new radio, and it was scrambled so no one could listen in. I told him what I had, and he said he'd send someone to pick it up."

Soon after, Rudy de Iongh, the newly appointed Dutch patrol officer in Agats, arrived. Van de Waal handed the remains over in a cloth sack. "He was very afraid; he came with a patrol vessel and a heap of policemen armed with machine guns.

"That was the end of the story," he said. "I stayed two more weeks, and then Eibrink Jansen said I could leave and go back to Pirimapun, and that's what I did."

He never heard another word about the bones or anything else connected to Michael Rockefeller, except from a Dutch ironwood dealer who had accompanied de Iongh to collect the bones. The dealer told him that the remains had been given to Eibrink Jansen, who'd given them to a dentist in Merauke before sending them to Utrecht, in Holland. It was now June 1962.

"The political situation was becoming awkward," van de Waal said. Indonesian paratroopers landed in Merauke at the end of the month to pressure the UN to make the Dutch government withdraw, and all women and children were sent home to Holland.

The struggle for control of West Papua was ending. The Dutch were capitulating, and van de Waal was soon sent to Merauke. "I was never asked to make a report of my time in Otsjanep," van de Waal said, and in meetings with Eibrink Jansen, "we never, ever, touched upon my investigation."

Today no records in the Dutch government archives mention van de Waal's assignment to Otsjanep, his time there, or the bones he turned over—the only written mention of it appears to be in van de Wouw's letters and in a highly aggrandized account by de Iongh in a colonial history of the Netherlands published in the 1990s.

"Why are there no government records?" van de Waal asked. "If there was no proof, it would have cost the government nothing to just tell the truth—that we'd spent three months in Otsjanep and had tried. But they did nothing, because [the truth] would have been very bad for the Dutch case, and that's why they wanted to keep it secret."

In September 1962, the UN ratified the New York Agreement, which transferred Dutch New Guinea to a United Nations Temporary Executive Authority (and then Indonesia eight months later). The Netherlands had lost its colony, and van de Waal sailed for home. "I never talked about it publicly," he said in Tenerife, shrugging his shoulders, holding a cassowary bone dagger. "I guess no one's going to be hurt by it now."

PART III

November 2012

THE CROWD WAS surging, hot bodies pressed against the railing in the hotter sun, as the *Tatamailau* eased up the Asawets River toward the dock in Agats. It was five p.m., and the river and the sky and the jungle and even the stilted shacks of Agats glowed softly in the light of the setting sun. Longboats and canoes and speedboats buzzed out to meet the twice-a-month ship that plied the coast of Indonesian Papua—the ship that was the only connection with the outside world for most people who lived there. The crowd shrieked, shouted, pointed, waved. I had been traveling for a week

VILLAGERS OF PIRIEN/JISAR COMPLETING THE ROOF OF JISAR'S NEW JEU.

already; I hadn't been able to get a seat on the Tregana flight out of Timika and had been forced aboard the four-hundred-foot-long *Tatamailau* at three a.m. for the fourteen-hour journey to Asmat.

I'd tried repeatedly to reach Amates and Wilem from the United States but could never get through, until Wilem finally received one of my text messages when I hit Timika, telling him that I was inbound again, seven months after leaving. He said he'd meet me at the boat.

We were still five hundred feet from the dock, just beginning to edge in, when I felt a hand on my shoulder. Wilem, barefoot and beaming, had jumped on the moving ship and found me. "Mister Karo!" he said, giving me a hug. "You are back and you speak Bahasa Indonesian!"

In the seven months since I'd left Asmat, I'd been riddled with doubts.

The pieces of the puzzle I'd unearthed fit, and fit well. Michael Rockefeller had swum away from the catamaran on the morning of November 19, 1961, with two flotation aids; René Wassing had witnessed his departure. Wassing said they had been close enough to see the shore, even if faintly, and the curvature of the earth was easily checked in routine maritime-distance-to-horizon tables: if the trees on the flat shoreline were fifty feet tall, then he and Michael were no more than nine and a half miles from shore—far away, but not an unreasonable distance for a fit, determined twenty-three-year-old male to swim in warm, calm water with a set of ad hoc water wings. And they might have been closer.

The village of Otsjanep had a long tradition of violence and had been reluctant to give up its traditions, and a large group of men from the village had left to return from Pirimapun on the afternoon of the nineteenth; Wim van de Waal had seen them there, and seen them leave. By any calculation, that observation put them at the mouth of the Ewta early on the morning of the twentieth. I knew within a mile or two where Michael and Wassing had lost

power on the eighteenth, and I had the latitude and longitude of where Wassing had been first spotted on the afternoon of the nineteenth and where he'd been picked up on the morning of the twentieth, so their location when Michael left the catamaran was clear. Had he swum at a half-mile an hour, he would have arrived close to the mouth of the Ewta early in the morning on the twentieth. I had the tide tables along the coast for that morning, and the water near the Ewta had reached its highest point at eight a.m., which also meant the tide was helping him toward shore at the point when he'd been the most exhausted.

The men from Otsjanep who would have been there at about the same time were related—though I wasn't yet sure exactly how—to the men killed by Max Lapré in 1958, just three years before, and those deaths had never been reciprocated. Seventeen men, women, and children had been killed in the past decade, eight by crocodile-hunting Chinese Indonesians (considered white by the Asmat) and five by Lapré, and Michael had found seventeen bisj poles still in the jeus. The Asmat were known to be opportunists, preferring victims to be alone and unprotected, and Michael would have been exhausted, vulnerable in a way they'd never encountered in a white before. And he'd been to the village already; they would have known him and may have remembered his name, an important factor in choosing a headhunting victim.

As for the two priests who felt certain he had been killed, both Father van Kessel and Father von Peij spoke Asmat, were close to the villages, and more than anyone else had deep experience with the culture. Everything von Peij had told me—that he and van Kessel wrote reports to the government and their superiors in the Church, that they were forbidden to speak publicly about their reports, that they had lists of names of men from the village, that Max Lapré had made a heavy-handed raid in reprisal for Otsjanep's and Omadesep's massacre of each other—I'd verified through official documents and letters in the archives of the

Dutch government and the Order of the Sacred Heart (the order to which van Kessel and von Peij belonged), as well as from the villagers themselves. I'd found no anomalies, nothing that couldn't be explained within Asmat cultural logic, and no inaccuracies or tall tales from any of the living witnesses.

And yet. For all of van Kessel's and von Peij's certainty, their stories were secondhand; not one of the accused had confessed directly to either priest, nor had either of them seen any concrete physical evidence. Bishop Sowada's chief concern—that no Asmat had ever killed a white—couldn't be easily dismissed. It nagged at me. How could that have happened? Van de Waal had photos of the skull he'd been given, but when he'd shown the photos to a forensic pathologist, the conclusion was that it was "most probably not of European origin." And the more I knew of Asmat, the more certain I was that, if the men of Otsjanep had killed Michael, the bones and skull would have been sacred objects that could never have been surrendered to a Westerner. After all, my offer of $1,000 for the glasses—a fortune in Asmat—had turned up only a fake. I was sure the skull and bones of Michael Rockefeller weren't sitting in some museum file drawer in Holland.

Then there was the question of reliability. The Asmat were expert liars. They had depended on deception to gain advantage over their enemies, to elude and placate the spirits; accounts of them saying whatever whites wanted to hear were abundant. Cannibalism is the apex of Otherness, the greatest transgression, the thing that makes people less than human, and maybe the missionaries wanted to believe the Asmat had killed and eaten Michael. It certainly strengthened their case for evangelizing them.

And maybe I wanted to believe too. Maybe that belief was what we all wanted. It confirmed our image of the Asmat as both horrific and exotic and reflected back on us, made us seem bolder, more intrepid, braver—we were cavorting with cannibals! It was what anthropologist Gananath Obeyesekere called "cannibal

talk"—our need to believe that these people existed and that we were among them. Even more so because Michael was so rich and his family so powerful; in a perverse way, it seemed to level the playing field that this scion of American power could have been not just killed but consumed, cooked and digested and shat out by his opposite—wild men who had nothing, no power, no money, no influence. Maybe all of the things hinted at that made van Kessel and von Peij suspicious had been in their own heads, projections of their own biases and needs, and maybe Asmat from other villages had just made the story up.

Von Peij's initial report had come in Omadesep, Otsjanep's longtime traditional enemy; maybe the story had been spread just to get Otsjanep in trouble. And the swim, though possible, was extremely difficult. To have reached the shore, Michael would have had to swim six to ten miles over twenty-four hours, some of it against strong tides, all through offshore waters where sharks were known to swim. Doable though it was, it was still a feat of will and physical strength—and luck.

Finally, there was the consistent denial to my face by the men in Otsjanep and Pirien. They never said the village hadn't done it, never directly denied it, but they were consistent in telling me they knew nothing about it one way or another—except in the dark of night to Amates and my crew. Would they really just lie about it to me now, after so many years, when none of the original perpetrators were even alive? Why wouldn't Kokai and Tapep, their sons, simply own up to it?

Struggling with these questions and the whole cultural logic of cannibalism, I'd turned to Peggy Reeves Sanday, an anthropologist and professor emeritus at the University of Pennsylvania, and the author of *Divine Hunger,* a weighty book on cannibalism that I'd read. It turned out that she lived an hour from me, and we began a series of long days together, reviewing the reports and evidence, my notes, and all of the ethnographic and anthropological

literature relating to Asmat. Sanday, too, was disturbed by Sowa-da's concern that Asmat had never killed a white before. But one thing was clear and irrefutable to both of us: all of Asmat "knew" the story that Otsjanep had killed Michael Rockefeller. And the men of Otsjanep and Pirien themselves had said, at various times, even as they vacillated and prevaricated to the missionaries (and denied it to me), that they had killed him, or that they'd seen a giant snake or a crocodile at sea that morning.

If Michael had drowned or been consumed by sharks and never made it to shore, it seemed unlikely that they would fabricate such a specific and consistent story. If the men from Otsjanep had never seen him the morning of November 20, every conversation with von Peij or van Kessel, every story and detail, was a lie, was made up. Although the details were sometimes different, the basic facts hadn't changed in fifty years: the involvement of Fin, Pep, and Ajim; the stabbing with a spear; the killing at the Jawor River, a quiet, hidden place that even today carried a sacred power. The description of the shorts—that detail in particular stood out. The specificity of Fin having the head. Von Peij's and van Kessel's later reports of the skull being placed in the jungle, and then the whispered reports to me from Amates, fifty years later, of the head being placed in a tree in the jungle.

To make it all up and then to sustain the lie for a half-century seemed more impossible and more illogical than what was a simple and straightforward tale: Michael had swum to shore, he had encountered the men from Otsjanep, and they had killed him to balance the chaos that Lapré had unleashed. And the constant thread of deception woven into the fabric of Asmat life raised another question. If the men from Otsjanep had killed Michael, it would have been a huge transgression, a thing that had never been done before in all of Asmat, something incredible and unbelievable. In van de Waal's experience, he told me, no villagers either within Otsjanep or outside of it would have believed the story if

they hadn't seen some concrete proof, if they hadn't seen bones or body parts or the skull.

Sanday felt it was significant that, when questioned by van Kessel, the men had all said they'd seen something big and unusual in the sea that morning. She raised another possibility. It was important, she believed, that the story had persisted so long in Asmat, among the Asmat themselves.

"The Asmat," she said, "are trying to tell us something." What was important to her was not that Michael Rockefeller might have been killed and eaten, but that a people were suggesting they had done so. Even if they hadn't killed and eaten Michael Rockefeller, they could have done so, they might have wished they had, and they had been thinking about killing a white man for years. She thought there might be significance in their backtracking explanations to van Kessel that all they'd seen was a giant mythical snake, or a crocodile. Why those animals? Every story had Michael being mistaken first for a crocodile, an animal of great symbolic importance within Asmat. The crocodile, which represents an eater of men, is carved into the bottom of almost every bisj pole.

Sanday also believed it was too much to make up if they had never encountered him at all. But she postulated that they might have seen him killed by sharks or crocodiles near them. Or that he had died at sea and his already dead body had washed ashore— that fact and fiction, the physical and the spiritual, had intermingled, as they tended to do in Asmat. In Sanday's opinion, the body theory solved the nagging question of what enabled them to kill a white man, and it fit into nativistic scenarios in which tribal people seek to reclaim their past power, influence, status. In a world where these white men were interfering with their culture, once-powerful men like Ajim and Fin could propagate their own power within their communities by not just finding the body, but saying they had killed him, eaten him, headhunted him.

Over the past fifty years, missionaries had recorded several ex-

amples of cargo cult–like eruptions in various Asmat villages—
men claiming supernatural powers and being able to produce
tobacco or other objects of white affluence, their traditional beliefs
strangely distorted by contact with the modern world. In the most
striking example, in 1966 a twenty-seven-year-old man in the vil-
lage of Ewer had begun breaking into the pastor's storeroom and
stealing tobacco, clothing, and money. Handing out the cargo to
others in Ewer, he told them he received the goods from Tuan
Tanah, the "Lord of the Earth," who'd given him a secret key with
which he was able to unlock a hole in the ground. Everyone who
believed in Tuan Tanah would eventually become white and rich
with goods. By the time the pastor caught the man, he and his fol-
lowers had become the most powerful figures in the village. Could
the "killing" of Michael have been a nativistic story that a few
men had promulgated to increase their status and power in a rap-
idly changing world?

I ALSO HAD been thinking about Michael's family, wondering what
they'd done to find closure, especially as rumors surfaced that he
might not have drowned. They had begun the legal steps necessary
to declare him dead within months of his disappearance. Through
the Museum of Primitive Art, they'd moved quickly to ship ev-
erything he'd collected back to New York—some five hundred
objects in total, valued by insurance appraisers in August 1962 at
$285,520. It was a stunning sum, a quarter of a million dollars in
value created via a few fishhooks, fishing line, axes, and lumps of
tobacco, off the talents of men who were illiterate and penniless.
As the centerpieces today of the Michael C. Rockefeller Wing of
the Metropolitan Museum of Art, their value in attracting visi-
tors and funding is incalculable, not to mention the priceless cache
(and hefty tax deductions) their donation to the museum must
have brought Nelson Rockefeller and his family. In 2012 the Met
hosted six million visitors, with a recommended voluntary entry

fee of $25; if the average visitor paid $15, the Met brought in $90 million in entry fees alone, while the grandson of the man Michael regarded as one of the best artists in all of Asmat, Chinasapitch, the man who carved the lovely canoe that holds prominence in the Met, sweeps the floor of the Asmat museum in Agats in bare feet. Until I told him, he had no idea what had ever happened to that canoe. Had priceless land or millions of dollars' worth of mineral rights been acquired from illiterate villagers via a few lumps of brown weed and bent wire, cries of injustice might have rung out, with demands that a people unable to understand the deal they'd agreed to be fairly compensated.

In September 1962, not even a year after Michael had swum away from his catamaran, the Museum of Primitive Art mounted a spectacular exhibit in New York in a specially constructed pavilion across from the museum that was meant, read the press release, "to evoke in part the spirit of Asmat life."

Featured among the artifacts were the bisj poles Michael had collected. "When an Asmat warrior is slain by an enemy villager, a bisj ceremony is called to honor the dead man and to invoke feelings of vengeance." The details of how that vengeance was supposed to manifest itself were omitted from the program. "After days of ceremony, a bisj pole, over twenty feet high, intricately designed, and studded with human figures, is carved. . . . To the beat of war drums, the singing of songs, and a mock battle dance, the bisj pole is then raised in front of the ceremonial house. Within a few days, the bisj is laid to rest in the sago forests that surround the village. The soft wood soon rots, and according to Asmat tradition, the spirit of the victim thus honored goes into the sago palms, and thence, into the people who eat sago." The public version had been cleansed of any mention of actual vengeance, reciprocation, killing, or cannibalism.

The exhibition was a resounding success. The museum's Committee on Membership, Publicity, and Publications reported that

by February 1963 stories about the exhibit had appeared in more than six hundred newspapers and magazines "with a combined circulation of 30,000,000 readers. This is as close to national and local saturation as any art story ever had."

In an effort to identify some of the objects before the exhibition, the museum had even written van Kessel in Pirimapun in May 1962, at the height of van de Waal's investigation. The letter found, not van Kessel, who had returned to Holland, but Father van de Wouw, who answered in June. It is an eerie correspondence. Patrol officer van de Waal, with van de Wouw's help, was living in Otsjanep officially investigating the case, but van de Wouw never mentions it. Just as eerie is a letter van Kessel himself wrote to the museum in 1974, in which he requests a copy of *The Asmat: The Journal of Michael C. Rockefeller,* which the museum published in 1967. He laments Michael's loss and mentions "sad memories," but not his certainty that Michael had been killed and eaten; to the Rockefellers, at least, the priests kept their word to never discuss the killing.

But what the Rockefellers privately knew was a mystery. In the archives of the Dutch government are cables and letters from Nelson Rockefeller to various officials, thanking them for their efforts. There is the cable from the Dutch ambassador to the United States asking his superiors about rumors that Michael was killed, and there is Foreign Minister Joseph Luns's response—that those rumors had been fully investigated and found to be untrue. There are letters between Rockefeller's lawyers and the Netherlands asking for a recap of the search effort, in order for a US court to declare Michael legally dead by drowning, which the court finally did on February 1, 1964, valuing his estate at $660,000. Those letters, too, are surreal, since they were sent during the very months when letters were flying back and forth between the Dutch government and van Kessel, von Peij, and the Church, all while van de Waal was in Otsjanep investigating. In one letter, between the law offices of Milbank, Tweed, Hope and Hadley and the Dutch consul

general in New York, Rockefeller attorney William Jackson writes: "It would be of great assistance if we could be provided with duly authenticated copies of any reports made by or to any official of the Netherlands Government with respect to the nature, extent and results of the various searches made in New Guinea in the effort to find Michael Rockefeller." But there is no trace of any correspondence between the Dutch and the Rockefellers or their lawyers that mentions or addresses his killing by Otsjanep or the official investigation happening at that very moment. The Dutch government and the Catholic Church appear to have kept silent, both in public and in private, even as they were actively communicating with Michael's family. At least through the 1960s there may have been no reason for Nelson to doubt that Michael had drowned.

In 1974, Milt Machlin, a magazine editor in New York, published *The Search for Michael Rockefeller*. The book is mostly the tale of a wild-goose chase: a mysterious Australian appeared in Machlin's office one day in the late '60s, claimed he was a smuggler who'd been working in the remote islands of Oceania, and said he had spotted Michael alive, held hostage by a tribe in the Trobriand Islands, a thousand miles away from Asmat. Most of the story details Machlin's fruitless search, which he began in 1969, but toward the book's end Machlin chases down the original rumors leaked to the press in early 1962 and finds van Kessel in the Netherlands, who tells him his tale. He then dispatches an unnamed assistant, who travels to Asmat and interviews a number of others. Whether it was still too early and too close to the events, or whether Machlin just didn't look, he never saw any of the supporting documents from the Dutch government or Catholic Church; he never saw Lapré's reports; he never found von Peij or van de Waal; and it appears he never even saw van Kessel's original memos. The theory that Michael made it to shore and was killed comes off as all wild speculation by a rogue priest, and Machlin's book has so few details and so little documentation that

it feels unbelievable. Nevertheless, it was a beginning, and he had explained his findings in a letter to the Rockefellers, whose lawyers sent Machlin a boilerplate response thanking him and saying nothing further.

Shortly after Nelson Rockefeller became vice president, during a meeting at the White House with the prime minister of Australia, Gough Whitlam, he publicly thanked Australia for its help in the search for Michael. "When Mr. Whitlam remarked that the disappearance had never been solved," reported the *New York Times,* "the Vice President said: 'I believe there is no question— you can't swim 12 miles against the current.'"

Then there's the story of Frank Monte. An Australian private investigator, Monte claimed in his memoir, *The Spying Game,* that shortly after Nelson's death in 1979 he was contracted by Michael's mother, Mary Todhunter Clark Rockefeller, to investigate rumors that Michael had been killed, after being prevented from doing so for years by her ex-husband. The fame-seeking, celebrity name– dropping private eye seems like the last person any Rockefeller would hire. His account reads, at best, like a hyped-up blend of fact and fiction. That he may have looked into the case seems possible—he cites enough detail about the rescue of Wassing to have found some documents or news reports—but searching for the most important papers, he wrote, "I discovered something odd. The records had vanished. Through his vast and powerful connections . . . Rockefeller had actually had anything written or published about his missing son destroyed. He'd employed people to go through files everywhere removing anything relating to the disappearance."

That, of course, was untrue; I was able to find hundreds of pages of cables and memos.

Monte then relates the story of a wild trip to the village that killed Michael with a gang of bloodthirsty Indonesian army commandos who leave a trail of dead bodies in a weeks-long, Kurtz-like voyage far inland, with a guide from Otsjanep. None of it makes

sense. He mixes up the names of rivers and geography, describes villagers wearing penis sheaths (which the Asmat don't wear), writes about dragging rubber rafts for days across the swamps—these details indicative, if he went anywhere near the area, not of the Asmat but of the Korowai, who produce little art, live far up-river, and never received a visit from Michael. Monte's conclusion—that Michael was killed after being caught trying to steal a sacred "totem pole" decorated with skulls (which bisj poles do not have), in the dead of night with the son of the chief, with whom he was having a homosexual relationship, and that Wassing and the over-turned catamaran were just a fabrication to hide the truth—is absurd. As is his claim that he brought three skulls home to Mary, was paid $100,000, and was later told by the mysterious Rockefeller go-between that one of them was positively identified as Michael's.

After my first trip to Asmat, I'd made an effort to contact Mary Rockefeller Morgan (formerly Mary Rockefeller Strawbridge), Michael's twin sister. Through a friend, I began a correspondence with a woman married high in the clan in the hope that she might introduce me to Mary, and the woman agreed to have lunch with me in New York. Though enthusiastic in our initial writings, by the time we met she'd had a long conversation with her husband and couldn't help in any way; it was something the family didn't speak of, at least not publicly. In May 2012, Mary self-published a memoir, *Beginning with the End: A Memoir of Twin Loss and Healing,* which is a sad and gracefully written account of her long efforts to heal from her twin brother's death. As the title suggests, Michael's disappearance in Asmat is but the beginning of the book. She writes: "Rumors and stories of Michael's having made it to shore—of his having been found, captured and killed by headhunting Asmat villagers—have persisted for over forty plus years. Even today, those rumors fuel the imagination and help to line the pockets of storytellers, playwrights, filmmakers, and the high-adventure tourist trade. This speculation has never

been substantiated by any concrete evidence. Since 1954, the
Dutch government had enforced a ban forbidding tribal warfare
and the resulting headhunting that would avenge the death of an
important tribal figure. In 1961, we were told that tribal warfare
and headhunting had not been entirely eradicated but were rare.
All the evidence, based on the strong offshore currents, the high
seasonal tides, and the turbulent outgoing waters, as well as the
calculations that Michael was approximately ten miles from shore
when he began to swim, supports the prevailing theory that he
drowned before he was able to reach land."

My letter to Mary, in which I offered to share all of my research
with her, went unanswered. The writer Peter Matthiessen, who
remains close to Mary and wrote a blurb for her book, told me,
"The family refuses to believe any version of the story beyond his
drowning."

The documents I had were public; if I had found them, so
could the Rockefellers, or anyone working on their behalf. That
said, I knew they'd never talked to either von Peij or van de Waal.
It hadn't been hard for me to track them down, but the Rockefell-
ers had never tried.

Either Mary and her family knew something and refused to
acknowledge it in public, or she and her father had left Merauke
and never looked back, clinging to a version of events that was
tragic, but neat and clean—if unlikely. Whatever the case, I knew
they had never undertaken the one thing I would have done if
my child or sibling had disappeared amid rumors of murder, the
thing that might lead to some clearer understanding: to learn the
language, go there, and personally investigate the crime scene. It
was ironic that a family of enormous wealth and resources sneered
at the efforts to solve Michael's death and accused anyone who did
so of exploiting the family name for profit, but it was the family's
own failure to address the rumors and reports that forced others
to do the investigating for them. The more I knew about Asmat,

the more I couldn't stop imagining Michael in the Asmat cosmos: that he was like one of those men whose spirits his people had not done enough to push on to Safan, to the land beyond the sea. All the speculation continued because his family had failed to fully seek closure and no one else had managed to gather the essential information. That no Rockefeller had ever been to Asmat, except for a few hours in an official Dutch delegation via PBY Catalina, surrounded by phalanxes of officials, boggled my mind.

WITH SO MANY nagging questions, I knew I had to go back again. My first trip to Asmat had taken two months, but much of it had been spent in transit, or waiting in Agats to set things up, or cruising the rivers so I could see the place, grasp it, as a whole. I had been to Otsjanep and Pirien twice, but the first visit had been for twenty-four hours and the second for just four days. Amates had then brought Kokai out to Agats, but that had been a tense, forced conversation. Beatus Usain, the man who with Kokai had finally told me the story of Pep's killing Michael, had been Pep's nephew. His father, Pep's younger brother, had married a woman from Biwar Laut, where Usain had grown up. He had been able to tell the story because he wasn't from Otsjanep—but that meant I still didn't have any sort of confession from anyone in the village.

And throughout I had been totally surrounded by and dependent on an entourage—Amates or Hennah for translation, Wilem and his assistants for food and logistics and sleeping arrangements. They had all been filters, and I'd never known what was actually being said, what I didn't hear, what I wasn't privy to, or if my questions were even being translated as I'd asked them. I'd been guilty of the same sins for which I was critical of Michael and the Rockefellers themselves—passing through Asmat too quickly, assuming that I was so important that I could pepper them with questions and out would pour their deepest secrets, not heading back after new questions had been raised. After all, the story of

Michael Rockefeller wasn't just another story. It was the tale of a murder, a heinous, bloody crime that ended not just with death but with the most egregious taboo—cannibalism—a practice the Asmat knew was inconceivably wrong in our eyes, a practice that had unleashed more ships and airplanes and helicopters and policemen in their world than they'd ever seen before, a practice that they now, fifty years later, knew was viewed as shameful by the pastors and priests of their now Catholic religion. If they'd done it, it was a secret held as deep as a secret could be. The sons of the men accused were afraid. Afraid of the spirits. Afraid of God. Afraid of the Indonesian military and police. Afraid of America. Afraid of the Rockefeller family, who had an obligation, in their minds, to avenge his death.

If I wanted to solve the mystery of Michael Rockefeller, I had to get to know them. Without filters, translators, guides, cooks. I had to speak their language. I had to have a much deeper understanding of Asmat life than I could ever get from a few weeks on the river or a few days in the village or than I could ever get from books or theses on Asmat culture.

My plan was to go to either Otsjanep or Pirien and find a family to stay with for a month—ideally, with one of the sons of the men named by van Kessel, someone older and powerful. Maybe Tapep, son of Pep, in Otsjanep, though he had been especially reluctant to speak and the others had always clammed up when he appeared. Or maybe Kokai, who had been alive when Michael disappeared, who had witnessed Lapré's raid and been willing to talk about it, who Amates said had been a village chief and was related to Dombai, the man van Kessel's report had named as having the glasses. In my wildest dreams, I hoped that in a few weeks they'd just confess everything to me, take me into the jungle and show me the skull—that it would all become completely clear. But if not that, I at least wanted to have a much better understanding of the village structure: who was who, how they were

related, who the men Lapré had killed were, and how they were related to the men named in van Kessel's and von Peij's reports. I wanted to hear their stories and songs, understand more clearly the importance of snakes and crocodiles and sharks in their cosmology. And from the archives of the Metropolitan Museum of Art in New York, I had copies of photos Michael had taken on his first trip to Otsjanep. They were beautiful black-and-white portraits of naked men draped in dog and pig teeth, posing with carvings and the magnificent bisj poles Michael had bought, paddling in huge groups and drumming in their houses. Had Michael met the men who killed him? Had he photographed them? I hoped to show the photos to men in the village and for them to identify the men named in van Kessel's reports, and perhaps even to find out who the poles had been carved for.

I needed to know if the story fell apart or grew stronger.

NOW I WAS BACK. As the ship bumped against the dock, Wilem grabbed my bag and pulled me through the crowd, down the gangplank, and over to his longboat. I could already tell things were different. Wilem spoke about ten words of English, and on my last trip I had spoken about the same number of words in Bahasa Indonesian, which was rapidly replacing the native Asmat language. Despite all the time we'd spent together, Wilem and I had been limited to our few common words and a pantomime of hand and facial gestures. But at home in Washington, DC, I'd found an Indonesian teacher whom I'd met with three times a week. I'd never worked so hard at a language—and as languages go, Indonesian was relatively easy. By the time I left for Asmat, I was far from fluent, but I was surprised at how much I knew. Wilem and I had been texting for three days, and as he gunned the engine and we sped toward the main part of town, we were chitchatting like old friends—without a translator. It was as if a heavy veil had been lifted.

Wilem and I walked across the rickety boardwalks of Agats toward my hotel. Everything was the same and yet different. People recognized me, waving and saying, "Hi, you're back!" and I replied, this time in their own language. It had been seven months, but even the hotel desk clerk remembered me. Wilem and I sat in the front of my room, and I told him my plan.

"Kokai is here in Agats!" he said. "Tomorrow I will find him and bring him to your hotel."

We shook hands, and as he left night closed in, the skies opened, and the rain pounded down. I fell asleep to that rain, mosquitoes buzzing in my ears.

I woke early, at dawn, and headed out, glad to be breathing the balmy air. The boardwalks were puddled and steaming. By the wharf I passed a man and did a double take. It was Kokai. He recognized me, and his eyes widened with surprise. I'd forgotten how wild he looked. Agats was full of Indonesians from all over the archipelago, as well as the much poorer Asmat; even the destitute of Agats looked citified, had an air of belonging, wore flip-flops. But Kokai had that reek of sweat and smoke that I'd forgotten. He was barefoot. His hair stuck out in willy-nilly tufts. The hole in his septum was the size of a dime. A woven bag thick with the feathers of cockatoo and cassowary hung over his chest. And his eyes—dark and brown, darting back and forth, taking everything in and giving nothing away.

Few Westerners came to Asmat, and certainly the vast majority who did never came back. They appeared, snapped photos, and were gone. But here I was again. I could sense the significance—I had never seen Kokai smile before, and now he did—and I could speak to him. I asked him what he was doing, when was he returning to Pirien.

"I came to see my son," he said, "but I don't know when I'm going back. I need a boat, and I don't have any money."

It was too good to be true, and I couldn't help it, it all just

poured out: I wanted to come to Pirien for a month, to live in his house, with him. Could I? We could go together, and get Wilem to take us.

"My house? For a month?" And then I couldn't understand anything else, he was ripping along too fast in a gravelly slur.

"Wilem will find you," I said, "and bring you to my hotel and we can talk." He turned and walked away.

HE AND WILEM showed up a few hours later. Wilem and I could understand each other well; Kokai was a different matter. He spoke Indonesian fluently, could read and write, but it wasn't his first language; he had a strange accent, and he couldn't seem to grasp just how slowly he needed to speak when talking to me. I repeated my request—could I come live with him in Pirien for a month? No problem, he said. I could live with him, in his house.

"But what will he eat?" he said, looking at Wilem.

"Whatever you eat," I said.

"Sago?" he said.

"Yes, sago. And whatever else."

"I'll go to the store," said Wilem. "We'll get some rice and SuperMi [the instant ramen noodles the Asmat love] and coffee and sugar and tobacco."

It was done. Kokai never asked me why I wanted to come, but I'd told him I wanted to learn about Asmat culture, to know about the language, carving, everything. Though the last time we'd met I'd been asking about Michael, neither of us mentioned him. I handed a wad of cash to Wilem, a down payment for the boat and $100 for food. I had a satellite telephone; I told Wilem I'd call him when I wanted to be picked up, and that if he didn't hear from me in three and a half weeks, he should come anyway. We would leave the next morning at six a.m.

November 2012

THE WORLD IS always more beautiful at dawn and dusk, but nowhere more so than in the tropics. There the sun is so hot and bright

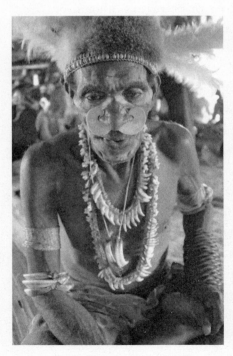

SAUER, THE HEAD OF THE JISAR JEU, DRAPED IN THE TEETH OF DOGS AND WILD BOARS.

and glaring you want to flee from it most of the day, and dawn and dusk are times of softness, when the blanched world becomes infused with color. As we slipped into Wilem's boat, a wispy mist lay over the Asawets, sky blue in the morning light. Dawn, too, is windless in Asmat, and the river, a half-mile across here, was placid, not a ripple. Kokai was his usual inscrutable, silent, wild-eyed self; Wilem took the bow and his buddy the throttle. Piled amidships was a case of ramen, a thirty-pound bag of rice, two cases

of Lampion (the loose-leaf tobacco the Asmat favored), five pounds of sugar, and a plastic sleeping mat sporting brightly colored Mickey Mouses that Wilem had bought for me.

We sped down the river straight out to sea—the day was so calm we were taking the direct ocean route, the same that Michael and Wassing had navigated almost exactly fifty-one years before. It felt good to be out on the water, the sky huge and arching overhead, the sea as still as a pond, and I thought of Michael on that last day, here in this same spot, and how good he, too, must have felt heading south to meet van Kessel in Basim. He was still so young, and though he was making mistakes and he never could have been here without his family's money, I couldn't help admiring him. There were a million places easier than Asmat, especially in 1961, for a child of wealth and privilege. He'd had a vision and was following his passion, striving for something original and deep, carving out a place for himself that was of his father, his family, yet was different too, that was his own. If one wave had been shaped differently, if the wind had been softer, if he'd taken the inland route, who knows how long he would have stayed in Asmat, how many times he might have returned, how much he might have understood and perhaps even given back to the place and its people.

But the world is in motion, we are but small pieces, and control is an illusion. We make our own luck, our own destiny, but only to a point, and we never know what could happen at any moment— that was the lesson of middle age I thought about as we sped toward Otsjanep and I tried to calm my nerves. Asmat was like no other place I'd ever been. The men could be so friendly and so closed. I longed for a rawness, for this thing I called "primitive" in my mind and had been romantic about for so long, this thing I had experienced during short plunges but never for a month straight. And I still didn't even really know what it meant—to be primitive, although I was beginning to understand that word's inadequacy. I hoped my month living in Pirien among these people who had been

headhunters and cannibals just a generation ago, and who still lived largely removed from the developed world, would help me understand them better. And to be there to investigate a possible murder, to ask about secrets—I wondered if they'd remember me and what I'd been pursuing before. Would they shun me because of it? Would I be able to communicate with them? How would they react to my questions? Otsjanep and Pirien had made my hair stand up during my previous, albeit short, visits.

Yet even as I felt anxious, if not a little frightened, to be heading toward a remote village with such a fearsome reputation, in a world of mud and heat, I had to remember that van Kessel had been there in 1955, van de Wouw had been in and out between 1962 and 1968, van de Waal was there in 1962, and Tobias Schneebaum in the 1970s and 1980s. Otsjanep-Pirien was far away. It had no services, no electricity, no plumbing, no stores, but it was full of real people, and I was convinced that more than anything else it was my own fear I was afraid of. If I approached my stay with humility and grace, and could win over Kokai, everything would be all right. Somehow the answers were right here, waiting to be unraveled.

Michael had loved Asmat, and I felt incredulous that no one from his immediate family had made the effort to see it and know it for themselves.

A HUGE EAGLE with wide wings and great, sharp talons swept near the boat and gracefully plucked a fish from the sea, bringing me out of my reverie. We were zipping past the mouth of the Betsj, where Michael had capsized, and there wasn't a wave. I was writing Indonesian words in my notebook, and Wilem was writing their Asmat equivalents. At ten-thirty we turned inland, toward the mouth of the Ewta. Here, still a half-mile out, the sea looked like a toothpick farm: thin poles, with nets tied to them, stood out of the water, and women stood up to their necks in the shallow water, pairs of them walking along the bottom working oval shrimp nets.

The tide was beginning to ebb. When it was high, the sea inundated the land, and the river mouth itself was an indistinct opening. Now glistening banks of mud extended hundreds of feet from shore, the river still a narrow cut in the black ooze a hundred yards out. Egrets paced the flats, terns zipped overhead, and then the jungle swallowed us up.

We passed a hut where a man was lounging on the veranda. Wilem bellowed a short song; the man sang back. It all happened fast then. The narrow river, enclosed by a wall of green jungle and hanging vines, twisted and turned for three miles and then opened to a clearing of thatch and palm huts on stilts, the shouts of children jumping in the brown river, the smell of smoke, and we pulled up at a mud bank in front of a small wood plank house with a corrugated metal roof. Men, children, surged. Everything was grabbed, carried off, Kokai barking directions.

The house was three rooms without furniture, its bare walls gray with years of dirt, soot, grime. Traditional handwoven palm mats covered the floors. In the front room stood three six-foot-high shields, a six-foot-long bow and bundle of arrows, a handful of spears, and two twelve-foot-long paddles. A back door led to an open-sided, thatch-roofed kitchen, its floorboards spaced a couple inches apart, a smoldering fire on a square of river mud, one blackened pot. Stick-thin women emptied the front room of sleeping mats and swept it with a bundle of sticks.

"You can have my room," said Kokai.

"Come," said Wilem, thrusting a case of Lampion tobacco in my hands. "We must go to Otsjanep."

He and Kokai and I jumped back in the boat and headed five minutes upstream, past a brief no-man's-land, to Otsjanep. Even now, fifty years later, the other side had to be placated to keep antipathies at bay. Men surrounded us as we walked to a thatch house, climbed a ladder of notched logs, and entered.

"Mister Karo has come to Pirien for a month," Wilem said. "He

eats everything—fish and even sago—and he is interested in see-ing Asmat."

The thick press of men nodded, looked at me. I recognized many of them from when Amates and I had been questioning them about Michael. "Thank you so much for the big welcome," I said, handing them the box of tobacco.

We left quickly, and Wilem dropped us back in Pirien and left. I was alone. Unsure of what to do next. Then men started arriving. Old men like Kokai, barbed-wire thin and muscled, with holes in their septums and bags hanging from their necks and cuscus fur headbands with the ubiquitous white cockatoo feathers. Age was hard to tell in Asmat—people tended to look older than they were—but all had to be over fifty, some a decade or two older. All would have been alive when Lapré came to the village, when Mi-chael had swung through three years later, and when he vanished a few months after that. The chances were high that the oldest among them had probably consumed human flesh. I was dying to see inside their minds, to know what they knew, not just about Michael but everything—how they saw the world now and how much of the traditional world of the spirits remained. They each shook my hand, patted me on the shoulder. We sat cross-legged in a circle on the floor. Kokai brought out tobacco—the tobacco I'd given him—and the men divided it up further, each man taking a palmful. They talked and smoked, knocking the ashes onto the floor and into its cracks, adding to the dried mud and dust that covered everything. They talked and talked and talked, and I lis-tened, as best I could, catching only the occasional word. Though they mostly spoke in Indonesian, it was too fast, too colloquial, for me to understand. This time I had vowed to myself to not ask anything, to not mention Michael or Lapré or any of the events surrounding Michael's disappearance, for at least a week or more. I was just there, and it felt totally different from before and made me realize again how much of a mistake I'd made—and Michael

before me—by just swooping in for a quick visit. Now I belonged to Kokai, to the village itself. I was under their protection. I was their responsibility.

When they finally trickled away, Kokai's wife set out two plastic bowls of rice and ramen and a single spoon before disappearing into the back kitchen again. No salt. No seasoning. Kokai ate with his fingers. The light was dying, the sun setting. Flies buzzed and landed on my hands, arms, legs, the food. We sat alone.

"*Adik*," he said to me. Younger brother. "You are my younger brother." Then we smoked on the front porch.

Other than the passing of a boat once a day or so, there were no sounds of engines, just the constant shriek of children playing— and almost every day and night there was like this first one. A few men came by, sat and smoked with us. Packs of dogs loped along the boardwalks, through the swampy ground beneath the houses, sometimes attacked each other in a wild scrum of barking and howling and yelping. The air reeked of human shit—the moldy, always wet outhouse was in the kitchen and the hole dropped straight to the ground beneath the kitchen, with those widely spaced boards. There were houses next to Kokai's, behind it, and in front of it across a small creek, the houses were everywhere, and each one was filled with people shitting onto the ground. The rich, pungent smell pervaded the village, and I never quite grew used to it.

When darkness fell, small bats the size of mice poured out of the eaves and heavy-footed lizards hammered across the ceilings, sounding infinitely bigger than they were. Without a moon, the village was pitch-black; I could see nothing but the glow of Kokai's cigarette and the heat lightning that flashed across the horizon like a World War I artillery barrage. It was all a mystery to me, everything. When the mosquitoes grew intense, we went inside, to the light of a single kerosene flame, and sat amid a houseful of people, men and women and naked children, green, viscous snot pouring from their noses, their bellies distended.

People came and went in a constant stream. Time inched by, each minute like an hour. I was in a place without things. No chairs, beds, tables, books, no blankets or sheets, no pictures on the walls, never mind televisions or computers or radios or telephones. Kokai was an important elder, but he and his wife had nothing but a knapsack, a battered suitcase full of a few plastic bowls and cups, a sleeping mat, and a soiled pillow. No one had a bed. Slowly, they just sort of dropped off, falling to the floor and falling asleep, and I slipped into my room, hung my mosquito net from a nail, and fell asleep too.

DAWN HIT JUST before five a.m., and with it the children started screaming—as they did virtually every morning, pounding the floor with their feet, their fists, hollering and crying and bellowing, as if their limbs were being torn from their bodies, and they did so for an entire hour. Kokai hissed; their mothers and aunts hissed; but as I soon learned, it didn't matter much whether they were put to the breast or struck or hugged and cradled—they screamed uncontrollably, and nothing could be done about it. It figured into my deepening understanding of what I came to call the inside-out people, and it exemplified who the Asmat were, a vestige of the consciousness that underlay the cannibalism they'd practiced for hundreds and perhaps thousands of years: a consciousness of emotional extremes, a bipolar duality. The Asmat have no inherent balance in their lives, no synthesis. Children and parents share an intense closeness. Parents—men and women both—hold and cuddle their children constantly, carry them in their arms, on their backs, lounge with them, sleep with them, and laugh when their children pee on them, and women nurse their children until they are three and four years old. They sing to their children, but they also wallop them like prizefighters on their backs and chests, so hard it's difficult to believe no bones are broken. Adults and children howl with laughter and

scream in despair. They fight with each other and can yell and stomp their feet for hours.

I saw boys fight, viciously, smashing their fists into each other's faces, or they walked and leapt holding hands, hugging each other. I saw a woman strike her husband with a two-by-four. I watched a man stand outside of a house and shout for two hours straight, until Kokai finally went out and shouted back at him. These confrontations seemed inches away from turning deadly. If they had tobacco, they'd smoke it all right away until it was gone and then pace in despair and withdrawal. If they had sugar, they'd pour it into coffee or tea, so much that it would be gone in a day. They would drum and sing all day and all night, and then sleep all the next day or crash on the floor at sunset. To achieve any sort of balance always required the opposite. To right a death had required another death. If they seemed to have no boundaries, perhaps their boundaries were so porous they tumbled right over them, becoming themselves only by consuming the other. It was all part of the same thing.

BY SIX, I'D given up on sleep, and I emerged to find Kokai slipping three-foot-long tassels of cockatoo feathers over the tops of the paddles he'd carved. His wife brought us coffee, and he introduced her—Maria, his third wife; his first two were dead. She was about twenty-five, maybe younger, with a pretty, round face. They had two young boys. His oldest daughter from his first wife was also dead; his oldest son lived in Agats, and then he and wife number two had three other children: a son who had died; a daughter who lived in the house with us with her three children; and a slightly mentally retarded son who looked normal but wasn't and who lived in Otsjanep, though no one knew why. Kokai would sell the paddles, the shields, the spears in Agats, his only way of earning money.

Though we spent hours and hours together, it was often in the

morning that we spoke the most, when he opened up a little, patting the space next to him for me to sit, as we munched on dry, flavorless sago and small fish and smoked our first cigarettes and drank our coffee—a luxury for him, since I had provided it from Agats. Pointing to the weapons, he gave them their Asmat names. *Amun,* bow. *Jamasj,* shield. *Po,* paddle. Then he said, "Look!" and showed me a scar on his forearm the size of a quarter. "From an arrow!" He slapped his forearm, slapped his thigh and groin— four wounds, one of which was from an arrow that entered his groin and came out the other side. "Otsjanep!" he said. He jumped up, grabbed a shield, hid behind it, advanced, ducked, advanced, screamed, pantomimed shooting an arrow.

In a world without photographs or television or recorded anything, the Asmat are wonderful storytellers, expressive and dramatic with their voices and bodies, their stories full of the chopping of heads and the shooting of arrows and the driving home of spears. When Kokai talked about canoes or paddling, he'd bend forward and spread his arms wide, become a canoe gliding over the sea, a canoe I could see. Once he imitated a fruit bat: he scrunched up and made a creepy face, exposing his teeth, screeching, holding his hands like he was clinging, and he *was* the bat—I could see it hanging upside down in a tree.

I'd already heard the story of the split between Otsjanep and Pirien, but I asked him again: Why? What happened?

He pantomimed grabbing someone, struggling over them, pulling and pushing. Made a circle with his index finger, started thrusting the index finger from his other hand in and out—a struggle over women, sex. Now I knew who was who, and the story's details came alive. It had been Dombai, the father of Ber, whose house stood in front of Kokai's, who had been cuckolded— and he'd been head of the jeu, the most important man in the clan. The man who'd slept with his wives had been Fin, the head of Otsjanep. It had been a brazen piece of treachery, a direct chal-

lenge, a grave insult to Dombai and every member of the jeu, sure
to provoke violence.

Pirien and Otsjanep were deeply complex places. On a nightly
basis, ten of us were sleeping in Kokai's house—he and his wife
and their two children, his daughter and son-in-law and their
three children. But it was so few only because I was there. More
people began trickling back the longer I stayed; after a few weeks,
on any given night there might be twenty. Pirien itself was di-
vided into five subvillages, each with a name, based around five
principal families, who themselves formed a larger clan and be-
longed to the same jeu. Five houses, at least fifty people, lived in
Ufin, all directly related to Kokai, and he was the patriarch—he
had, in fact, served as *kepala desa* (the headman) of Pirien for
five years. It was essentially an elected position—he was like the
mayor and had received a small salary (which was how he had
been given a plank house). But there was another headman too,
who was variously called the *kepala perang* or *kepala adat*—the
war leader or head of custom. This was the most important posi-
tion of all, and most men served for life. They were the head of
the jeu, of which there were five in the twin villages: Otsjanep,
Kajerpis, and Bakyer in Otsjanep; Pirien and Jisar in Pirien.

Strangely, although every village I'd ever been in had a jeu—
the massive, one-hundred-foot-long houses that served as the cer-
emonial centers of village life—neither Otsjanep nor Pirien did, a
mystery for which I could never get a direct answer. The lack of
a jeu was related, I suspected, to the two villages' long history of
violence, and maybe even to Michael Rockefeller's death. For all
of the disruption imposed on the Asmat by the Dutch, Indone-
sian officials had been far more extreme. While the Dutch had
banned headhunting and warfare and brought Christianity, Indo-
nesian government officials had burned all the jeus and banned all
carving and feasting. The few Dutch missionaries who remained
behind were supplanted by a wave of Crozier priests from the

United States. Tensions between the missionaries and the Indone-
sians grew so tense that Father Jan Smit was shot to death by an
Indonesian official in Agats in 1965. Only in the early 1970s did
Indonesia begin softening its position and slowly allow traditional
Asmat customs to flourish again, under pressure from and sub-
tle manipulation by American missionaries. But even today vil-
lages had to get a building permit from the government to erect
a new jeu, and I suspected that officials remained apprehensive
that the most visual manifestation of traditional spiritual life—
five big jeus in a village that had been riven with power struggles
for decades—might bring out old prides and animosities, allowing
violence to bubble forth.

Of course, as had been shown by the earliest Dutch efforts to
quash headhunting, traditions didn't die so easily. My question
about the lack of a jeu in Otsjanep and Pirien was complicated by
the fact that whenever I asked it, no one understood what I was
asking. There were five jeus in Otsjanep and Pirien, they'd say, and
everyone knew who belonged to which jeu, even if there wasn't
a traditional building per se. Of course! It wasn't the buildings
themselves—the churches, so to speak—that counted.

One day Kokai pointed to a house across from his and said,
"That's the jeu." "Oh," I said, "can I see it?" When we went inside,
it turned out to be the house of Ber, Pirien's current kepala desa.
Otsjanep and Pirien didn't have formal, traditionally built jeus,
but that didn't matter in the least.

As it turned out, however, the men of Jisar had convinced the lo-
cal authorities that a new jeu might foster tourism, and permission
had been given to begin construction. A few days after my arrival,
Kokai's son-in-law, Bouvier, took me out to look. Pirien consisted
of about thirty houses, nine of them plank, along the banks of the
Ewta. Although I could see no dividing line, another twenty at the
downriver side of the village were technically in Jisar, perhaps a
quarter-mile down a rough, three-foot-wide boardwalk.

In a clearing along the riverbank a Stone Age fantasy was ris-
ing. Resting atop a foundation thirty-three poles wide, each pole
three feet apart, was the framework of a new jeu. From each of the
poles in the front row, looking out to the river, gazed a carved face.
The floor was already built, a springy layer of narrow, inch-wide
poles, and above it stood the framing—a rough rectangular out-
line to which the walls and roof would be attached. All jeus had a
high, pitched roof descending from a central beam that lay across
a series of notched support logs, and it was these logs that thirty
men at a time were driving into the mud. The men worked fast,
singing, chanting, clutching the poles with their arms and driving
them downward with their feet, deep into the mud. It reminded
me of a hive of bees or an ant farm: with no central "architect," no
blueprints, no big pieces of machinery, gangs of men worked in
some mysterious harmony, driving logs, hoisting the top beams
into place, tying it all together with strips of rattan.

"More! A little more!" voices called, and the men heaved and
chanted, until everything lined up perfectly. No nails. No wire.
They worked with nothing but a handful of axes and machetes,
and though not a single pole was uniform in width or length or
was even straight itself, the jeu looked as true as if they were work-
ing with levels and power tools.

DURING THE HEAT of the day, almost no one moved except the chil-
dren, but toward late afternoon the village sprang to life, and the
next evening I found a different scene altogether. The jeu had no
walls, no roof, but the Asmat couldn't help themselves. It was the
first jeu rising in years, and the feasting and celebrating had be-
gun and would continue until it was finished.

I walked over alone, trailed by the thirty or so children who
followed me everywhere, constantly laughing at me. Men sat and
lay throughout the unfinished structure, and a circle of men with
drums was in the center. They called out to me, waved me over,

and an old man at the head of the circle moved aside and patted the floor, motioning me to sit next to him. "We will be finished in two weeks," he said, "after the Bupati [the district governor] comes from Agats. We must cover the walls with gabagaba and the roof with *atap* [palm fronds] on the day he is here."

Then, until the sun set, and for many afternoons after, I became lost in tribal reverie. A fire burned on a lump of mud. The glow of the light, the jungle soft green, the air hot and moist and still, the river flowing, always flowing by like grains of sand dripping through an hourglass, the sun a blazing yellow circle to the west. The men were decked out, claiming their history, dripping with dogs' teeth and the tusks of boars around their arms, cockatoo feathers sprouting from their hair and fur headbands, their faces painted—some ochre, some black—cassowary bone daggers through rattan bracelets around their biceps. The older men sported pig bones or shells in their septums. Sauer, the old man I sat next to, was the kepala perang of Jisar, with the classic Asmat high cheekbones and physique of raw muscle and bone and black skin, smeared with war paint.

In the Asmat creation myth, Fumeripitsj drummed the Asmat to life from his carvings, and Sauer and his jeu mates began drumming themselves into existence, reconstituting themselves as what they were, how they saw themselves. Months before, when I'd contacted an American woman who was closely involved with Asmat art and the Crozier order and told her about my project, her response had been cold. Not more about primitive headhunters and cannibals, she'd said. "That's so been done. It's the past. There are so many problems there, real problems, and the Asmat need to be seen as they are today, suffering from AIDS, poverty, the lack of access to education and health care."

I understood her point, but it was as fanciful as my own, as full of Western ideals and preconceptions. If I saw them through her eyes, I'd see them as poverty-stricken victims in rags, covered in

ringworm, subject to exploitation from Indonesia. Which they are. The Asmat are a people who live in palm shacks in the outback on the outermost fringes of human civilization without plumbing or electricity, dressed in our castaway and holey T-shirts and tattered gym shorts, substantially illiterate, with little future in a dynamic and technological global economy.

I didn't see them that way, though, and, watching them come to life, I saw that they didn't feel that way either. My American contact wanted them to be victims, requiring our help and our pity, but their dignity and pride and sense of self lay in what they had been, and still were in their own minds: warriors. Former headhunters deeply enmeshed in a rich spirit world. Take that away and they were but victims dwelling in a ghetto swamp. Though they were now Catholics and often crossed themselves before meals, and though they ducked away from directly answering questions about killing and cannibalism, what was taking place before me—and in every story and song I would hear over the next weeks—revealed the Asmat as they saw themselves.

They drummed sitting down, and they drummed standing up, two hundred beats a minute, and they sang, and men danced and children danced, and sweat poured from their bodies, and other men blew eerie, aching-sounding horns, and the floor of the jeu pulsated. They moved to the ground between riverbank and jeu, and more men appeared, and women too, some topless in grass skirts, bouncing and shaking, knees flapping in and out, and they danced with weapons, with bows and arrows and spears, and the sun dipped lower, and smoke curled around the sweating bodies, and in their sameness each was dressed a little differently, and they howled and bellowed and hooted, a wild free-for-all of unadulterated joy and abandon, of culture that stretched back beyond memory.

I welled up in tears. It was powerful and beautiful and unfiltered; it was pure and rich and of the earth and the river and the mud. Huge clouds dangled from the sky, and one young man

with ochre stripes across his face and blazing orange gym shorts, clutching a spear, went wilder than everyone else, kicking his legs up high, fluttering his hands, shouting, "Wha! Wha! Woooweee!" The people followed the drummers in rows back and forth in front of the jeu, and just before the sun dipped below the tangled green horizon, giant birds appeared, birds that weren't birds at all, but bats. Giant fruit bats the size of eagles, hundreds of them, thousands, rising from their resting places near the sea and flying a few hundred feet overhead in a single direction—away from the sun, toward the east. They flew not like bats but like birds, each flying alone, two wingbeats a second, slowly, steadily, and I thought of Hitchcock or the monkeys flying in *The Wizard of Oz*. They looked purposeful; they didn't glide or soar, they were just pulsing wings and bulbous bat bodies, two tiny feet trailing behind.

The drumming and singing and dancing continued for the next two weeks, until the big day when government officials were to come and the men would finish the jeu by installing the roof and lighting the family hearths that lined the jeu's back wall. My Indonesian was growing stronger, and I was beginning to understand more. It helped that Kokai was getting used to speaking slowly and simply with me. The pattern of the days began to unfold. The house and the village woke at dawn. Though there was a primary school, the teacher hadn't been there for two months. Children played all day, chasing each other, fighting, climbing trees over the river and plunging in. The boys made small bows and arrows, caught snakes and mice; together boys and girls built small forts out of scrub and sent the girls off to collect wood, and then they'd build a fire. The teenagers chased each other, swam, plaited each other's hair, played vicious games of soccer in a foot of thick mud on the "field" by the schoolhouse. Just after sunrise, women paddled their canoes to the sea, where they fished or shrimped or chopped wood for the kitchen fires all day.

Women did everything. They washed the tattered clothes in

the muddy river and made all the food, a never-ending diet of sago pancakes and sago balls, of rice and ramen and small fish and tiny, krill-like shrimp, which they wrapped in palm leaves and baked on the fire. Mostly the food and wood in Kokai's house came from other family members in other houses. I never saw a green vegetable or fruit, save for coconuts. If the men weren't drumming or singing or carving, they did nothing, except occasionally helping their wives cut down sago in the jungle. They were warriors with no war to fight. In the old days, if they hadn't been fighting, they would have been hunting or protecting the women, but that was no longer necessary, and during my time there I never saw anyone hunt—though they must have, for there was a never-ending supply of cassowary bones and feathers and cuscus fur and cockatoo feathers in the village. To bathe they jumped in the river, fully clothed; no one used soap. The river repelled me. It was brown with muddy silt, and at high tide it flooded the villages and their outhouses—and the whole village of Otsjanep lay upriver. But it was that or nothing. One day, just as I was about to jump in, a log of shit floated by.

Kokai's son-in-law often escorted me wherever I went, and I was never sure if it was because he wanted to hang out or if he was being tasked to do so. He was young, handsome, and probably in his twenties. He could read and write—he'd been to primary school. Once I asked him how old he was. He thought for a long time and then said, "Fifteen."

At any time of day or night, there was always a child screaming and a song wafting over the mud and breeze, intermingling with the omnipresent smoke and smell of shit. Kokai's daughter and nieces and extended family, always coming and going from one house to another, sang beautifully, sweetly—even Kokai's sister, a rail-thin, nearly toothless old woman with a gravelly voice who lived next door, sang well. Listening to these human sounds, I realized that back home so much of every conversation or experi-

ence takes place over headsets or telephones, over computer screens or televisions, through email or SMS message. Much of our experience is prerecorded, heavily produced, often divorced from the immediate source. The West is a place of all these overlapping and competing realities. But everything in Asmat is immediate, present, touchable, live. If you want music, you have to create it. If you want to talk to someone, you have to find that person. If you want a story, someone has to tell it and you have to be next to the person creating it.

Everything in Asmat is raw, that constant emotional intensity of joy or sadness, of fighting or hugging, and everyone is so close, knows their place, is so connected, to family, neighborhood, jeu, village. I'd been thinking a lot about my obsession with what I'd called the primitive, the thing that had driven me to Asmat and Michael's story in the first place. Part of it was simple romance— the romance of the jungle and open fires, of drumming and spears and bows and arrows and dogs' teeth necklaces. But it was also the hope of seeing something, understanding something, about myself, and the recognition of what was lacking in my own life, a yearning for something. My father's family were Orthodox Jews, a people who always saw themselves as separate from mainstream America. Yet whatever greater connection to that community my grandparents and aunts and uncles might have felt, my father had rebelled, had rejected it all, had declared himself an atheist to my grandmother at the age of seventeen. Then he'd married my mother, a WASP, and she herself was a quiet reader and lover of books, not much of a joiner. Neither liked to watch or play sports; we didn't go to church; we lived in a predominantly Catholic neighborhood that was filled with enormous families—the Murrays next door had eleven children, the Hagues around the corner twelve, the Hannapels across the street six, the Vieths a few blocks away sixteen. We were nothing like them. My parents had even told my sister and me, from the beginning, that there was no such

thing as Santa Claus or the Easter Bunny. I'd grown up with no tribe, no belief, no ritual, belonging to nothing, never able to surrender to a larger group.

In Asmat behavior I recognized a truth. I had always longed for more connection, even as I'd fled from it, and in Pirien, despite its strangeness, I never felt lonely. In love I had little balance, either keeping intimacy at bay, people at a distance, or tipping wildly in the other direction, falling crazy in consuming love, wanting everything all the time, wanting to consume the other, to eat them up. I felt like I understood the Asmat's dualism, their lack of balance, and I recognized that sometimes I was but a step away from it myself, at least metaphorically. What I called primitiveness wasn't really about living in a house or a hut, or dancing wildly in a nightclub or under the moon in a swamp by an open fire, but about your consciousness, your sense of self. Kokai and his family, all of the Asmat in Pirien, were connected to each other and their village in a way I could barely fathom, and there was a huge part of me that wanted to be like them. Their unfiltered, immediate experience of life appealed to my own primitiveness, even as I couldn't quite throw off my inhibitions and join them completely.

Tobias Schneebaum had felt the same longing, had been driven to Asmat for many of the same reasons. "Throughout my life," he wrote, "I have been searching for a way to connect with other human beings. Suddenly, I find myself in a forest among the Asmat, living in their world, where I lose my insecurities and am content."

25

December 2012

AS THE SECOND WEEK melted into the third, it was time to start asking questions. I was comfortable in the village, and the village seemed comfortable with me. I was welcome, and expected, in the drumming at the rising jeu in Jisar. Men, and even women, greeted me on my daily walks along the boardwalk, and I no lon-

ME WITH KOKAI (*STANDING BEHIND ME, IN A BASEBALL CAP*) AND HIS FAMILY, IN PIRIEN.

ger attracted a crowd of onlookers for my daily bath in the river.
I had made three trips in a small boat owned by one of Kokai's
nephews to Basim, an hour away, which had a few stores where
I'd continually supplied the household with rice and ramen, to-
bacco and sugar, even lollipops and a soccer ball for the kids. I
was feeding a family of fifty—we'd already been through ninety
pounds of rice—and the more I bought, the faster it disappeared
throughout Kokai's fiefdom of Ufin. Within a family there was no
private property; everything belonged to everyone and everything
was shared, and the more important you were the more you were
expected to give.

Ideas were beginning to form in my mind about Michael, about
what could have happened, and how and why.

Kokai and I spoke more and more in the early mornings over
our coffee and cigarettes, amid smoke and the tromping of chil-
dren's feet and their shrieks and cries. He often spoke of himself
in the third person. "My grandfather and my father told me the
history of Asmat, the history of the village. Songs, so many songs.
Songs of the jeu, songs of sago, songs of paddling, songs about
birds and fish and about bisj. Kokai listened. Always listened and
watched." Kokai's father, it turned out, was Fom, one of the men
named by van Kessel as having taken one of Michael's ribs. If Fom
had participated in the killing of Michael, Kokai knew it. I had
no doubt.

Kokai told me how hard it had been to find a new wife. He
hadn't had any luck in the village of Pirien, where the women were
afraid of him, he said, maybe because he was so old. He had found
Maria in Basim, but it had taken a great deal of sago and sugar
and dogs' teeth necklaces to convince the men in the jeu to acqui-
esce. "They made Kokai wait and wait and wait," he said.

He told me how boys' septums were pierced by a sharp piece
of bamboo as they lay on the ground, and how the hole was grad-
ually widened over time. Change shadowed every story. No one

pierced their septums anymore, and Kokai refused to join any of the drumming and singing. Instead, he would put on his feathers and cuscus headband and sit singing to himself and rocking back and forth for hours.

Kami is my love
You are my beloved
After your death you give me only memories
For my pride.
Kami is my love
And I long for you
For everything.
And Kami my wife
You are my first wife
Why did you die this time?
I need you.
But now you're not living with me.
It's a long time I live alone
Without you in my life.
I love you forever.
But my life is forever because
I am your beloved.
Forever in my life.

"I am sad," he said. "In the past we had feasts for weeks and weeks. Gathering sago, gathering fish, and I would give and give and give, tobacco and sugar and sago and fish, and we would drum and sing for weeks, months. But now I sit and cry. I feel sad and tears stream down my face. I spread mud along my forehead and my hairline, and I cry and remember. Today I sing for my first daughter; she is dead and buried there," he said, pointing toward a grave behind the house.

Bis is my wife
You are a beautiful wife
Now where have you gone?
Are you looking for sago?
Or are you looking for fish?
Why have you not come home?

Here, I am waiting for you.
Crying for you.
Because you're my wife, my beautiful wife.
I am your husband crying for you
Forever.
And I will cry until I die.
Because you have made my life so difficult
And I cry, cry forever
And die for you.

I told Kokai I had some old photographs. Would he like to see them?

"Yes!" he said emphatically.

I brought them out, a stack of fifty or so photocopies of black-and-white shots Michael Rockefeller had taken during his trip to Otsjanep in the summer of 1961. We were sitting on the ash-covered floor, by the door to the kitchen. By the time I'd handed them to him the space was crowded, the women and children rushing over, and almost instantly men appeared from all over the village, including Kokai's brother. Each photo had a few accompanying words of description—the place and sometimes a jeu were identified, but the men in them were almost all unnamed. They were naked, proud, smiling, their hair in long ringlets, and the shells of triton hung on the abdomen of some—the sign of a great headhunter. Other photos showed men drumming naked in jeus,

or elaborate bisj poles, both on the floor of the jeu and erected on scaffolding outside it.

The women and girls giggled and twittered at the nakedness, but Kokai became silent. Reverent. He stared and stared, held the photos up to the light, as if gazing through a doorway to a past that was long gone, that he must have pictured in his memory but that he hadn't seen in a half-century.

"Hmmm," he mumbled, tracing the lines of the men with his long fingernail. Then he began naming people. Dombai, with heavy eyebrows and a flashing smile and a pig's bone in his nose, named in van Kessel's original report, the former kepala perang of Pirien, the man who had been cuckolded, the father of Ber, who lived fifty feet away. (Kokai called Ber "my brother," though exactly how they were related I could never quite untangle; both of their parents were different, and they lived in different clans within the village.) Tatsji, one of the Omadesep and Otsjanep go-betweens and one of the men who had reported to von Peij that Michael had been killed. The chief from Omadesep, Faniptas, who had started it all by convincing the men from Otsjanep to accompany him to Wagin in 1957. Mighty he looked: in his late forties or early fifties, naked and tall and thickly muscled, his hair lengthened with sago fibers to his shoulders, covered with dogs' teeth and boar tusks and dangling shells and ornaments, wearing a thick rattan bracelet to protect his left wrist from the bowstring. Kokai pointed out Jane and Bese, also named in van Kessel's report. Kokai knew which jeu was which, and he knew the jeu to which every man he recognized belonged.

I asked him about Faniptas. "After the trip to Wagin," Kokai said, "he gave one of his daughters to Dombai to make peace." Faniptas and his men had murdered six from Otsjanep, and the men from Otsjanep had massacred dozens of men from Omadesep, but balance had been restored. The Asmat had not needed Max Lapré or his government. They had done it themselves, and I thought

of Father Vince Cole's words: despite (or perhaps because of) their constant warfare, the Asmat had always created some connection, some strategy, that left open avenues of communication, that cemented relationships and kept them from all being annihilated.

"And what about these bisj poles?" I said. "Why are they still in the jeu?"

"The bisj festival was not finished."

"Who were the poles for?"

"I don't know," he said.

Word swept through Pirien and Jisar quickly. Over the next few days, amid the drumming and singing in the jeu, and in Ber's house in Pirien itself, where the men of Pirien had also begun drumming and singing in celebration of Jisar and a new idea—that they, too, would build a new jeu—the men wanted to see the photos.

They identified six of the fifteen men named by van Kessel and von Peij as having parts of Michael's skeleton, which confirmed that the men named by both priests had, in fact, met him. Which meant that if Michael had made it to shore, he had encountered men who knew him, knew his name. I asked again and again about the bisj poles, and always the answer was the same: the bisj festival wasn't finished, and they didn't know who the poles had been made for. That was possible; it was fifty years ago. But it seemed unlikely. They remembered everything, knew hundreds of songs by heart, knew their family lineages back generations, knew how to carve a drum or a spear or construct a one-hundred-foot-long, thirty-foot-high longhouse without a nail or a drawing.

One afternoon I walked to Otsjanep. Pirien was spread down one side of the river, only a couple of houses deep; Otsjanep, much more spread out, lay on both sides of the Ewta. Pirien had grown used to me. Every house I passed had men and women and children sitting on its front porch, and everyone waved, said "good afternoon" or "good evening" to me. But Otsjanep was silent, the

people staring. Near the river I encountered an old man with one eye sitting on the boardwalk. I sat down with him, brought out some tobacco. His name was Petrus. A few other men sat down with us. I told them I was living with Kokai in Pirien. They nodded, said little. I left a few minutes later.

I returned the next afternoon with the photos. The village boardwalks were deserted. In the afternoon heat, it was as still as still could be, the only trace of movement and sound coming from a few children following me. I decided to head back. I was nearly at the village edge when the boys caught up to me. They grabbed me, pointed to a man a few hundred yards away. "He wants to talk to you." I turned around, walked back, found Petrus coming toward me. "Do you like sago?" he asked.

"Yes," I said.

"Come to my house."

I followed him to a traditional palm-and-gabagaba structure entered by climbing up a notched log. Smoke rose from two fireplaces. It was dark, full of languishing bodies and their acrid sweet smell, babies latched on to drooping breasts. We sat cross-legged, I handed out some tobacco, and we smoked, sweat rolling off my forehead. A woman brought two rolls of sago. It was warm, gummy and dry and slightly nutty, hard to get down. I took the photos out of my knapsack, and somehow the word went out. Men, women, and children streamed in from all directions. *Crack!* There were so many crowding into the house that the floor broke, shifted, dropped three inches under me. "Sorry! So sorry!" I said.

"*Tidak apa apa!*" Petrus said, laughing, pulling me away. "Never mind!"

We went outside, and a hundred people clustered around, the pages flying away in a sea of hands and pressing bodies. An old man edged in and was fixated on one of the photos of the bisj poles, tracing his fingers over them. "He carved that pole," someone said.

"You carved that?" I said.

He looked at me. It was crazy. There was so much jostling, so many people, I could barely stand my ground. I tried to stay close to him, tried to keep track of the photos so I wouldn't lose them. I pushed closer to him. It wasn't an ideal time, but I had to ask.

"Which pole did you carve? Who was it for?"

He looked at me again. Caught my eyes for the briefest moment. Turned, pushed through, walked away, and disappeared. I couldn't follow him—everyone had the photos and I was caught in the bodies.

There was that wall again, that doorway that wouldn't open, that I couldn't get through, still. I just couldn't believe that the men, especially the old ones, could know so much, could so readily identify men and jeus in fifty-year-old photos—even men from Omadesep, a different village—and know nothing about the bisj poles themselves. But whatever they knew, they wouldn't say. None of them.

OTHER PIECES WERE falling into place. As we sat smoking, my chest feeling like I'd soon need a lung transplant, I asked Kokai and Ber about the men killed by Lapré. I wanted to know exactly who they were, what their positions in the village had been, and how they'd been related to the men named as having taken body parts of Michael. Their answers were remarkable. Foretsjbai had been kepala perang of Kajerpis. Osom was kepala perang of Otsjanep. Akon the kepala perang of Bakyer, and Samut the kepala perang of Jisar. Of the five people Lapré had shot, four had been the most important men in the village, the heads of four out of the five jeus. Either he'd targeted them or they had been out front, the most visible and perhaps threatening—to him at least. He had killed, in effect, the president, the vice president, the speaker of the house, and the president pro tempore of the Senate. It was hard for me to fathom how the village must have felt. Many of the strongest,

most able warriors of one of the strongest, most traditional villages in all of Asmat, killed in an instant. By an outsider no less.

And the men who had taken their places? Fin replaced Osom as the head of the Otsjanep jeu. Ajim and Pep replaced Akon; Kokai said (and Amates later agreed) that it wasn't uncommon for two men to hold the position if both were powerful. Not only that, but Pep had married Osom's widow. Sauer, the kepala perang of Jisar, who I sat next to nearly every day, had replaced Samut. And Jane, one of the men named by van Kessel as having one of Michael's tibia? He was married to Samut's sister, and Samut had been married to Jane's sister. Dombai was already kepala perang of Pirien, the only jeu from which Lapré had killed no one—and the jeu that van Kessel and von Peij reported had been against Michael's killing.

Not every death could be avenged, not every death could have a full bisj ceremony. A bisj required months of feasting and carving, during which the carvers could not hunt or go into the jungle to collect sago. To support a bisj festival required power, influence, the ability to organize men and inspire them and take leadership, and then, ultimately, to plan and lead an attack. The kepala perangs were the most powerful men in the village, and the men who took their places were related to them and would have had the power and the drive and charisma (tes) to respond. Even more, they had an obligation to do so; their whole standing as men desirable to women and as leaders who commanded the respect of others depended on it.

Yet they were rendered impotent by their inability to respond. It must have been a festering wound that wouldn't, couldn't heal. Even starker: in the six years before Michael arrived in Otsjanep, seventeen people had been murdered. Eight by the crocodile hunters, four by Omadesep, and five by Lapré. Michael had reported finding seventeen bisj poles in the jeus, seven of which he'd "bought" and only three of which had been delivered. Perhaps one of those three had

been satisfied by the killing of Sanpai in September 1961, a partial revenge against Lapré by taking one of the men from Atsj who'd accompanied him. Taken together with the political and sacred positions of the men killed by Lapré and their relationship to the men at the mouth of the Ewta the morning Michael swam to shore, the motive for Michael's killing felt increasingly solid.

Early the next morning a man named John dropped in for a visit. I'd met him on my second night in Pirien, and he seemed different from the others in the village. The Asmat asked me nothing about who I was or what America was like other than how long I was staying and whether I would return. But in the darkness on Kokai's front porch, John had peppered me with questions: What city I was from. Whether it was night in America right now. What the weather was like. What I did for work. All the normal questions that people, anywhere in the world, always asked. And then he'd asked me the strangest thing of all, for an Asmat: would I like to come over to his house for dinner the next evening?

Which I'd done, and everything about it was different from everything else in Pirien. He lived in a claptrap wooden frame house that sat alone in the no-man's-land between Otsjanep and Pirien. It was spotless inside, as was his outhouse. A few photos hung on the walls; a longboat with an outboard engine floated in the creek out front. His wife greeted me openly, with a big smile, and he lined up his three children and they looked me in the eye and shook my hand. They cuddled the puppies tumbling around the house instead of kicking them. For dinner, John's wife served eggs and green vegetables, grown in a garden behind the house. They had a pig in a wooden pen on the side porch. I could easily understand John's Indonesian. And craziest of all, John had a generator the size of a car engine that powered not only a few electric lightbulbs but a TV hooked up to a satellite dish.

The explanation turned out to be simple: John and his wife weren't Asmat. They were Bofun Digul people, and John's father

had come to Pirien as the catechist in the early 1970s. John had been born in Pirien, had grown up there, but the contrast between him and the other villagers was shocking. Every few weeks he worked for a logging company, which brought him astounding riches (relative to everyone else in the village), and without fifty family members surrounding him, whatever he earned stayed with him. He watched the BBC and CNN; he ate vegetables; he acted curious. I often dropped in at his house to chat.

This morning he and Kokai and I were talking, and somehow I asked Kokai about the first time he'd seen white people. His response was strange, something about "tourists."

"No," I said, "long before tourists—maybe the first pastor or policeman who came here long ago, when you were a boy."

He and John started speaking quickly to each other, and I couldn't keep up. I heard the words "tourist" and "Pep" and "Dombai," the word "*mati*"—dead—and then "Rockefeller." I froze. I was sure Kokai was telling the story of Michael Rockefeller. Finally! I didn't want to interject, to tell him to slow down, I was afraid he might clam up. He was speaking more to John than to me, and I just wanted it to roll out. Kokai pantomimed shooting an arrow, and I heard the word "*polisi*," and he was talking about helicopters coming in and people running into the jungle to hide—Kokai in his dynamic storytelling was a boy hiding behind a tree, the jungle, peering out into the sky in fear. Not for the first time I imagined how frightening and otherworldly those throbbing, powerful machines in the sky must have seemed. Without missing a beat, he segued into the next part of the story, an event that I knew about but had never connected before to Michael. From the helicopter and hiding in the jungle, Kokai talked about the cholera epidemic that swept through all of Asmat and hit Otsjanep particularly hard. "Dead, dead," Kokai said, repeatedly placing one hand over the other, a demonstration of the bodies piling up on top of each other. "So many dead. *Bensin*," the Indonesian word for gasoline.

It was true. When cholera hit Asmat in October and November 1962, a year after Michael's disappearance, the dead of Otsjanep were still laid out to decompose on raised platforms in the center of the village. Only when the flesh was gone could the skull be removed from the body to be preserved and decorated and made an object of veneration. It's hard to imagine the smell, the flies, the gruesomeness of a single body rotting openly in the tropical sun, and cholera was killing dozens. If so many bodies rotting in the village wasn't awful in itself, being near dozens of rotting cholera victims was suicidal. Cholera produces violent and unstoppable diarrhea, and victims essentially starve to death. Van de Wouw's photos are heartrending—men, women, children who were nothing but skin and bones, lying naked and ashen, hooked to jury-rigged IV bottles. By early November 1962, more than seventy men, women, and children were dead in Otsjanep, rotting on platforms. "Now and then you could see dogs walking around with parts of a foot or hand which—after sufficient rotting—fell off the platforms," wrote van de Wouw. "Some of the corpses were more or less entirely eaten by dogs that were able to climb on the platforms via stumps and shrubs. Because more and more people died, the corpse platforms had become very slovenly." Van de Wouw's description of what happened next is worth quoting in its entirety.

"On November the tenth Gabriel gave a remarkable explanation to all the kepala kampongs. He truly is a gifted speaker. He spoke for at least a half hour and explained to the people that the corpses were sources of new infections and that it was difficult to bury them with such high water. What to do? He left it to the kepalas to come up with a solution. When they weren't able to find a way out, he came up with a proposition from 'the mighty doctor who lives under the surface of the water.'

"After the kepalas had agreed, all the involved family members were called. It appeared there were two families in which the man, wife and children had died. Furthermore there was a single man

whose wife and two children had passed away. It was intensely sad to see how devastated this man was.

"In the meanwhile jerry cans with petroleum had arrived from Basiem [*sic*]. It was agreed upon that the involved family members would take care of sufficient firewood under each platform for to-morrow.

"When Sunday November the tenth came, I had to do the most exceptional Sunday mass I ever served and will ever serve. While I carried out the holy ceremony, the folks of the village were search-ing for firewood. This firewood was put under the platforms of the dead. Starting at the back of the village, I ploughed through the mud. But as it turned out the people were scared to death. Compared to their veneration of the dead, this treatment of their deceased was very cruel. It was sufficiently made clear though that only under these exceptional circumstances this could be done and that it was not going to happen again.

"The male family members were gathered near the corpse plat-forms and before the petroleum was poured over the corpses, it was asked again if they agreed to this. Every time I was the one who then personally set it on fire. And at every new death plat-form it was asked again if the family agreed.

"As soon as the firewood was burning well, the rattan that tied the corpse down was chopped loose and the platform and the corpse descended into the fire.

"It took the entire day—because of the mud behind the houses—to discover and burn all the corpse platforms. At the end of the ceremony, the catechists tried to come closer wearing a handkerchief over their noses and mouth. But when they came close, they immediately turned around and went back. The vil-lagers repeatedly made remarks about how strong my stomach had to be. I knew better, but this had to be done so I had to go through with it. When all the platforms were burned and a hor-rible disgusting smoke and smell was hanging over the village, I

jumped into the river as fast as I could, after an enormous yell.

"The catechist repeatedly told me during that day that the villagers wanted to kill me. But soon after everything was done it turned out this wasn't true. In fact, they came to give me arrows, bows, rocks, axes etcetera, because they were convinced that the disease was expelled from Otanep [*sic*] forever now."

It was a huge moment in Otsjanep's history, a sad and tragic blow, not just the deaths of so many men, women, and children, but the burning of their ancestors. Kokai had moved from one story into the next as if they were part of the same event, and it hit me: what if the cholera had been seen as the spirits' punishment for killing Michael Rockefeller? Even more significant, Australian army helicopters had been dispatched to aid in the cholera fight, which meant that the only two times the Asmat had ever seen helicopters were within days of Michael's death and as more death, faster than they'd ever experienced, swept through their villages.

That evening I went to talk to John. I asked him to tell me what Kokai had told him. He seemed nervous and told me that Kokai had merely told the same old story—that Michael had come to the village, had left, was returning when his boat capsized and he swam away and disappeared, and then cholera came. The names Pep and Dombai, the shooting of the arrow—he wouldn't explain. "They are afraid," he said.

I WAS FINALLY beginning to be convinced, especially because of the positions of the men killed by Lapré and their relation to the men van Kessel and von Peij named as having killed Michael. I'd been all along the coast and had never seen a shark or crocodile; the crocs were inland, not along the ocean shore, and certainly not out at sea. Sharks were in deeper water; I'd never heard a single story of a human being attacked by one in Asmat, and their presence was so minimal they rarely figured in Asmat carvings. Sanday's idea that Michael might have made it close to shore only to be attacked

by a shark or crocodile, within sight of the men from Otsjanep gathered there, didn't make sense. And if he'd been killed at sea, his body would have drifted and been blown farther south, not come straight inland.

If he'd made it to shore, he would have met the men from Otsjanep—they were there and that was fact. Max Lapré's raid had killed the most important men in the village, spread across four out of five jeus, which meant that nearly every person in the village was related to the men killed—even more so Pep, Fin, and Ajim, who had taken over the dead men's leadership positions. Bisj poles had been carved, a lot of them, and they were still sitting in the jeus when Michael arrived, which meant that the ceremonies had not been completed. And though he had bought and ultimately even taken delivery of some of them, other poles had failed to appear.

As for Bishop Sowada's point that "it seems quite improbable at this early stage in their development that the Asmat people would wish to kill, and further, possess the courage to kill a white man," well, that was condescension at its worst, I was finally realizing. It was the height of Western conceit. It limited the Asmat, made them less than human, relegated them to a people incapable of operating outside of their normal cultural boundaries, as if remote tribal societies could only follow the script of their myths and didn't possess the creativity or passion to ever deviate from them.

I had been living with Kokai now, watching the men in the village drum and sing and dance and tell stories, for almost a month, I had traveled with Amates and Wilem, and I had seen human beings. Individuals. If most of them danced the same dance, there was one man who flapped his hands and danced on one foot. If every elder danced and drummed and sang in celebration of the new jeu, Kokai sang alone to himself, enveloped in sadness for those he'd lost.

It all rolled over me. Human beings follow no script. Human

history is the story of people breaking away from patterns and doing things that aren't traditional, that no one else has ever done. Sailing across the ocean to the New World. Sailing across the Pacific to new islands. Falling in love with someone from the wrong tribe, the wrong caste. White Englishmen throwing on Arab *dishdashas* to unite disparate tribes of Bedouin. Black men having the gall to run for president. There is always someone doing something different, breaking the pattern—in this case, killing a white man. The fascinating stories aren't the ones about people following patterns, but about people doing the unpredictable. How can you ever explain men who snap and murder their wives and children? Jealousy. Anger. Rage. Love. Sadness. Envy. Curiosity. Pride. People love and yet do violent, even savage things; we humans are all savages at different times and in different ways. The Asmat are the strangest people I've ever seen, their secrets deep, their cultural boundaries seemingly rigid. But they are men, and I saw those elemental human feelings in every one of them, feelings that were the stuff of literature and poetry, not logic and reason.

Whoever had embedded that spear in Michael Rockefeller—Pep, Fin, Ajim—had done so because he could. Because he was a man. A warrior. Because Michael was probably the first white man he'd ever encountered who was powerless, perhaps the least powerful man in all of Asmat when he'd completed his epic swim. Exhausted. Unarmed. With no family, no connections to his world. And he knew Michael wasn't a spirit, but a man just like them. He was conquered. Consumed. In taking Michael's life, he had confirmed his own, had triumphed over death in a fragile world, where at any moment anyone could be felled by an enemy or fatally injured by a cut from a bad ax swing, and he affirmed life no differently than any Indy car driver or mountain climber who feels more alive the closer he comes to death.

To kill is to claim, own, take. Killing is rage and passion. A

man kills his wife not because he hates her but because he loves her so much he hates her. The serial killer preying on women takes what he wants the most and can't have: love, nurturing. The Asmat that day killed Michael Rockefeller out of passion and love, love for what they had lost and were losing—Ipi, Foretsjbai, Samut, Akon, and Osom, their culture and traditions, head-hunting—as modernity and Christianity closed in from every direction. The killing fit tightly and seamlessly into Asmat cultural logic. It helped to send the souls of their jeu leaders on to Safan. It righted an imbalance in their cosmic world. They took a man's power, became him, and perhaps thought that since he was white they might acquire a power they didn't have in the world of white men. But it went beyond that, to something more elementally human: an effort to avenge their own impotence against the intrusion of the West. In that, the killing probably did fit some of Sanday's nativistic theory—it was an attempt to reclaim power in the flash of a moment. An assertion of pride.

In the end, however, the killing only hastened the change hurtling toward them. For the Asmat of Otsjanep, driving that spear into Michael was catastrophic. It was the end of one life, the beginning of another. It unleashed planes, ships, helicopters, policemen, and more technology and power than they'd ever seen in their lives. The spirits retaliated, and almost 10 percent of the village died of cholera. Moreover, that epidemic ended hundreds, perhaps thousands, of years of funerary practices. It increased the role of van de Wouw and accelerated the end of headhunting and cannibalism and the introduction of Christianity and its shame. Soon after, Indonesia took over, sending government representatives to every village, where they burned every men's house and forbade all feasting and carving for a decade.

In 1964 tensions in Otsjanep reached a crescendo when Dombai was cuckolded—the story I'd heard on my first visit to Pirien now had a context—and the jeus went to war with each other. On

December 4, Ajim was shot by an arrow and died a few days later. Pep, who most claimed had driven the spear into Michael Rockefeller, demanded the shooter's nine-year-old sister so he could kill her and balance the conflict. The priests intervened, but the two sides of the village fought for a month. Father van de Wouw wanted to arrest Pep. "Somebody has to interfere," he wrote in his diary. "I can keep threatening, but if nothing happens, we will not be able to keep this under control." And it seemed increasingly likely that a disagreement had arisen that day at the mouth of the Ewta between Dombai, the head of Pirien, and Pep, Fin, and Ajim of Otsjanep about the wisdom of killing Michael. If so, the cholera epidemic must have ratified the fear of Dombai and those close to him, which would have profoundly exacerbated the tensions between the jeus.

Six years after Father van de Wouw's involvement in the cholera epidemic, in September 1968, it was finally time for him to leave Asmat and return to Holland. After six years of deep intimacy with the place and its people, he'd become convinced about Michael's fate. "Although the two sides of the villages are not yet back together," he wrote his superior, "they are now close to each other. I only build temporary houses for the catechist and the school in hopes that after a year or so Pirajin [*sic*] will go back to the former place. During my last visit to Otsjanep I once again brought up Rockefeller. It is difficult to interrogate the Asmat, especially because the enmity between the two halves of the village is quite strong and it is possible that the one side blames the other. However, it is clear that [he] came to the shore alive."

In the end, that village split had never healed, and Otsjanep and Pirien were connected by a no-man's-land that still stood today—where only John, an outsider, lived.

The craziest, weirdest thing about all of it was that Michael had photographed so many elements important to his own murder. He had shot Faniptas, whose trip to Wagin would start the

chain of events that led to Lapré's killing of Otsjanep's jeu leaders. He'd shot the bisj poles that would be carved as a result of that raid and that promised and foretold what would ultimately be his own murder. And he'd shot the men who would do it.

ALTHOUGH MOST OF the celebrating had been taking place in Jisar, Pirien and Jisar were two parts of a whole, and Pirien had to celebrate too. I spent a whole day in Ber's house, which served as Pirien's jeu, and sat, my legs aching, as Ber and Bif (Pirien's kepala perang) and the other men drummed and sang and sang and drummed, from the early morning until an hour or so before sunset, the day punctuated only by smoking breaks and drum-tuning over the open fire, which filled the room with smoke, and lunch, when women streamed in bringing logs of sago mixed with the larvae of the Capricorn beetle, baked in long tubes of palm leaves. This was sacred food, and the sago worm was synonymous with the human brain. "Take a photo, take a photo!" they yelled when the women started to arrive. They lined the logs up in the center of the circle, then broke into drumming and singing and hooting. Then pulled chunks off for every man, Ber feeding me, a mark of honor. Sago was dry and tasteless, as was all food in Asmat, but biting into the chunks of larvae released hot squirts of flavor and fat. It tasted like buttery, liquid pistachios, like explosions of bacon and ice cream after nothing but sago and rice and ramen and small fish for weeks.

After we'd eaten, Marco, a man I guessed to be in his late sixties or early seventies, began telling a story in the Asmat language. Everyone listened, some lying down and even falling asleep. I lay down too, noticing a soot-blackened rattan bag at the top of Ber's roof, round, covered in cobwebs, like it was holding a ball. *A skull?* I wondered. Although I couldn't understand the words, and the story wasn't for me, I watched the drama unfold as dogs scraped around in the swamp below the house. There was the firing of arrows, the powerful side-arm stabbing of someone with a spear. I

heard the words Otsjanep and Dombai. Marco walked. Stalked. Stabbed again. Pulled his pants legs up tight, thrust his hips forward, not like he was having sex, but as if he were peeing or having his penis sucked. Men grunted. Nodded. "Uh! Uh!" Finally, an hour into it, I picked up my camera and switched it to video and began filming. But the theatrics were over; he just talked and talked, and after eight minutes, running low on power with no way to recharge, I stopped.

Although I didn't know it yet, it was perhaps my most important moment in Asmat.

They broke just before sunset, then resumed outside on the boardwalk at eight p.m. The moon was only a sliver; it was so dark I couldn't see my feet, but a fire burned on a bed of mud on the boardwalk and cigarettes glowed and vast numbers of stars cut the blackness overhead, the Milky Way thick, heat lightning rolling across the horizon. At first there were five or six drummers and a handful of men, but a voice called into the darkness, booming, echoing, half song, half call, and soon a hundred had gathered. The drums cut through the night, and the deep, chanting songs called forth the spirits—Kokai had told me they were a "bridge" to their ancestors, and the men of Pirien rocked the boardwalk. Spirits were here, swirling around us in the dark. I couldn't see them, but they were here, as surely as the mosquitoes and lizards and crickets, filling the night. The air reverberated. The men, their deep voices, the beat of the drums, their imaginations and the images that appeared to them, were as much a part of the jungle as the insects and the lightning and the moist air and the trees and the river a few yards away. It was all gathered in one consciousness; you couldn't separate any of it out. The drums and voices knitted it all into a wholeness, a wholeness that stretched back years, generations, maybe centuries and even millennia. And I couldn't help it: I imagined Michael's spirit among them, swirling overhead in the jungle night, threading through the palms, the stars, a ghost

who was finally free now that I was understanding the mystery of his disappearance.

Around midnight, women began streaming in, bearing huge bowls of rice, piles of pale yams, sago, even two bowls of green vegetables. The men divided them into five piles, one for each section of Pirien, and ate. Bif placed a pile by me. "For Kokai," he said. It was a huge moment of respect and acceptance. I was Kokai's representative.

Their stamina was amazing. Without alcohol or drugs, they went on and on, and around three I finally collapsed, climbing over and around the sleeping bodies of women and children when I got to Kokai's house and falling fast asleep to the rhythmic voices echoing through the darkness and over the swamp.

I HAD BEEN in Pirien a month, and Wilem was set to arrive anytime. It felt strange to be leaving. Time had passed so slowly at first, but then it had stopped existing at all. The days had passed into a blur of heat and rain and smoke and sameness, the river rising and falling and always flowing by. Ber popped in for a visit, and over my last coffee and smoke I looked at him and Kokai and said: "Why are the men in Otsjanep so afraid to talk about killing Michael Rockefeller?"

Kokai looked at me, his eyes dark, his face as expressionless as a face could be. Ber shook his head. "We don't know anything about that," said Kokai. "There is a story in Asmat that Michael Rockefeller died at the Kali Jawor and all the Asmat people say that he was speared by Fin and Pep, but I don't know anything about it." That's all he would say. Ber too.

We were staring at each other when the sound of an engine cut the silence. Bouvier, Kokai's son-in-law, burst in. "Wilem is here!"

The intimacy that I'd slowly built over the last month evaporated into chaos. Wilem leapt off the boat, along with Amates, who'd just arrived back in Agats as Wilem was preparing to fetch

me. Villagers swarmed from every direction, crowding into Kokai's house, filling the porch, leaning in the door and window. They'd left at five a.m. and battled high waves and wind while crossing the mouth of the Betsj, where Michael and Wassing had floundered. "I was so scared!" said Amates. "I kept yelling, 'Wilem, we must go into shore!' Just last week, a boat broke right there, and seventeen men and women and children died. Only one man lived."

"We have to wait an hour," Wilem said. "For the wind to die down. Then we must go."

Kokai's wife brought out sago, and we ate and talked and laughed, surrounded by bodies. Then Kokai said, "We must go to Jisar. You must give money to the jeu."

I grabbed 300,000 rupiah, about $30, and Kokai and I and Wilem and Amates, trailed by a throng, walked through the morning sunlight to Jisar. Sauer, the kepala perang, and a half-dozen other men were there, the fires smoldering. It was the first time, as far as I knew, that Kokai had been to the jeu. Sauer stood, and I handed him the bills. The men broke into song, a powerful chant, punctuated with grunts and shrieks. Sauer said that I was welcome to come back anytime. I spoke as eloquently as I could in Indonesian, thanking them for a warm welcome, for always making me feel at home, for letting me share sago with them, and apologizing that my Indonesian was so bad. They chanted again, and Amates said, "They are saying a prayer for you, Mister Carl, so that you will travel safely on the sea."

We shook hands, leathery and warm, and I took my last breaths of the jeu, always rich with the smell of bodies and smoke and grass.

We walked back to Kokai's, and it all happened so quickly I couldn't slow it down. Men grabbed my bags and threw them in the boat, and Wilem jumped in after. "Photo," I yelled. "Of the family!" Kokai and his brood stood like statues in the hot sun

while Amates snapped a few pics of us, and then Kokai took my hand, said, "Adik" (younger brother), rubbed my hand along his hot, scratchy cheeks, and turned away. The last time I'd left Pirien I had been feeling frightened, relieved to escape, under the inscrutable glare of wooden faces. This time everyone was yelling and screaming and calling good-bye and waving as Wilem drifted into the current, gunned the engine, and took me away.

I was feeling overwhelmed, sad to be leaving, elated to be heading for a bed and toilet and hot shower and as many green vegetables as I could eat. I still had so many questions—more all the time, really, the more I learned. The children exchanged between Omadesep and Otsjanep. More specifics about the split between Otsjanep and Pirien, and its role in Michael's death. Whether Sauer, the kepala perang of Jisar, who had replaced his father, Samut, after Lapré's raid, had been present at the killing. But I could turn over rocks forever, and once again I was out of time. I'd already overstayed my visa.

As we sped toward the sea, I pictured Kokai sitting on his mat, singing in a voice that might have been issuing from the depths of the earth, rocking back and forth as the river flowed past. The world had been one way when Michael Rockefeller came to Asmat, another by the time he was dead. Kokai spanned both worlds, had lived in both, though I couldn't help but feel that he wasn't quite fully in either. And I wondered. That very morning, which itself already seemed like another era, I had been sitting with Ber and Kokai, the son of Dombai and the son of Fom, both named as having been present at Michael's murder by van Kessel, and both were kepala desas, patriarchs, leaders, repositories of I couldn't imagine how many songs and stories and memories—the whole history of Pirien and Otsjanep. Both men had fed me sago, had brought me into their homes and their lives, had sung songs for me. Would they really lie about what had happened to Michael? Did they really know nothing? If their fathers had done it, why not just admit

it and tell it to me? Could they, after so much time, look me in the eye and pretend they knew nothing, remembered nothing?

BACK IN AGATS, I showed Amates the eight minutes of video I'd shot of Marco during the drumming and singing in Ber's house. What I filmed after he told the story was a stern warning to the men gathered around him:

"Don't you tell this story to any other man or any other village, because this story is only for us," said Marco. *"Don't speak. Don't speak and tell the story. I hope you remember it and you must keep this for us. I hope, I hope, this is for you and you only. Don't talk to anyone, forever, to other people or another village. If people question you, don't answer. Don't talk to them, because this story is only for you. If you tell it to them, you'll die. I am afraid you will die. You'll be dead, your people will be dead, if you tell this story. You keep this story in your house, to yourself, I hope, forever. Forever. I hope and I hope. If any man comes and has questions for you, don't you talk, don't talk. Today. Tomorrow and for every day, you must keep this story.*

"Even for a stone ax or a necklace of dogs' teeth, do not ever share this story."

ACKNOWLEDGMENTS

Savage Harvest wouldn't exist without Erik Thijssen. The letters, cables, telexes, reports, journals, diaries, tide tables, and other information from archives in the Netherlands are its foundation, and Erik, my researcher in Amsterdam, unearthed it all. Over nearly two years, he doggedly poked his nose everywhere, made telephone calls, found documents and translated them, and even interviewed several people for me. Without him, I would never have found two of the most important sources for the story, Hubertus von Peij and Wim van der Waal, not to mention Cornelius van Kessel's widow, Mieke van Kessel, and others. Not only that, but he put me up on his sofa in Amsterdam. I can never thank him enough.

A huge thank-you to my friends who spent long hours reading early copies of the manuscript: Keith Bellows, Christian D'Andrea, Iwonka Swenson, Scott Wallace, Spencer Wells, and Clif Wiens. Their suggestions and comments made the book stronger in every way, and I'm equally thankful for their counsel, laughter, and friendship, which I could never have survived without.

Iwonka Swenson also deserves an extra thanks for everything.

A special thanks to Liz Lynch for her friendship and photos.

I owe a huge debt to Peggy Sanday. Her questions, doubts, insights, experience, patience, and wise counsel were incredibly

important to my thinking and perception of the Asmat, Asmat cannibalism and cosmology, and its intersection with Michael Rockefeller. Even better, she became a friend, and I appreciate her deeply.

My second trip to Asmat was profoundly important, and I never would have been able to afford the journey without the generous support of so many people who contributed to my Kickstarter campaign, specifically: James Angell, Tim Buzza, Juli Hodgson, Diane Hoffman, and Alida Latham. And there never would have been a Kickstarter campaign without Kris Arnold, who spent hours filming and editing the all-important video, not to mention providing good friendship.

A huge thanks to Uppy Zein Yudhistira for teaching me Bahasa Indonesian, letting me pay her what I could, and spending so many hours and afternoons patiently working with me. My stay in Pirien would never have been possible without Uppy's help.

Everyone needs a veteran sea captain to pester with questions, which I did to David Erickson, who never failed to answer my queries and whom I have to thank for the distance-to-horizon tables and a host of answers to questions about tides and currents.

I owe a huge debt to Jennifer Larson at the Metropolitan Museum of Art's Visual Resource Archive in the Department of the Arts of Africa, Oceania, and the Americas. Thanks to her and the Met, I have Michael's field notes, letters, accounts, photos, and a host of other details.

A thanks to Alain Bourgeoise, who granted me access to the papers of his father, Robert Goldwater, at the Smithsonian Archives of American Art.

A huge thanks to Amy Fitch, archivist at the Rockefeller Archive Center in Sleepy Hollow, New York.

Incalculable help was provided by Wim van de Waal, who did more than just tell me his story. He patiently answered my many, many questions over dozens of emails, showed me photos, confirmed facts and spellings, and told me to look for certain docu-

ments and a host of other details that only someone who was there would know about. It's hard to imagine trying to write this book without him.

Thank you to Jasper van Santen, who translated René Wassing's lengthy report from his first journey to Asmat with Michael Rockefeller, and to Tanya McCown for her help with the papers of Eliot Elisofon in Austin, Texas.

My children, Lily, Max, and Charlotte, are inspirations every day, and now they even pick me up at the airport. I love you and thank you. Thanks to my sister Jean for her unfailing support, and to my mom, who doesn't like it when I go away.

Where would I be without my agents Joe Regal and Markus Hoffmann? Joe's encouragement and insight and friendship, all above and beyond the business wizardry he and Markus do, have been a huge part of my career for more than a decade now. A special thanks to Joe's edits, which were hard to find time for but which tightened the book immensely. I owe Joe and Markus and everyone at Regal Literary a huge thank-you.

Every writer should have an editor and supporter as smart and enthusiastic as Lynn Grady. She always made me feel in good hands. Thanks, too, to everyone else at Morrow, especially Sharyn Rosenblum and Kimberly Liu.

Thanks to Terry Ward and Chris Jackson for their warm hospitality in Bali, to Carla van de Kieft for hospitality in Amsterdam, and to Daniel Lautenslager for his translations.

I owe big thank-yous to Tim Sohn for sharing his thoughts about travel in Asmat, and to Blair Hickman for her web services.

Thanks to Leticia Franchi.

And thank you to everyone in Asmat who helped me, put up with my questions, kept me safe and fed, in particular: Amates, Wilem, Kokai, Harun, Ber, Sauer, and Bif.

A NOTE ON SOURCES

This is a work of nonfiction. Anything between quotation marks was taken from documents or letters or was told to me by an eye-witness in an interview. I spent almost two years researching the story and made two trips lasting a total of four months to Asmat, Indonesian Papua, including living for a month in the village of Pirien in the house of a key Asmat informant. In a few cases I have used my most informed guess to reconstruct a scene, based on my close observations and experiences in the exact spot where the original events took place or on anthropological and ethno-graphic reports documenting Asmat cultural practices. Complete information on sources is in the notes.

NOTES

1. NOVEMBER 19, 1961

3 *It was eight a.m.:* Netherlands naval communication, November 22, 1961, National Archive of the Netherlands, Ministry of Education, Culture, and Science, The Hague, Netherlands.

3 *The tide was high:* Tide tables for Dutch New Guinea (Getijuen Stroomtafels voor Nederlands New Guinea), 1961, Hydrographisch Bureau, Archief Dienst der Hydrografie, Koninklijke Marine, Ministerie van Defensie, The Hague, Netherlands.

3 *white cotton underpants:* Author's interview with Hubertus von Peij, Tilburg, Netherlands, December 2011. Also, Wassing's description of Michael removing his pants and shoes prior to making the swim is detailed, among other places, in Mary Rockefeller Morgan, *Beginning with the End* (New York: Vantage Point, 2012), p. 24.

3 *He had two empty gasoline cans:* Netherlands naval communication, November 22, 1961, National Archive of the Netherlands.

3 *a hazy line of gray:* René Wassing is widely quoted as saying he estimated they were three miles off the coast, but that seems too close, given the time they'd been drifting and the position where the catamaran was found that afternoon. What does seem certain is that they could see the shore, at least faintly; otherwise, Wassing would never have made the three-mile statement and Michael would never have swum away from the vessel, since he wouldn't have known which way to swim. The coast is low and flat, and trees onshore are no more than fifty feet tall. Based on distance-to-horizon tables, that would put them no more than nine and a half miles from the coast.

4 *the tides weren't evenly spaced:* Tide tables for Dutch New Guinea.

4 *he would speed along the Maine Turnpike:* Milt Machlin, *The Search for Michael Rockefeller* (New York: Akadine Press, 2000), p. 154; Morgan, *Beginning with the End,* p. 221.

5 *"Stewardship" was the word:* Morgan, *Beginning with the End,* p. 223.

5 *he and his Harvard classmates had rolled their eyes:* Author's interview with Paul D'Andrea, Harvard class of 1960, February 2013.

5 *Luckily the wind:* Author's interview with former Dutch patrol officer Wim van de Waal, who was at sea that night looking for Michael Rockefeller, Tenerife, Canary Islands, Spain, December 2011.

5 *Heat lightning flashed:* During the four months I spent in Asmat, if it wasn't raining, lightning flashed along the horizon every night.

6 *the sky lit, white:* Author's telephone interview with Rudolf Idzerda, the pilot who dropped the flares, January 2012. Also described by Ben van Oers, who saw the flares from the shore; see *HN* magazine (December 1996), National Archive of the Netherlands.

2. NOVEMBER 20, 1961

7 *They saw him:* Report of Cornelius van Kessel to Herman Tillemans, January 23, 1962, archives of the Order of the Sacred Heart (OSC), Dutch Heritage Monastery Life Center (Erfgoedcentrum Nederlands Kloosterleven), AR-P027, archive inventory of the Missionaries of the Sacred Heart (Archiefinventaris Missionarissen van het H. Hart), St. Agatha, Netherlands (hereafter "OSC Archives").

7 *It was six a.m.:* This is a reasonable, approximate time. Van de Waal saw them leave Pirimapun for the trip back to Otsjanep on the evening of November 19; every report and account of Michael's death—including van Kessel, report to Tillemans, January 23, 1962, OSC Archives; Hubertus von Peij, report to Tillemans, December 1961, OSC Archives; and author's interview with Beatus Usain, Agats, Papua, March 2012—places the men from Otsjanep at the mouth of the Ewta in the morning. According to the Dutch tide tables of 1961, high tide was at eight a.m., so the men would have wanted to be paddling the three miles upriver before the outflowing tide turned against them.

7 *"Look, an ew!":* Author's interview with Hubertus von Peij, Tilburg, Netherlands, December 2011; author's interview with Beatus Usain, Agats, Papua, March 2012; Cornelius van Kessel's letter to Cor Nijoff, December 15, 1961, and his report to Tillemans, January 23, 1962, both in the OSC Archives.

7 *The men reached:* Ibid.

8 *Michael was swimming:* Ibid.

8 *"No," said Fin:* Ibid.

9 *"Now is your chance":* Ibid.

9 *Ajim was the head:* Author's interview with Kosmos Kokai, Pirien Village,
 Papua, March 2013; see also van Kessel, report to Tillemans, January 23,
 1962, OSC Archives.

9 *He had killed more people:* Van Kessel, report to Tillemans, January 23,
 1962; see also Kees van Kessel, "My Stay and Personal Experiences in
 Asmat: A Historical Review" (unpublished memoir), 1970.

9 *He howled and arched his back:* Author's interview with Beatus Usain, Agats,
 Papua, March 2012; my observations of many Asmat telling stories about
 men being speared.

9 *A few miles south:* Author's interview with Hubertus von Peij, Tilburg,
 Netherlands, December 2011; van Kessel, report to Tillemans, January 23,
 1962, OSC Archives.

10 *The cockatoos ate fruit:* The detailed descriptions of Asmat headhunting
 and cannibalism come from Gerard Zegwaard, "Headhunting Practices
 of the Asmat of Netherlands New Guinea," *American Anthropologist* 61,
 no. 6 (December 1959): 1020–41. Other good sources include Tobias
 Schneebaum, *Where the Spirits Dwell* (New York: Grove Press, 1988);
 The Asmat of New Guinea: The Journal of Michael Clark Rockefeller, edited,
 with an introduction, by Adrian A. Gerbrands (New York: Museum of
 Primitive Art, 1967), pp. 11–39.

10 *"This is my head!":* Zegwaard, "Headhunting Practices of the Asmat
 of Netherlands New Guinea." We'll never know exactly how Michael
 Rockefeller was killed, but if he was killed by Asmat, they would have
 followed the sacred traditions laid out by Zegwaard, on whose account the
 remainder of this chapter is based.

3. FEBRUARY 2012

17 *As for sharks, despite their fearsome reputation:* Author's interview with
 George H. Burgess, Coordinator of Museum Operations and Director,
 Florida Program for Shark Research and International Shark Attack File,
 Florida Museum of Natural History, Gainesville, FL, August 2012. See
 also the International Shark Attack File's website, which maintains the
 best statistics on shark attacks: http://www.flmnh.ufl.edu/fish/sharks/
 attacks/perspect.htm.

18 *maintained a gravesite:* Morgan, *Beginning with the End,* p. 62.

18 *His twin sister, Mary:* Mary Rockefeller Morgan's book *Beginning with the
 End* is about her efforts to heal from the loss of her twin brother.

19 *At night, to me, it was dark and locked tight:* Author's interview with Father
 Vince Cole, Agats, Papua, March 2012.

4. FEBRUARY 20, 1957

22 *Temperatures in New York City: Farmers' Almanac,* weather history results for
 New York, NY, February 20, 1961, www.farmersalmanac.com.

22 *black tie:* Copy of original invitation, Robert John Goldwater Papers, Archives of American Art, Smithsonian Institution, Washington, DC.

23 *John D. was the richest man on earth:* Joseph Persico, *The Imperial Rockefeller: A Biography of Nelson A. Rockefeller* (New York: Washington Square Press/ Pocket Books, 1983), p. 10.

23 *Down East patrician drawl:* "Rocky as a Collector," *New York Times,* May 18, 1969.

23 *"exuded an exuberant self-assurance":* Persico, *The Imperial Rockefeller,* p. 2.

23 *"Not a social arrogance":* Ibid., p. 3.

23 *guests began arriving at 8:30 p.m.:* Original invitation, Goldwater Papers, Smithsonian Institution.

23 *which one critic said was "so tasteful":* "The Fetish and the Water Buffalo," *The Reporter,* May 2, 1957.

23 *There was Rene d'Harnoncourt:* Guest list, Mr. and Mrs. Nelson A. Rockefeller, February 20, 1957, Rockefeller Archive Center, NAR Personal Papers, project series, folders 1642 and 1664, Sleepy Hollow, NY.

23 *Henry Luce, who founded* Time *and* Life *magazines:* Ibid.

23 *Henry Ochs Sulzberger:* Ibid.

24 *A carved paddle from Easter Island:* Museum of Primitive Art, *Selected Works from the Collection* (catalog), Spring 1957, Department of the Arts of Africa, Oceania, and the Americas, Visual Resource Archive, Metropolitan Museum of Art, New York (hereafter "MMA Archives").

24 *atop stark white cylinders and cubes:* Photos in the collection of the MMA Archives.

24 *As the guests nibbled on canapés:* Esquire (July 1957).

24 *"It is our purpose to supplement their achievement":* Museum of Primitive Art, press release, February 20, 1957, MMA Archives.

25 *one of those cabinets in 1599:* Shelly Errington, *The Death of Authentic Primitive Art and Other Tales of Progress* (Berkeley: University of California Press, 1998), p. 9.

25 *Every seed, leaf, and plant collected:* Ibid., p. 12.

25 *the collection of Sir Hans Sloane:* Ibid.

26 *His father, John D. Rockefeller Jr., loved porcelain:* Suzanne Loebl, *America's Medicis: The Rockefellers and Their Astonishing Cultural Legacy* (New York: HarperCollins, 2010), p. 8.

26 *"If you start to cultivate your taste and eye so young":* "Rocky as a Collector," *New York Times,* May 18, 1969.

26 *In 1930 Nelson and his new bride:* Persico, *The Imperial Rockefeller,* pp. 18–19.

26 *"widely varying expressions of individuals":* Loebl, *America's Medicis,* p. 310.

27 *"had the ambience of a museum after hours":* Persico, *The Imperial Rockefeller,* p. 2.

27 *"Everywhere," wrote Carl Sandburg:* Sally Price, *Primitive Art in Civilized Places,* 2nd ed. (Chicago: University of Chicago Press, 1989), p. 26.

28 *"Far more striking than any common denominator":* "Month in Review," *Arts* (May 1957): 42–45.

29 *"The ancestor's spirit lives in the shield":* Tobias Schneebaum, *Where the Spirits Dwell: An Odyssey in the Jungle of New Guinea* (New York: Grove Press, 1989), p. 52.

29 *Nelson himself told an interviewer:* Kathleen Bickford Berzock and Christa Clarke, eds., *Representing Africa in American Art Museums* (Seattle: University of Washington Press, 2011), p. 125.

30 *It's hard not to wonder if:* Nelson Rockefeller, letter to Robert Goldwater, Goldwater Papers, Smithsonian Institution.

5. DECEMBER 1957

31 *Pip, Dombai, Su:* Author's interview with Kosmos Kokai, Basim, Papua, February 2012.

32 *Moving south with them were 118 other men:* Various accounts of this journey can be found in many places. It first appears in Max Lapré's patrol report of February 17, 1958, to the governor of Netherlands New Guinea, "Patrol Report Otsjanep, re: the headhunting on Omadesep Ultimo December 1957," at the National Archive of the Netherlands. Additional details are available in "Oral History Project Collection: Memories of the East: The Lapré Interview," tape-recorded interview with Max Lapré, 116.2a (track 11–) and 116.2b (tracks 1–2), August 1997, Koninklijk Instituut voor Taal, Land- en Volkenkunde (KITLV), Royal Netherlands Institute of Southeast Asian and Caribbean Studies, Leiden, Netherlands. See also van Kessel, report to Tillemans, January 23, 1962; and van Kessel's unpublished journals, all in OSC Archives. The story is well remembered in Asmat today, and additional details come from interviews with Kosmos Kokai, Basim and Pirien, Papua, February 2012, and with Everisus Birojipts, Omadesep Village, Papua, February 2012.

33 "Seabird coming": These are traditional Asmat songs sung while canoeing, provided by Kosmos Kokai and Amates Owun, translated by Owun.

35 *David Eyde believed that all Asmat warfare:* David Bruener Eyde, "Cultural Correlates of Warfare Among the Asmat of South-West New Guinea" (PhD dissertation), Yale University, 1967, p. 304.

35 *In a study of cannibalism:* Peggy Reeves Sanday, *Divine Hunger: Cannibalism as a Cultural System* (Cambridge: Cambridge University Press, 1986), p. 15.

35 *Desoipitsj was older and unable to hunt:* Zegwaard, "Headhunting Practices of the Asmat of Netherlands New Guinea." All of the story in the following paragraphs comes from Zegwaard's article.

38 *In parts of Asmat, men had sex with each other:* The amount of homosexual
 contact between men in Asmat has been controversial, in part because it
 was hidden from Catholic priests and government officials until a gay man,
 Tobias Schneebaum, first wrote deeply about it. Though some claim that
 Schneebaum overemphasized its prevalence and role, I tend to side with
 Schneebaum. For more, see Schneebaum, *Where the Spirits Dwell: An Odyssey
 in the Jungle of New Guinea* (New York: Grove Press, 1989), and *Secret Places:
 My Life in New York and New Guinea* (Madison: University of Wisconsin
 Press, 2000); and Bruce M. Knauft, *South Coast New Guinea Cultures: History,
 Comparison, Dialectic* (Cambridge: Cambridge University Press, 1993).

38 *they sometimes drank each other's urine:* Story told by a group of men in Pirien
 Village, February 2012, translated by Amates Owun.

38 *acts of deep intimacy and submission:* Cornelius van Kessel, "A Few Notes
 About the Casuarinen Coast" (unpublished), OSC Archives.

39 *"monsters and hell creatures":* Kirkpatrick Sale, *The Conquest of Paradise:
 Christopher Columbus and the Columbian Legacy* (New York: Knopf, 1990),
 pp. 76–78.

39 *Pip and his jeu mates weren't savages:* Jared Diamond, *Guns, Germs, and Steel:
 The Fates of Human Societies* (New York: Norton, 1999), pp. 38–40.

39 *They knew that a red sunset:* Zegwaard, "Headhunting Practices of the
 Asmat of Netherlands New Guinea," p. 1038.

40 *That was, after all, how they had come to be:* Adrian A. Gerbrands, ed., *The
 Asmat of New Guinea: The Journal of Michael Clark Rockefeller* (New York:
 Museum of Primitive Art, 1967), p. 21.

40 *"There is a bird on the sea":* Traditional Asmat songs provided by Kosmos
 Kokai and Amates Owun, translated by Owun.

40 *bound for the village of Wagin:* Lapré, "Patrol Report Otsjanep, re: the
 headhunting on Omadesep Ultimo December 1957"; van Kessel, report
 to Tillemans, January 23, 1962; van Kessel's unpublished journals.
 Additional details come from author's interviews with Kosmos Kokai,
 Basim and Pirien Village, Papua, February 2012; and with Everisus
 Birojipts, Omadesep Village, Papua, February 2012.

40 *but they had been lured into a trap:* Author's interview with Kosmos Kokai,
 Pirien Village, Papua, February 2012; also described in van Kessel, report
 to Tillemans, January 23, 1962.

41 *"Hello, my brothers and sisters":* Author's interview with Kosmos Kokai,
 Pirien Village, Papua, February 2012.

41 *"There are many dogs' teeth in Wagin":* Ibid.; also author's interview with
 Everisus Birojipts, Omadesep Village, Papua, February 2012.

41 *This particular doorway had a guardian:* Author's interviews with Kosmos
 Kokai, Basim and Pirien Village, Papua, February 2012; and with Everisus
 Birojipts, Omadesep Village, Papua, February 2012.

41 *Faniptas and his mates from the jeu Desep:* Ibid.

6. FEBRUARY 2012

44 *Francis Chichester, who, passing Cape Horn:* Sir Francis Chichester, *Gipsy Moth Circles the World* (New York: Coward-McCann, 1968), pp. 179–80.

7. DECEMBER 1957

55 *The warriors stayed well offshore:* Author's interview with Everisus Birojipts, Omadesep Village, Papua, February 2012. This story has many variants. Birojipts said that 500 men in fifty canoes had gone to Wagin and stayed a year before returning, and that 250 men had been slaughtered, but that doesn't make sense; the Asmat also tend to exaggerate dates and numbers. The contemporaneous reports of Lapré and van Kessel say 124 men, so I've gone with that.

56 *In the driving, chill rain, Emene:* Ibid.

56 *One man from Omadesep died and four from Emene:* Ibid.

56 *In the morning they found their canoes destroyed:* Ibid.

56 *In Baiyun six died, three from Omadesep:* Ibid.

56 *Pip took a steel ax blow to his abdomen:* Ibid.

56 *"Father," he said, staring at the dead man:* Ibid.

56 *"No, he's dead," said Birojipts's father:* Ibid.

56 *He wasn't dead:* Ibid.; author's interview with Kosmos Kokai, Basim and Pirien Village, Papua, February 2012.

56 *At the Ewta, Pip encountered his kinsmen:* Ibid.

57 *they drummed and sang:* Ibid.

57 *Two hundred men in twenty canoes:* Ibid.

57 *The Portuguese touched the island in 1526:* Gavin Souter, *New Guinea: The Last Unknown* (Sydney, Australia: Angus and Robertson, 1963), p. 18.

57 *In 1595 the Netherlands sent an expedition:* Howard Palfrey Jones, *The Possible Dream* (New York: Harcourt Brace Jovanovich, 1971), p. 27.

58 *the southwest coast even more so:* Knauft, *South Coast New Guinea Cultures,* p. 26.

58 *When Jan Carstenz landed in 1623:* Souter, *New Guinea,* p. 7.

58 *"Their Arms were ordinary darts":* Gerbrands, ed., *The Asmat: The Journal of Michael Clark Rockefeller,* p. 83.

58 *When that first contact was over:* Schneebaum, *Where the Spirits Dwell,* pp. 59–60.

58 *In 1902, under pressure from British authorities:* Knauft, *South Coast New Guinea Cultures,* p. 33.

59 *The Japanese briefly established a post:* Gerard Zegwaard, "1953 Data on the Asmat People," in *An Asmat Sketchbook No. 6,* edited by Frank Trenkenschuh (Hastings, NE.: Asmat Museum of Culture and Progress, 1977), pp. 20–21; van Kessel, "My Stay and Personal Experiences in Asmat," OSC Archives, p. 2.

59 *Raids could happen at any time:* Van Kessel, "My Stay and Personal Experiences in Asmat"; see also Zegwaard, "1953 Data on the Asmat People"; Eyde, "Cultural Correlates of Warfare Among the Asmat of South-West New Guinea."

60 *Far preferable were sudden ambushes:* Zegwaard, "Headhunting Practices of the Asmat of Netherlands New Guinea."

60 *Even among warring villages:* Ibid.

60 *Village ambushes were associated with ceremonies:* Ibid.

60 *For the Asmat, ancestors are involved:* Ibid.; van Kessel, "My Stay and Personal Experiences in Asmat"; Schneebaum, *Where the Spirits Dwell.*

61 *To the west lies Safan:* Ibid.

61 *Raids usually took place just before dawn:* Zegwaard, "Headhunting Practices of the Asmat of Netherlands New Guinea."

62 *ten canoes of a hundred Asmat came ashore:* Frank A. Trenkenschuh, ed., *An Asmat Sketchbook Nos. 1 and 2* (Hastings, NE.: Asmat Museum of Culture and Progress, 1982), p. 26.

62 *By 1947, the raiding and warfare in Asmat:* Zegwaard, "1953 Data on the Asmat People."

63 *"There is a tendency to minimize":* Ibid.

64 *In the village of Sjuru in 1947 and 1948:* Ibid.

65 *Anything outside of that tangible immediacy:* Van Kessel, "A Few Notes About the Casuarinen Coast."

65 *Upon a death in the village, women rolled:* Schneebaum, *Where the Spirits Dwell,* p. 45.

65 *An airplane was* opndettaji: Van Kessel, "A Few Notes About the Casuarinen Coast."

66 *Yet they also carried out* papisj: Trenkenschuh, ed., *An Asmat Sketchbook Nos. 1 and 2,* p. 22.

66 *He had a deep wanderlust:* Interview by author's researcher Erik Thijssen with Mieke van Kessel, widow of Cornelius van Kessel, Leeuwarden, Netherlands, October 2012.

66 *"The mission had no motorized vessel":* Van Kessel, "My Stay and Personal Experiences in Asmat," p. 7.

66 *"In each village I left":* Ibid.

67 *He was deeply pious:* Erik Thijssen, interview with Mieke van Kessel, Leeuwarden, Netherlands, October 2012.

67 *He believed unequivocally in heaven:* Ibid.

67 *He loved cigars:* Ibid.

67 *He didn't think religion could:* Ibid.

67 *He was reprimanded for not baptizing:* Ibid.; see also "Subject: Behavior Father Van Kessel," letter 13/54, National Archive of the Netherlands.

68 *In October 1953, a group of Chinese:* Van Kessel, report to Tillemans, January 23, 1962.

68 *"I could have mown them down":* Ibid.

68 *"We were welcomed most heartily":* Ibid.

68 *"The village became wildly enthusiastic":* Ibid.

68 *In September 1956, Omadesep killed another four:* Ibid.

69 *Van Kessel traveled to Amborep:* Van Kessel, "My Stay and Personal Experiences in Asmat," p. 10.

69 *In the village of Ajam, in May:* Ibid.

69 *Van Kessel kept a list of the violence:* Ibid., pp. 97–99.

69 *Von Peij, too, had heard the calling early:* Author's interview with Hubertus von Peij, Tilburg, Netherlands, December 2011.

70 *"So, I leave":* Ibid.

70 *And so, on that day toward the end of 1957:* Ibid.

71 *As the last stragglers from Omadesep:* Author's interview with Everisus Birojipts, Omadesep Village, Papua, February 2012; author's interview with Kosmos Kokai, Basim and Pirien Village, Papua, February 2012; van Kessel, report to Tillemans, January 23, 1962.

71 *Van Kessel called it the Sylvester Massacre:* Van Kessel, "My Stay and Personal Experiences in Asmat," p. 24.

9. FEBRUARY 1958

76 *On February 6, 1958:* Lapré, "Patrol Report Otsjanep, re: the headhunting on Omadesep Ultimo December 1957."

76 *Accompanying him were eleven Papuan policemen:* Ibid.

77 *Mauser M98 bolt-action rifles:* Author's interview with Wim van de Waal, Tenerife, Canary Islands, Spain, December 2011.

77 *Lapré felt afraid:* Van Kessel, report to Tillemans, January 23, 1962.

77 *three canoes of warriors from Atsj:* Lapré, "Patrol Report Otsjanep, re: the headhunting on Omadesep Ultimo December 1957."

77 *he was determined to teach the natives a lesson:* "Oral History Project Collection: Memories of the East: The Lapré Interview."

77 *Max Lapré's relatives had been:* Ibid.

77 *His father was a soldier:* Ibid.

77 *When he was three, the family moved:* Ibid.

77 *"There was this Japanese store":* Ibid.

78 *"You go teach them a lesson":* Ibid.

79 *He would say in later interviews that he didn't:* Ibid.

79 *After meeting him, van Kessel lamented:* Van Kessel, "My Stay and Personal Experiences in Asmat," p. 19.

79 *Soon after Lapré arrived in Asmat:* Ibid.

79 *an action that van Kessel called "unproportionate":* Ibid., p. 20.

79 *Dias and a force descended on Omadesep:* Lapré, "Patrol Report Otsjanep, re: the headhunting on Omadesep Ultimo December 1957."

79 *Otsjanep wanted nothing to do:* Ibid.

80 *"Maybe they saw it as an opportunity to smack":* "Oral History Project Collection: Memories of the East: The Lapré Interview."

80 *Lapré would say:* Ibid.

80 *"They are the best people in the world":* Sale, *The Conquest of Paradise,* p. 100.

81 *The violent savages' response:* Tobias Schneebaum, *Keep the River on Your Right* (New York: Grove Press, 1970), pp. 65–69.

81 *used to reading footprints:* Edward L. Schieffelin and Robert Crittenden, *Like People You See in a Dream: First Contact in Six Papuan Societies* (Stanford, CA: Stanford University Press, 1991), p. 79.

82 *"We jumped with surprise":* Ibid., p. 73.

82 *They screeched and "bawled":* Lapré, "Patrol Report Otsjanep, re: the headhunting on Omadesep Ultimo December 1957."

82 *On the sixth of February, he dispatched:* Ibid.

83 *Lapré grabbed the tiller himself:* "Oral History Project Collection: Memories of the East: The Lapré Interview."

83 *The villagers, men and women, were:* Lapré, "Patrol Report Otsjanep, re: the headhunting on Omadesep Ultimo December 1957."

84 *On the left a group approached:* Ibid.

84 *An Asmat named Faratsjam was hit in the head:* The details of the shooting of Faratsjam and the other men in Otsjanep come from the author's interview with Kosmos Kokai, Basim Village, Papua, February 2012.

84 *"Stop shooting!" Lapré yelled:* "Oral History Project Collection: Memories of the East: The Lapré Interview."

85 *Lapré's explanation to van Kessel:* Van Kessel, report to Tillemans, January 23, 1962; see also van Kessel, "My Stay and Personal Experiences in Asmat," p. 92.

85 *Lapré spent the night offshore:* Lapré, "Patrol Report Otsjanep, re: the headhunting on Omadesep Ultimo December 1957."

85 *Lapré had left five dead:* Author interview with Kosmos Kokai, Basim Village, Papua, February 2012. Lapré's reports variously list three and four killed; van Kessel mentions four. The men in Pirien/Otsjanep today have clear memories that four men and one woman, Ipi, were killed, and another man wounded.

85 *When he visited Otsjanep three months later:* Lapré, "Patrol Report Otsjanep, re: the headhunting on Omadesep Ultimo December 1957."

10. MARCH 1958

87 *Cameras flashed:* Jones, *The Possible Dream,* p. 70.

88 *"Prince and pauper, patrician and coolie":* Ibid., p. 57.

88 *Sukarno emphasized Indonesia's:* Ibid.

89 *For the Dutch, keeping its Papuan colony:* Arend Lijphard, *The Trauma of Decolonization* (New Haven, CT: Yale University Press, 1966), pp. 39–48.

89 *Percy Spender, Australia's minister for external affairs:* "Australia's Attitude on
 West New Guinea Unalterable: Spender," *Canberra Times,* November 26,
 1954; Bilveer Singh, *Papua: Geopolitics and the Quest for Nationhood*
 (Piscataway, NJ: Transaction Publishers, 2008), pp. 65–67.

89 *winning 27 percent of the votes cast:* Jones, *The Possible Dream,* p. 73.

90 *"New Guinea had been the abandoned child":* Author's interview with Wim
 van de Waal, Tenerife, Canary Islands, Spain, December 2011.

90 *Jones's words to Sukarno notwithstanding:* Ibid., p. 70.

90 *"It is essential for the Netherlands to see to it":* John Saltford, *The United
 Nations and the Indonesian Takeover of West Papua, 1962–1969: The Anatomy
 of Betrayal* (London: Routledge, 2006), p. 10.

91 *The Dutch foreign minister, Joseph Luns:* Ibid., pp. 10–11.

91 *Returning West New Guinea to Sukarno:* Ibid.

11. MARCH 1961

95 *"I'm finally in New Guinea":* Michael Rockefeller, letter to Samuel Putnam,
 March 29, 1961, MMA Archives.

96 *Heider had arrived the day before:* Author's interview with Karl Heider,
 Columbia, SC, June 2011.

96 *Michael perched in the cockpit:* Michael Rockefeller, letter to Samuel Putnam,
 March 29, 1961, MMA Archives.

96 *Michael scrambled into his seat:* Ibid.

96 *As Abby had done with Nelson:* "Rocky as a Collector," *New York Times,* May
 18, 1969.

96 *when he was eleven:* Morgan, *Beginning with the End,* p. 215.

97 *By the time he was nearing the end:* Author's telephone interview with Betsy
 Warriner, then girlfriend and later the wife of Samuel Putnam, June 2011.

97 *to have a big adventure:* Ibid.

97 *Gardner ran the Harvard Film Study Center:* Robert Gardner, *Making Dead
 Birds: Chronicle of a Film* (Cambridge, MA: Peabody Museum Press, 2007).

98 *In 1959 he'd begun casting about for the right project:* Ibid., p. 7.

98 *Gardner contacted Victor de Bruyn:* Ibid., p. 8.

98 *De Bruyn suggested a film about the Dani tribes:* Ibid., pp. 12–19.

99 *The United States and the Soviet Union:* Author's interview with Jan
 Broekhuijse, Nieuwkoop, Netherlands, December 2011.

99 *like most observers fascinated with indigenous people:* Gardner, *Making Dead
 Birds,* pp. x–xv.

99 *At lunch one afternoon on Martha's Vineyard:* Author's telephone interview
 with Peter Matthiessen, November 2011.

99 *on the steps of the Peabody Museum:* Author's interview with Karl Heider,
 Columbia, SC, June 2011.

99 *Michael plunged in, learning everything:* Gardner, *Making Dead Birds,* p. 25.

100 *"My first reaction was one of terror":* Ibid., p. 33.

100 *"At least my typing will get a good practicing":* Ibid.

100 *"I have received all sorts of useful pointers":* Ibid., p. 34.

100 *"I can assure you that he knows":* Ibid., 35.

100 *"The flight in was spectacular":* Michael Rockefeller, letter to Samuel Putnam, April 2, 1961, MMA Archives.

101 *A few days later they brought hundreds:* Ibid.

101 *a strong first impression:* Outtakes from interview with Peter Matthiessen for *The Seekers of the Lost Treasure* (Discovery Channel, 1994).

101 *as beautiful as Michael described it:* In March 2012, I spent nearly a week in the Baliem Valley, where elderly Dani tribesmen who met and remembered their encounters with the Peabody expedition showed me the locations where Gardner and his team had worked.

101 *The team shared civilized meals:* Author's interview with Karl Heider, Columbia, SC, June 2011.

101 *Michael found them "emotionally expressive":* Michael Rockefeller, letter to Samuel Putnam, April 14, 1961, MMA Archives.

101 *"Polik, the warrior," he wrote:* Ibid.

102 *They were so close to the action that one day:* Author's interview with Karl Heider, Columbia, SC, June 2011.

102 *"They went to war with a set of rules":* Author's telephone interview with Peter Matthiessen, November 2011.

102 *He "shot wildly," he wrote:* Michael Rockefeller, letter to Samuel Putnam, April 14, 1961, MMA Archives.

102 *"Michael went away in tears":* Outtakes from interview with Peter Matthiessen for *The Seekers of the Lost Treasure* (Discovery Channel, 1994).

102 *"Mike was very quiet":* Author's interview with Karl Heider, Columbia, SC, June 2011.

102 *While Elisofon, the professional, would pose them:* Ibid.

102 *In the evenings Heider was astonished:* Ibid.

103 *"there is a large opportunity for me":* Michael Rockefeller, letter to Samuel Putnam, April 29, 1961, MMA Archives.

103 *"Michael's father had put him on the board":* Author's interview with Karl Heider, Columbia, SC, June 2011; see also minutes of Museum of Primitive Art's board meetings, MMA Archives.

104 *"Collecting along the Sepik":* Robert Goldwater, letter to Michael Rockefeller, May 5, 1961, MMA Archives.

104 *"looking forward to your coming up":* Ibid.

104 *The two linked up in the capital:* René Wassing, "Report from the Journey to the Asmat Region with the Gentleman M. Rockefeller," National Archive of the Netherlands.

105 *He'd finished high school late:* Author interview with Wim van de Waal, Tenerife, Canary Islands, Spain, December 2011.

105 *"Make contact":* Ibid.

105 *There wasn't much to do:* Ibid.

106 *As there would be for years to come: in 1970:* Trenkenschuh, ed., *An Asmat Sketchbook Nos. 1 and 2,* p. 37.

106 *and even in the early 1980s Schneebaum:* Schneebaum, *Where the Spirits Dwell,* p. 74.

106 *Still, van de Waal traveled undefended:* Author's interview with Wim van de Waal, Tenerife, Canary Islands, Spain, December 2011.

106 *their first encounter with Australian explorers:* Schieffelin and Crittenden, *Like People You See in a Dream,* p. 222.

107 *when Francisco Pizarro met the Inca emperor Atahualpa:* Diamond, *Guns, Germs, and Steel,* p. 68.

107 *When Englishman Charlie Savage arrived in Fiji:* Ibid., p. 76.

107 *an investigation of the Strickland-Purari patrol:* Schieffelin and Crittenden, *Like People You See in a Dream,* pp. 231–32.

108 *All of Asmat was based on reciprocation:* For Asmat culture and cosmology, see Schneebaum, *Where the Spirits Dwell;* Knauft, *South Coast New Guinea Cultures;* Zegwaard, "Headhunting Practices of the Asmat of Netherlands New Guinea"; Eyde, "Cultural Correlates of Warfare Among the Asmat of South-West New Guinea"; Trenkenschuh, ed., *An Asmat Sketchbook Nos. 1 and 2*; van Kessel, "My Stay and Personal Experiences in Asmat"; and Gerbrands, ed., *The Asmat: The Journal of Michael Clark Rockefeller.*

108 *Van de Waal showed Michael and Wassing around:* Author's interview with Wim van de Waal, Tenerife, Canary Islands, Spain, December 2011.

109 *Van Kessel, he wrote Goldwater a few days later:* Michael Rockefeller, letter (undated) to Robert Goldwater, MMA Archives.

109 *"There has been something mysterious about my arrival":* Michael Rockefeller, field notes, MMA Archives.

110 *But with the help of Gerbrands and Eyde:* Ibid.

111 *Michael was in ecstasy as hundreds of warriors:* Ibid.

111 *They left two days later at three p.m.:* Gerbrands, ed., *The Asmat: The Journal of Michael Clark Rockefeller,* p. 107.

111 *"First there was the quiet, leisurely departure":* Ibid.

111 *"I only wish I could have somehow recorded":* Ibid., p. 111.

112 *After seven hours, they arrived at a bivouac:* Wassing, "Report from the Journey to the Asmat Region," National Archive of the Netherlands.

112 *And when he asked to see carvings:* Michael Rockefeller, field notes, MMA Archives.

113 *"This was one kind of object that":* Ibid.

113 *Certain songs are so powerful:* Author's interview with Vince Cole, Agats, Papua, March 2012.

114 *"There is no magic involved and no offering":* Michael Rockefeller, field notes, MMA Archives.

114 *"an elusive personality":* Ibid.

115 *"This was an old, beautiful one of a kind":* Ibid.

116 *In the tangled knot of Asmat allegiances:* Ibid; Wassing, "Report from the Journey to the Asmat Region," National Archive of the Netherlands.

117 *he had given a daughter to Dombai:* Author's interview with Kosmos Kokai, Basim and Pirien Village, Papua, February 2012.

117 *"It was a marvelous paddle upstream":* Gerbrands, ed., *The Asmat: The Journal of Michael Clark Rockefeller,* p. 127.

117 *The river twisted and turned and narrowed:* Wassing, "Report from the Journey to the Asmat Region," National Archive of the Netherlands.

117 *Tatsji let out a long, melodious yell:* Ibid.

118 *"Now this is wild and somehow more remote country":* Gerbrands, ed., *The Asmat: The Journal of Michael Clark Rockefeller,* p. 128.

118 *Michael continued on in the morning:* Michael Rockefeller, field notes, MMA Archives.

118 *found seventeen bisj poles:* Ibid.; Gerbrands, ed., *The Asmat: The Journal of Michael Clark Rockefeller,* p. 141.

119 *Michael noted that the poles seemed to have been carved:* Michael Rockefeller, field notes, MMA Archives.

119 *In exchange for tobacco:* Wassing, "Report from the Journey to the Asmat Region," National Archive of the Netherlands.

119 *Michael gave them a partial down payment:* Ibid.; Gerbrands, ed., *The Asmat: The Journal of Michael Clark Rockefeller,* p. 142.

120 *"On our way to Biwar we had to cross":* Michael Rockefeller, field notes, MMA Archives.

120 *Three days later, they arrived at the rendezvous:* Ibid.; Gerbrands, ed., *The Asmat: The Journal of Michael Clark Rockefeller,* p. 142.

12. MARCH 2012

126 *Tobias Schneebaum romanticized the Amazonian:* Schneebaum, *Keep the River on Your Right,* pp. 100–110.

13. SEPTEMBER 1961

136 *"What time is it and where am I":* Gerbrands, ed., *The Asmat: The Journal of Michael Clark Rockefeller,* p. 44.

136 *"I think I can report with some confidence":* Michael Rockefeller, letter to Robert Goldwater, July 9, 1961, MMA Archives.

137 *"He arrived in Otsjanep and was immediately stabbed/shot":* Hubertus von Peij, letter to Herman Tillemans, February 3, 1962, OSC Archives.

138 *was "unique" for the United States:* Michael Rockefeller, letter to Robert Goldwater, July 9, 1961, MMA Archives.

138 *Goldwater wrote van Kessel:* Ibid.

138 *"Mr. Rockefeller is, as you know":* Robert Goldwater, letter to Cornelius van Kessel, July 27, 1961, MMA Archives.

138 *"for its lack of acculturation":* Michael Rockefeller, letter to Robert Goldwater, July 9, 1961, MMA Archives.

139 *Although Gaisseau was able to get the village:* Tony Saulnier, *The Headhunters of Papua* (New York: Crown, 1963), pp. 69–92.

139 *"with equally as talented sculptors":* Michael Rockefeller, letter to Cornelius van Kessel, June 10, 1961, MMA Archives.

139 *"I will not exclude Otsjanep":* Cornelius van Kessel, letter to Michael Rockefeller, August 1961, MMA Archives.

139 *"objectives; themes of investigation":* Michael C. Rockefeller, field notes, MMA Archives.

140 *After a few days in Hollandia:* Gerbrands, ed., *The Asmat: The Journal of Michael Clark Rockefeller,* p. 44.

140 *"The key to my fascination with the Asmat":* Ibid.

141 *"Nights here are really the most fun":* Ibid.

141 *There was a single government vessel:* Author's interview with Wim van de Waal, Tenerife, Canary Islands, Spain, December 2011.

141 *The catamaran was great on the rivers:* Ibid.

141 *"The sideboards were only ten":* Ibid.

142 *"He was stuck, flabbergasted":* Ibid.

142 *"I came in my own catamaran":* Ibid.

142 *"Will you sell it to me":* Ibid.

142 *He wanted to have a forty-five-horsepower outboard:* Ibid.

142 *At the local Chinese general store:* Accounts of M. C. Rockefeller, MMA Archives.

143 *"Both Rene Wassing and I":* Michael Rockefeller, letter to Cornelius van Kessel, October 7, 1961, MMA Archives.

143 *They made a quick swing south first:* Michael Rockefeller, field notes, MMA Archives.

144 *"The evening was crystal clear":* Ibid.

144 *"The Asmat has a special shout":* Gerbrands, ed., *The Asmat: The Journal of Michael Clark Rockefeller,* p. 45.

144 *Over the next three weeks, he and Wassing:* Ibid., p. 46.

144 *He made intricate drawings of designs:* Michael Rockefeller, field notes, MMA Archives.

144 *"The only difference between Mark Twain and us":* Gerbrands, ed., *The Asmat: The Journal of Michael Clark Rockefeller,* p. 46.

145 *"making use of the Sisters' major contribution":* Ibid.

145 *"The Asmat is like a huge puzzle":* Ibid.

147 *Father von Peij got wind that two boys:* Author's interview with Hubertus von Peij, Tilburg, Netherlands, December 2011.

148 *On Wednesday, November 15, at five p.m.:* Ibid.

148 *They sipped their tea and sat in chairs:* Ibid.

148 *"I'm leaving for Atsj on Friday"*: Ibid.
148 *"I have to go to Per first"*: Ibid.

15. NOVEMBER 1961

157 *The catamaran was fully loaded:* Interview with René Wassing, as recounted in Morgan, *Beginning with the End,* pp. 22–24; Accounts of M. C. Rockefeller, MMA Archives.

158 *They spent the night:* Author's interview with Hubertus von Peij, Tilburg, Netherlands, December 2011.

159 *Wassing took the throttle:* Morgan, *Beginning with the End,* p. 22.

159 *Wassing throttled back:* Ibid.

160 *If we get swept out to sea, no one will find us:* Ibid.

160 *They weren't afraid:* Ibid., pp. 22–24.

160 *Michael and Wassing gathered what they could:* Ibid.

160 *It wasn't long until a wave:* Ibid.

160 *They salvaged what they could:* Ibid.

160 *they reached Agats at ten-thirty p.m.:* Dutch Navy, telex to patrol ship *Snellius,* National Archive of the Netherlands.

160 *the radio was buzzing:* Dutch Navy, telex to Ministry of Foreign Affairs, November 20, 1961, National Archive of the Netherlands.

160 *Dutch authorities in Agats scrambled the government vessel:* Ibid.

161 *But the boat had been inspected the day before:* Author's interview with Hubertus von Peij, Tilburg, Netherlands, December 2011.

161 *And it had no operating radio:* Dutch Navy, telex to Ministry of Foreign Affairs, November 20, 1961, National Archive of the Netherlands.

161 *They pried a couple of boards:* Morgan, *Beginning with the End,* p. 23.

161 *Michael with the motor's empty fuel tank:* Ibid.

161 *Wassing thought they were three miles off the coast:* Reuters report, dossier 39666, Ministerie Van Binnenlandse Zaken, National Archive of the Netherlands.

161 *"Let's try to paddle again":* Morgan, *Beginning with the End,* p. 23.

162 *"If you can make it, I don't do it":* Ibid.

162 *Michael had the one fuel tank already strapped:* Ibid.

162 *It was eight a.m. on November 19:* Dutch Navy, telex to Ministry of Foreign Affairs, November 20, 1961, National Archive of the Netherlands.

162 *He was swimming against the outflowing tide:* Tide tables for Dutch New Guinea.

162 *"I think I can make it":* Reuters report, dossier 39666, Ministerie Van Binnenlandse Zaken, National Archive of the Netherlands; Morgan, *Beginning with the End,* p. 23.

162 *until he became a dim form, three dots:* Ibid.

16. NOVEMBER 1961

164 *So it was that, on the evening of November 18:* Van Kessel, report to Tillemans, January 23, 1962.

164 *Ajim, a short, powerfully built man:* Cornelius van Kessel, photo, OSC Archives.

164 *He wore six-inch-wide rattan bracelets:* Ibid.

164 *There were Fin and Pep and Dombai:* Van Kessel, report to Tillemans, January 23, 1962.

164 *They paddled down the Ewta at slack tide:* Tide tables for Dutch New Guinea.

165 *They made Pirimapun on the morning:* Author's interview with Hubertus von Peij, Tilburg, Netherlands, December 2011; author's interview with Wim van de Waal, Tenerife, Canary Islands, Spain, December 2011.

17. NOVEMBER 1961

166 *At nine a.m. on Sunday, November 19:* Dutch Navy, telex to Ministry of Foreign Affairs, November 20, 1961, National Archive of the Netherlands.

167 *If that wasn't bad enough, the very next day:* Singh, *Papua,* p. 77.

167 *the Dutch Royal Air Force kept a squadron:* Author's telephone interview with Rudolf Idzerda, January 2012.

167 *The plane was the first designed:* See Military Factory, "Lockheed P2V Neptune Land-Based Patrol Aircraft/VP Transport," available at: http://www.militaryfactory.com/aircraft/detail.asp?aircraft_id=514; and Wikipedia, "Lockheed P-2 Neptune," available at: http://en.wikipedia.org/wiki/Lockheed_P-2_Neptune.

167 *a range of four thousand miles:* Ibid.

167 *At thirty-eight, the former fighter pilot:* Author's telephone interview with Rudolf Idzerda, January 2012.

167 *Late on the morning of November 19:* Ibid.

167 *Von Peij, waiting for Michael:* Author's interview with Hubertus von Peij, Tilburg, Netherlands, December 2011.

167 *Farther down the coast:* Van Kessel, report to Tillemans, January 23, 1962.

167 *After three hours, Idzerda's navigator:* Author's telephone interview with Rudolf Idzerda, January 2012.

168 *René Wassing spotted the plane:* Author's interview with Wim van de Waal, Tenerife, Canary Islands, Spain, December 2011.

168 *As soon as Idzerda located the boat:* Author's telephone interview with Rudolf Idzerda, January 2012.

168 *van de Waal received a radio call:* Author's interview with Wim van de Waal, Tenerife, Canary Islands, Spain, December 2011.

168 *It was dark and the sea was quiet:* Ibid.

168 *He was asleep in the men's house:* Ben van Oers, *HN* magazine (December 1996), National Archive of the Netherlands.

168 *"Fire has fallen from the heavens":* Ibid.

168 *Wim van de Waal was in it:* Author's interview with Wim van de Waal, Tenerife, Canary Islands, Spain, December 2011; also confirmed by Dutch cables, National Archive of the Netherlands.

169 *"Mike is gone," Wassing said:* Author's interview with Wim van de Waal, Tenerife, Canary Islands, Spain, December 2011.

169 *And now he was there, in the family home:* Morgan, *Beginning with the End,* p. 4.

169 *"wary and watching":* Ibid.

169 *He held a yellow cablegram in his hands:* Ibid.

169 *Nelson received a radio telephone call from Hollandia:* "Rockefeller in Honolulu," *New York Times,* November 21, 1961.

169 *"I'm headed out there," he told reporters:* Ibid.

170 *"I am extremely sorry to hear about your son":* Ibid.

170 *chartered a Pan American Boeing 707:* "Rockefeller Search Joined by Natives," *New York Times,* November 25, 1961.

170 *"We found ourselves within a new group":* Morgan, *Beginning with the End,* p. 7.

18. NOVEMBER 1961

172 *"In connection with the enormous publicity":* Ministry of Foreign Affairs, Cable 7425 to Ministry of the Interior, Hollandia, November 21, 1961, National Archive of the Netherlands.

173 *"As a consequence of the tragic disappearance":* Ibid.

174 *On Monday, November 20, a Dutch DeHavilland Beaver:* The search is detailed in cables and telexes between government officials and military personnel in the Netherlands and New Guinea at the National Archive of the Netherlands in The Hague.

174 *A PBY Catalina flying boat was brought in from Lae:* Ministry of Foreign Affairs, Cable 7425 to Ministry of the Interior, Hollandia, November 21, 1961, National Archive of the Netherlands.

174 *Ken Dresser and missionary pilot Betty Greene:* "Explorer Sought in Crocodile-Infested Jungle," *New York Times,* November 22, 1961.

174 *The Dutch patrol boats* Tasman, Eendracht, *and* Snellius: Government cables, National Archive of the Netherlands.

174 *In Biak a Dutch marine tied gerry cans to his waist:* Ibid.

174 *As a test, the navy dropped gerry cans into the water:* Ibid.

174 *cabled that he was overwhelmed:* Ibid.

174 *Nelson and Mary paused briefly in Biak:* Ibid.

175 *"My daughter Mary and I are very satisfied":* "Gouverneur Rockefeller naar erauke vertrokken (2)" (press report summary), November 23, 1961, National Archive of the Netherlands.

175 *"a flat, ugly little settlement":* Peter Hastings, "The Press, the Press, the Awful Press," *The Bulletin,* December 23, 1961.

176 *"The story we had all arrived to report":* Ibid.

176 *"He was," remebered Broekhuijse:* Author's interview with Jan Broekhuijse, Nieuwkoop, Netherlands, December 2011.

176 *"For the first time in my life":* Morgan, *Beginning with the End,* p. 18.

176 *"The coastline here is dismal":* Letter from Eliot Elisofon (undated, recipient unknown), Eliot Elisofon Papers, Harry Ransom Center, University of Texas–Austin.

177 *René Wassing was trotted out:* Morgan, *Beginning with the End,* p. 19.

177 *"mirrored my own deep anxiety":* Ibid., p. 20.

177 *"I can provide patrol planes":* CINC American Pacific Fleet, Netherlands naval communications cable to CINC Netherlands Navy New Guinea, November 23, 1961, National Archive of the Netherlands.

177 *"I am considering your kind offer":* Admiral Netherlands New Guinea, Netherlands naval communications cable to CINC American Pacific Fleet, November 23, 1961, National Archive of the Netherlands.

177 *"The Indonesian minister of Foreign Affairs has suggested Friday":* Reuters, November 24, 1961, in collection of press clippings sent by the attaché for New Guinea affairs, Dutch embassy, Canberra, Australia, National Archive of the Netherlands.

178 *"After consultations with Governor Nelson Rockefeller":* COSTRING Netherlands naval communications cable to BDZ, November 24, 1961, National Archive of the Netherlands.

178 *officials in Hollandia had "abandoned all hope":* Associated Press, November 23, 1961, in collection of press clippings sent by the attaché for New Guinea affairs, Dutch embassy, Canberra, Austrailia, National Archive of the Netherlands.

178 *"There is no longer any hope of finding":* "Dutch Rejoin Navy Hunt," *New York Times,* November 24, 1961.

178 *"I'm a realist," the governor said:* "Rockefeller Hunt Joined by Natives," *New York Times,* November 25, 1961.

178 *"If Michael reached shore":* Ibid.

178 *"for having inspired so much loyalty and affection":* Ibid.

178 *"Rockefeller enthusiastic about rescue action":* Hollandia, telegram to Department of Interior, The Hague, November 25, 1961, National Archive of the Netherlands.

179 *two Australian army Bell 47 G2-A helicopters:* Captain Dick Knight, "The Search for Michael Rockefeller," *Fourays Journal* 1, no. 1 (March 1995), available at: http://beckerhelicopters.com/oscar/oscar-joins-the-army/Oscar-looks-for-rockefeller.html.

179 *ninety miles along the coast and six miles inland:* Ibid.

179 *"a torrid, hostile wilderness":* Ibid.

179 *a red Johnson gasoline can for an outboard engine:* Dutch naval communications to Ministry of Interior, National Archive of the Netherlands.

179 *The tank was shown to Wassing:* "Rockefeller Search Joined by Natives," *New York Times,* November 25, 1961.

179 *Nelson looking like he was at a country club:* Photos in OSC Archives.

179 *"Is this yours":* Author's interview with Wim van de Waal, Tenerife, Canary Islands, Spain, December 2011.

180 *They landed briefly in the Catalina:* Morgan, *Beginning with the End,* pp. 30–31.

19. NOVEMBER 1961

182 *First, sharks rarely attack humans:* Author's interview with George H. Burgess, Gainesville, FL, August 2012.

183 *Van Kessel immediately sent his assistant:* Van Kessel, report to Tillemans, January 23, 1962.

183 *Gabriel saw nothing out of the ordinary:* Ibid.

183 *Van Kessel followed him:* Ibid.

183 *Van Kessel linked up with the* Tasman: Ibid.

183 *Gabriel, meanwhile, spent the entire day:* Ibid.

184 *The villagers fled into the jungle:* Ibid.; author's interview with Kosmos Kokai, Basim and Pirien Village, Papua, February 2012.

184 *the village emptied at the sight:* Van Kessel, report to Tillemans, January 23, 1962; author's interview with Kosmos Kokai, Basim and Pirien Village, Papua, February 2012.

184 *They said they knew nothing of Michael:* Ibid.

184 *In Atsj, von Peij watched as ship after ship:* Author's interview with Hubertus von Peij, Tilburg, Netherlands, December 2011.

184 *In Atsj, von Peij waited a week to let:* Ibid.

185 *"There are some men who want to meet you":* Ibid.

185 *"Let them come," he said:* Ibid.

20. DECEMBER 1961

186 *van Kessel started hearing:* Van Kessel, report to Tillemans, January 23, 1962.

186 *van Kessel sent Gabriel back to Otsjanep:* Ibid.

187 *"We saw a fierce giant snake":* Ibid.

187 *But Bere went on a rampage:* Ibid.

187 *Van Kessel sent a canoe:* Ibid.

187 *"Men of Otsjanep," Gabriel told them:* Ibid.

187 *Pep had a new dagger:* Ibid.

187 *He "saw they were acting":* Ibid.

187 *Van Kessel wasn't sure:* Ibid.

188 *On December 9, von Peij arrived in Omadesep:* Author's interview with Hubertus von Peij, Tilburg, Netherlands, December 2011.

188 *He felt unsettled:* Ibid.

188 *in walked four men:* Ibid.

188 *They wore shorts:* Ibid.

188 *"Okay," von Peij said, "tell me your story":* Ibid.

188 *Bit by bit, it spilled out:* Ibid.

189 *"Was he wearing glasses":* Ibid.

189 *Their answer burned in his memory:* Ibid.

189 "Fin-tsjem aotepetsj ara": Ibid.

189 *"What about his thigh bones":* Ibid.

189 *Pep had one thigh bone, Ajim the other:* Van Kessel, report to Tillemans, January 23, 1962.

189 *The killings in Otsjanep almost four years earlier:* Author's interview with Hubertus von Peij, Tilburg, Netherlands, December 2011.

189 *Von Peij was overwhelmed:* Ibid.

189 "Nda kapak to": Ibid.

190 *Von Peij scratched a note:* Ibid.

190 *On December 12, van Kessel arrived in Agats:* Van Kessel, report to Tillemans, January 23, 1962.

190 *On December 15, back in Basim, van Kessel:* Ibid.

191 *Gabriel took the note that night to Nijoff:* Ibid.

191 *Five days later, on December 20, Ajim, Fin:* Ibid.

191 *"THEY DID NOT DENY THE MURDER," van Kessel wrote:* Ibid.

191 *"Resident Merauke {Eibrink Jansen} received through controller Agats":* Ministry of Foreign Affairs, Cable 7740 to Ministry of Internal Affairs, December 21, 1961, National Archive of the Netherlands.

22. JANUARY, FEBRUARY, AND MARCH 1962

206 *On December 20, 1961, one month after Michael disappeared:* P. J. Platteel, cable to Dutch embassy, Canberra, Australia, December 20, 1961, National Archive of the Netherlands.

207 *"The entire area has been extensively searched":* P. J. Platteel telegram to Nelson Rockefeller, December 21, 1961, National Archive of the Netherlands.

207 *"All of us in the family will be eternally grateful":* "New Guinea Dutch End Search for Rockefeller's Missing Son," *New York Times,* December 22, 1961.

207 *Van Kessel and von Peij named fifteen men:* Van Kessel, report to Tillemans, January 23, 1962.

208 *Van Kessel had been pushing for a trip home:* Herman Tillemans, letter to Cornelius van Kessel, December 27, 1961, OSC Archives.

209 *"From the Resident I got approval to see":* Ibid.

209 *"I wrote my bishop":* Author's interview with Hubertus von Peij, Tilburg, Netherlands, December 2011.

209 *"In the matter of Mr. M. Rockefeller":* Herman Tillemans, letter to Hubertus von Peij and Cornelius van Kessel, February 1, 1962, OSC Archives.

209 *"What is most puzzling to me," Sowada wrote:* Alphonse Sowada, letter to Herman Tillemans, February 22, 1962, OSC Archives.

210 *"I received your letter in relation to":* Hubertus von Peij, letter to Herman Tillemans, February 3, 1962, OSC Archives.

211 *"Everywhere it's assumed that":* Herman Tillemans, letter to F. R. J. Eibrink Jensen, February 14, 1962, OSC Archives.

211 *"I want to ask you to make clear to Father van Kessel":* Herman Tillemans, letter to the Provencial, February 25, 1962, OSC Archives.

211 *"I rely on you to forbid van Kessel":* Herman Tillemans, letter to the Provencial, February 28, 1961, OSC Archives.

212 *December 2011 report by the Dutch Conference of Bishops:* "Catholic Church Involved in Abuse of Dutch Children, Report Finds," *Los Angeles Times,* December 17, 2011.

212 *the most common punishment was a quiet transfer:* Ibid.

212 *On March 4, Father van de Wouw sent Gabriel:* Anton van de Wouw, letter to Herman Tillemans, March 4, 1962, OSC Archives.

212 *"Gab did not pick up anything in Ocenep":* Anton van de Wouw, letter to Herman Tillemans, March 23, 1962, OSC Archives.

212 *"If you get new information on the case of Rockefeller":* Herman Tillemans, letter to Anton van de Wouw, April 4, 1962, OSC Archives.

213 *a Dutch priest working in Asmat, W. Hekman:* "Zendeling Hekman: Rockefeller Jr. is opgegeten; Wraak tegen moorden van politie," *De Waarheid,* March 29, 1962.

213 *"Press reports from the Netherlands":* Dutch embassy in Washington, DC, cable to Ministry of Foreign Affairs, The Hague, March 27, 1962, National Archive of the Netherlands.

213 *"Similar rumors also circulated":* Ibid.

214 *Nevertheless, the denials did the trick:* "Rockefeller Not Eaten by Cannibals," *Canberra Times,* March 29, 1962.

214 *"It must have been strange for the people there":* Author's interview with Wim van de Waal, Tenerife, Canary Islands, Spain, December 2011.

215 *"The answer," van de Wouw wrote:* Anton van de Wouw, letter to Herman Tillemans, May 15, 1962, OSC Archives.

216 *Van de Wouw also reported that Otsjanep:* Ibid.

216 *"I needed proof, not just names":* Author's interview with Wim van de Waal, Tenerife, Canary Islands, Spain, December 2011.

216 *"He was very afraid":* Ibid.

23. NOVEMBER 2012

223 *latitude and longitude of where Wassing:* Dutch Navy, telexes, National
 Archive of the Netherlands.

224 *Gananath Obeyesekere called "cannibal talk":* Gananath Obeyesekere, *The
 Man-Eating Myth and Human Sacrifice in the South Seas* (Berkeley: University
 of California Press, 2005).

228 *In the most striking example:* Frank Trenkenschuh, "Cargo Cult in Asmat:
 Examples and Prospects," in Trenkenschuh, ed., *An Asmat Sketchbook Nos. 1
 and 2,* pp. 59–65.

228 *valued by insurance appraisers in August 1962:* Insurance of the Michael
 Rockefeller Asmat Collection, Museum of Primitive Art, MMA Archives.

228 *In 2012 the Met hosted six million visitors:* Metropolitan Museum of Art,
 "Metropolitan Museum Announces 6.26 Million Attendance," July 16,
 2012, available at: http://www.metmuseum.org/about-the-museum/press-
 room/news/2012/attendance.

229 *the lovely canoe that holds prominence in the Met:* Author's interview with
 Asmat Museum of Culture and Progress, Agats, Papua, December 2012.

229 *"to evoke in part the spirit of Asmat life":* Metropolitan Museum of Art, press
 release, September 11, 1962, MMA Archives.

229 *"When an Asmat warrior is slain by an enemy villager":* Ibid.

230 *who answered in June:* Anton van de Wouw, letter to Metropolitan Museum
 of Art, June 26, 1962, MMA Archives.

230 *a letter van Kessel himself wrote:* Cornelius van Kessel, letter to Robert
 Goldwater, July 3, 1974, MMA Archives.

230 *letters between Rockefeller's lawyers and the Netherlands:* Letters between
 Rockefeller attorneys at Milbank, Tweed, Hope and Hadley and the
 Dutch government, February 8, April 18, May 3, June 6, and July 6, 1962,
 National Archive of the Netherlands.

230 *valuing his estate:* "Rockefeller Son Ruled Dead; Estate Valued at
 $660,000," *New York Times,* February 2, 1964.

231 *"It would be of great assistance":* William Jackson of Milbank, Tweed, Hope
 and Hadley, letter to Dutch consul general in New York, February 8,
 1962, National Archive of the Netherlands.

232 *had explained his findings in a letter:* Machlin, *The Search for Michael
 Rockefeller,* p. 193.

232 *"When Mr. Whitlam remarked that the disappearance":* New York Times, May 8,
 1975.

232 *"I discovered something odd":* Frank Monte, *The Spying Game: My
 Extraordinary Life as a Private Investigator* (Sydney, Australia: Vapula Press,
 2003), p. 180.

233 *"Rumors and stories of Michael's having made it to shore":* Morgan, *Beginning
 with the End,* p. 36.

234 *"The family refuses to believe any version of the story":* Author's telephone interview with Peter Matthiessen, November 2011.

24. NOVEMBER 2012

249 *Pirien itself was divided into five:* Author's interview with Kosmos Kokai, Basim and Pirien Village, Papua, February 2012.

249 *Indonesian government officials burned all the jeus:* Frank Trenkenschuh, "Some Additional Notes on Zegwaard from a 1970 Vantage," in Trenkenschuh, ed., *An Asmat Sketchbook Nos. 1 and 2*, pp. 31–36.

250 *Father Jan Smit was shot to death:* Frank Trenkenschuh, "An Outline of Asmat History in Perspective," in Trenkenschuh, ed., *An Asmat Sketchbook Nos. 1 and 2*, p. 32.

250 *Only in the early 1970s did Indonesia begin softening:* Ibid., pp. 31–36.

252 *Fumeripitsj drummed the Asmat to life:* Gerbrands, ed., *The Asmat: The Journal of Michael Clark Rockefeller*, p. 21.

257 *"Throughout my life . . . I have been searching":* Schneebaum, *Secret Places*, p. 3.

25. DECEMBER 2012

260 "Kami is my love": Kosmos Kokai, song translated by Amates Owun.

261 "Bis is my wife": Ibid.

266 *Fin replaced Osom as the head of the Otsjanep jeu:* Author's interview with Kosmos Kokai, Basim and Pirien Village, Papua, February 2012.

269 *Van de Wouw's photos are heartrending:* OSC Archives.

269 *By early November 1962:* The journals of Anton van de Wouw, De Kasuarinenjust (1962–1969), OSC Archives.

269 *"Now and then you could see dogs":* Ibid.

271 *Australian army helicopters had been dispatched:* Ibid.; author's interview with Kosmos Kokai, Basim and Pirien Village, Papua, February 2012.

272 *who had taken over the dead men's leadership positions:* Author's interview with Kosmos Kokai, Basim and Pirien Village, Papua, February 2012.

274 *tensions in Otsjanep reached a crescendo:* Anton van de Wouw, De Kasuarinenjust (1962–1969), OSC Archives.

275 *Ajim was shot by an arrow:* Ibid.

275 *demanded the shooter's nine-year-old sister:* Ibid.

275 *"Somebody has to interfere," he wrote:* Ibid.

275 *"the two sides of the villages are not yet back together":* Ibid.

SELECT BIBLIOGRAPHY

Anderson, Warwick. *The Collectors of Lost Souls: Turning Kuru Scientists into White-men.* Baltimore, MD: Johns Hopkins University Press, 2008.

Arens, William. *The Man-Eating Myth: Anthropology and Anthrophagy.* Oxford: Oxford University Press, 1979.

Avramescu, Catalin. *An Intellectual History of Cannibalism.* Princeton, NJ: Princeton University Press, 2011.

Bickford Berzock, Kathleen, and Christa Clarke, eds. *Representing Africa in American Art Museums.* Seattle: University of Washington Press, 2011.

Chichester, Sir Francis. *Gipsy Moth Circles the World.* New York: Coward-McCann, 1968.

Cook, James. *The Journals of Captain Cook.* London: Penguin Books, 1999.

Diamond, Jared. *Guns, Germs, and Steel: The Fates of Human Societies.* New York: W. W. Norton, 1999.

Errington, Shelly. *The Death of Authentic Primitive Art and Other Tales of Progress.* Berkeley: University of California Press, 1998.

Eyde, David Bruener. "Cultural Correlates of Warfare Among the Asmat of South-West New Guinea." PhD diss., Yale University, 1967.

Flannery, Tim. *Throwim Way Leg: Tree-Kangaroos, Possums, and Penis Gourds—On the Track of Unknown Mammals in Wildest New Guinea.* New York: Atlantic Monthly Press, 1998.

Gardner, Robert. *Making Dead Birds: Chronicle of a Film.* Cambridge, MA: Peabody Museum Press, 2007.

Gerbrands, Adrian A., ed. *The Asmat of New Guinea: The Journal of Michael Clark Rockefeller.* New York: Museum of Primitive Art, 1967.

Girard, Rene. *Violence and the Sacred.* Baltimore, MD: Johns Hopkins University Press, 1977.

Goldman, Laurence R. *The Anthropology of Cannibalism*. Westport, CT: Bergin and Garvey, 1999.

Heider, Karl. *Grand Valley Dani: Peaceful Warriors*. Belmont, CA: Wadsworth Group, 1997.

Hemming, John. *Red Gold: The Conquest of the Brazilian Indians, 1500–1760*. Cambridge, MA: Harvard University Press, 1978.

Jones, Howard Palfrey. *The Possible Dream*. New York: Harcourt Brace Jovanovich, 1971.

Kapuscinski, Ryszard. *The Other*. London: Verso, 2008.

Knauft, Bruce M. *South Coast New Guinea Cultures: History, Comparison, Dialectic*. Cambridge: Cambridge University Press, 1993.

Leahy, Michael J. *Explorations into Highland New Guinea, 1930–1935*. Tuscaloosa: University of Alabama Press, 1991.

Lijphard, Arend. *The Trauma of Decolonization*. New Haven, CT: Yale University Press, 1966.

Loebl, Suzanne. *America's Medicis: The Rockefellers and Their Astonishing Cultural Legacy*. New York: HarperCollins, 2010.

Machlin, Milt. *The Search for Michael Rockefeller*. New York: Akadine Press, 2000.

Malinowski, Bronislaw. *A Diary in the Strict Sense of the Term*. Stanford, CA: Stanford University Press, 1967.

Matthiessen, Peter. *Under the Mountain Wall: A Chronicle of Two Seasons in Stone Age New Guinea*. New York: Penguin Books, 1996.

May, R. J. *Between Two Nations: The Indonesia–Papua New Guinea Border and West Papuan Nationalism*. Bathhurst, Australia: Robert Brown and Associates PTY Ltd., 1986.

Monte, Frank. *The Spying Game: My Extraordinary Life as a Private Investigator*. Sydney, Australia: Vapula Press, 2003.

Morgan, Mary Rockefeller. *Beginning with the End*. New York: Vantage Point, 2012.

Obeyesekere, Gananath. *The Man-Eating Myth and Human Sacrifice in the South Seas*. Berkeley: University of California Press, 2005.

Persico, Joseph. *The Imperial Rockefeller: A Biography of Nelson A. Rockefeller*. New York: Washington Square Press/Pocket Books, 1983.

Price, Sally. *Primitive Art in Civilized Places,* 2nd ed. Chicago: University of Chicago Press, 1989.

Sale, Kirkpatrick. *The Conquest of Paradise: Christopher Columbus and the Columbian Legacy*. New York: Knopf, 1990.

Sanday, Peggy Reeves. *Divine Hunger: Cannibalism as a Cultural System*. Cambridge: Cambridge University Press, 1986.

Saulnier, Tony. *The Headhunters of Papua*. New York: Crown, 1963.

Schieffelin, Edward L., and Robert Crittenden. *Like People You See in a Dream: First Contact in Six Papuan Societies*. Stanford, CA: Stanford University Press, 1991.

Schneebaum, Tobias. *Keep the River on Your Right.* New York: Grove Press, 1969.

————. *Secret Places: My Life in New York and New Guinea.* Madison: University of Wisconsin Press, 2000.

————. *Where the Spirits Dwell: An Odyssey in the Jungle of New Guinea.* New York: Grove Press, 1988.

Singh, Bilveer. *Papua: Geopolitics and the Quest for Nationhood.* Piscataway, NJ: Transaction, 2008.

Smidt, Dirk. *Asmat Art: Woodcarvings of Southwest New Guinea.* Amsterdam, Netherlands: Periplus, 1993.

Souter, Gavin. *New Guinea: The Last Unknown.* Sydney, Australia: Angus and Robertson, 1963.

Zubrinich, Kerry. "Cosmology and Colonisation: History and Culture of the Asmat of Irian Jaya." PhD diss., Charles Sturt University, 1997.

INDEX

NOTE: Page references in *italics* refer to photos.

ASMAT TRIBAL AREA
OF
NETHERLANDS NEW GUINEA
CIRCA 1961

Sagapo

Pupis

Wejo

Tjemor

Agani

Monu

Bu

Sawa

Erma

Manep

Komor

Jipajer

NORTH WEST R.

Jamas-Jeni

LORENTZ R.

Ajam

Jaun-Jufri

ASEWETS R.

Betjew

Ewer

Biwar-on Sor

FLAMINGO BAY

JETT R.

Agats

SIRETSJ R.

Per

KAMPONG R.

Atamut

Amanamkai

Biwar Laut

BETSJ R.

Ambisu

Omadesep

FARETSJ R.

EWTA R.

Otsjanep

CASUARINEN COAST

Buepis

Yaptambor

ARAFURA SEA

0 10 20 30 KM

0 5 10 15 20 MILES

Pirimapun